Ten percent of the profits from this book will be donated to Faith Tabernacle Missionary Baptist Church, an African American Baptist church in Stamford, Connecticut, "The City That Works."

I would like to express my deep gratitude to Reverend Tommie Jackson, Dr. Boise Kimber, Dr. Joseph Ford, and all present and past leaders of Faith Tabernacle Missionary Baptist Church along with the members of Faith Tabernacle for the willingness to have me worship alongside them and to share their vibrant Christian faith with me.

The message of "Life, Love, Liberty," as found in the weekly worship bulletin for the sermon, has been an inspiration and an eye-opener. It was so inspirational that it motivated me to run for governor in the state of Connecticut in 2017–2018. In time, it has become the five *ls: life, love, liberty, listen, and learn.* Rev. Tommie Jackson was the minister at Faith Tabernacle and was instrumental in adopting life, love, and liberty for the bulletin. Dr. Boise Kimber served as the interim pastor after Rev. Tommie Jackson left. Dr. Kimber was gracious enough to meet with me for countless Thursdays to go over the policies and platforms of my campaign for governor. Dr. Joseph Ford became the full-time minister of Faith Tabernacle in 2019, and he, too, has listened to me and advised me as I proposed policy changes after the killing of George Floyd and Breonna Taylor in the spring of 2020. I am grateful for the generosity of each of these ministers, for their positive message, and for their patience to sit with me. Ralph; Betty; Emma; Leon; Deacons Brevard, Dupree, McClintock, Elliott, and Homer; and the late Jack Bryant have all extended a warm hand of fellowship. To the leadership of President Guy Fortt and my fellow executive committee members of the Stamford NAACP, I also express my gratitude for allowing me to participate and for sharing your feedback. And so my education continues.

I would like to acknowledge the many Democrats who have also been willing to sit with me and offer feedback and refinements, but the intolerance of the intolerants and cancel culture is so great that they may suffer a backlash from the intolerants if identified by name. Nonetheless, I thank you for your generosity of time and insight.

100 Questions after the Killing of George Floyd and Breonna Taylor

———

With Policy Recommendations

———

And

———

The Chicago Tragedy

———

Our Silence on the Daily Violent Death of Young Black Men, Boys, and Bystanders Nationwide

———

PETER THALHEIM

FULTON BOOKS
Meadville, Pennsylvania

Contents

PART 1

THE CHICAGO TRAGEDY

———

*Our Silence on the Daily Violent Death of Young
Black Men, Boys, and Bystanders Nationwide*

Chapter 1

The Chicago Tragedy

"THE CHICAGO TRAGEDY" has been happening in Chicago, Illinois, and in other American cities, annually for years and hit its apogee in 2016 in Chicago, when there were 762 murders reported in Chicago alone. That worked out to more than 2 people killed per day. Now, apologists will point out that on a per-100,000-person basis, Chicago had a lower murder rate than cities like St. Louis, Detroit, and New Orleans. But 762 murders in one year works out to 2 violent murders per day. "The victims were mostly black and in their teens, while many of the suspects had prior arrest records. And increasingly, much of the violence occurred in just a handful of neighborhoods."[1] Josh Sanburn and David Johnson, writing for *Time* magazine, wrote that most of the murder increase happened on Chicago's South and West Sides. The murder rate for 2019 was less. By July 2019, 270 people had been killed, versus the 366 in 2016. Instead of 2 people being killed every day, it was closer to 1.5 people per day. To get some perspective of the death toll in these larger cities, the average murder rate in the United States was about 5.3 people per 100,000 in 2017. The 2016 murder rate in

---

[1] Josh Sanburn and David Johnson, "See Chicago's Deadly Year in Three Charts," *Time*, January 17, 2017.

Chicago was 27.7 per 100,000. What makes it noteworthy is not that it is above the nationwide average but that most of the people dying were young African American males, men and boys. There were certainly women and children that also suffered a violent death as a bystander in a park, walking one's children on a public street or sleeping in their own bed or crib and being hit by a stray bullet. But the larger picture is that the victims are concentrated among poor black males. What you die from if you are black, young, and a male in Chicago is, disproportionately, violence. Yet we as a nation are not allowed to discuss it and try to change that reality on the ground.

In 2017 St. Louis had the most per capita homicides at 66.1 per 100,000 citizens. St. Louis and Baltimore both had more than 50 citizens killed per 100,000 every year, which is almost ten times the national average. After Hurricane Katrina and a resulting decrease in population for people who left New Orleans, New Orleans hit 94.7 victims per 100,000 citizens.[2] When the national average was 5.3 violent deaths per 100,000 people, 94.7 victims per 100,000 should require changes to try to ameliorate this tragedy for these young men, the innocent bystanders, and the local community! When the leading cause of death for young black men between the ages of fifteen and nineteen in 2015 was homicide, something is seriously wrong. In 2015, 49.5 percent of the deaths of young black men between the ages of fifteen and nineteen was caused by homicide, for young black men between the ages of twenty and twenty-four, the homicide rate was 49.7 percent, and for ages twenty-five to thirty-four, it was 35.5 percent. That is a real problem. The next category for dying for these young men was "unintentional injuries" at 23 percent, 22.3 percent, and 22.3 percent, respectively. "Unintentional injuries" are also known as "accidents" in the statistical tables.[3] This is alarming, but not new, that the leading cause of death for young black males in the United States was and is murder (see Appendix A: Center for Disease Control and Prevention, "Leading Causes of Death by Age

---

[2]   John Gramlich and Drew Desilver, "Despite Recent Violence, Chicago Is Far from the US 'Murder Capital,'" Fact Tank, November 13, 2018, pewresearch.org.

[3]   Center for Disease Control and Prevention, "Leading Causes of Death by Age Group, Black Males- United States, 2015," Health Equity 2015.

Group, Black Males-United States, 2015"). The Chicago Tragedy is the public face of this tragedy.

An argument has been made, and should be made, that the right to not die a violent death is a civil right. What can we do about it? Why do we tolerate it? Because these victims are male and of color, they are invisible to much of the nation. There are three principal reasons for this invisibility: they are male, they are of color, and they die in cities long controlled by Democrats. If young women of color were dying a violent death in Chicago at the rate of two per day, we would hear about it. The media elite would have had shows on it. They would have reporters in the streets. Both before and after the killing of African Americans George Floyd and Breonna Taylor at the hands of police officers, if a police officer were involved in the fatal shooting of an African American citizen, the nation would hear about it. If young African American women were dying a violent death of two women per day in Chicago or another American city, our nation would be asking politicians how this could happen. Oprah Winfrey might even have a show on-site to shine a light on such a tragedy.

But with reference to the Chicago Tragedy, this has not happened and is unlikely to happen, because it is young men. And young men just aren't cool anymore. Instead, the leading progressives vilify men. The media elite regularly vilifies and diminishes men, just because of their gender. You have a free pass in these days of political correctness and cancel cancer[4] to vilify men. Go ahead. Do it. Nobody will question it. In fact, if you are a man and white, you are sometimes told that you have done something wrong. Perhaps

---

[4] "Cancel cancer" was popularly known as "cancel culture" in the early 2020s but a culture is alive, like the culture in a petri dish in your chemistry class, or a lively culture of art, music, literature, philosophy, academics, architecture, and generally a free and open society, while cancer is vigorous on the outside as it consumes its host and is dead on the inside. Cancel cancer tries to extinguish the professional and personal life of an individual who questions the orthodoxies of the intolerants so that the person may not work again and is permanently reviled in their society so as to silence not just that person but anyone else foolish enough to question the political orthodoxies of the elites as well. Cancel cancer is deadening and is another version of the struggle sessions that the Maoists of China would use to vilify a citizen onstage before their fellow citizens for hours for being the son of a "rich" landlord or wealthy farmer or counterrevolutionary or bad type, to either be castigated, executed elsewhere, or beaten to death onstage with farm implements to intimidate the rest of the citizens.

a politician or activist might say that that person has "white priv-ilege," to use a Marxian term. *Privilege* is a Marxian term that has been substituted for the more obvious *bourgeois* or *petit bourgeois.* Since it would appear retrograde to call people bourgeois, the same result can be achieved by calling someone privileged. But it is the same, a label to vilify someone with and to shame them. It is a term used to dehumanize the individual as not an individual but rather an object of scorn. The effect for the Marxist is the same: division and dehumanization.

After having determined and written that white males are guilty of "white privilege," to then try to make the distinction that it is really only white men who are bad, as opposed to all men, is a tough one to parse, so the intolerants just paint with a broad brush and vil-ify all men as a class. This does not help young men of color in poor neighborhoods. We have forgotten our younger brothers in many of our nation's cities.

The protests in the summer of 2020 following the killing of George Floyd and Breonna Taylor, among others, briefly shone a light on the travails of young black men, but mostly as the victims of police shootings. The Chicago Tragedy, which has claimed the lives of hundreds more young black men, women, and children, however, was not examined. The killing of unarmed black men and women by police is clearly a reason for public protest and demands for account-ability. When some in the political realm interjected that the high death rate of young black men by a violent death other than at the hands of police ought to be included in the subsequent discussion, it was waved off. Reporter Molly Stellino did a fact-check on a claim by political commentator Charlie Kirk that a total of 8 unarmed black men had been killed by police in 2019, writing, "Police killed more unarmed Black men in 2019 than conservative activist claimed." According to the news story, Mr. Kirk had relied on data collected by *The Washington Post.* "Even though data on fatalities at the hands of police is underreported and the actual number is likely higher, the Washington Post's database has reported 13 instances of police shoot-ing and killing unarmed Black men (plus one instance of police shooting and killing an unarmed Black woman) in 2019."[5] It is a truism that any death is a tragedy. The Chicago Tragedy in Chicago in 2016 was of 762 citizens! Reporter Stillino also referred to 25 police killings of unarmed black men as reported by Mapping Police Violence, a "crowdsourced database that includes deaths by vehicle, tasering or beating in addition to shootings."[6] Reporter Stillino pointed to the likely underreporting of the shooting of unarmed civilians by the police, as some jurisdictions "fail to file reports or omit justifiable homicides committed by police officers," or that "there were virtually no incentives for police departments to submit this information to the government." Citing an analysis by *The Washington Post*, reporter Stillino wrote that "police have killed around the same number of people each year—about 1,000—since it began collecting the data. The data for 2020 appear on par with previous years."[7] That would mean neither increasing nor decreasing, but the number of people shot by the police has been declining every decade. Her story concludes that 13 unarmed black men were killed in 2019 by police and not 8; therefore, her fact-check found this political pundit had undercounted.

And she was right, and no citizen takes solace in any unarmed citizen, black or white, getting shot in a confrontation with the police; ergo, there were sizable demonstrations and protests sparked by the killing of African American George Floyd in Minneapolis, Minnesota, by police officer Derek Chauvin kneeling on Mr. Floyd's neck for over nine minutes while Mr. Floyd said that he couldn't breathe. Both these men had also worked at the same club in Minneapolis and may have known each other. The demonstrations and protests across the United States focused on accountability by the government for the actions of police officers. Some pointed out that government rules and public union contract rules made it difficult to monitor problem police officers that had higher incidences of complaints by citizens and may have exceeded lawful tactics. Calls to

---

5   Molly Stellino, "Fact Check: Police Killed More Unarmed Black Men in 2019 Than Conservative Activist Claimed," *USA Today*, June 23, 2020, accessed October 26, 2020.

6   Ibid.

7   Ibid.

"defund the police" or to dismantle police departments were heard in these protests. The city of Minneapolis, however, ultimately did not defund or dismantle its police department by the fall of 2020 as it did not have the support of its citizens, as citizens, white and black, rich and poor, and everyone else in between, need to be secure in their person and property in order to exercise their civil rights and go about their daily lives.

The amorphous phrase "Black lives matter" became a topic for daily conversation and was highlighted in written and spoken reports in the need to reform police work and in demonstrations in the street. *Amorphous* is defined as "(1) lacking definite form; having no specific shape; formless: (2) of no particular kind or character; indeterminate; having no pattern or structure; unorganized."[8]

"Black Lives Matter" showed up on signs and T-shirts at protests. It was written in graffiti with spray paint on public and private spaces. Handcrafted signs with "Black Lives Matter" sprouted on front lawns, on shop and apartment windows, and along roadways. One needs to differentiate between a leading Black Lives Matter organization that has been successful in raising money but has also been alleged to be Marxist-led and other organizations or individuals that support the concept that black lives matter. Others said that Black Lives Matter was just that: black lives matter not to the exclusion of other lives but as a simple statement of fact. My local National Association for the Advancement of Colored People president stated it quite succinctly: "We are tired of dying." And that was said with a sense of exasperation. How many times do we have to go through this?

There were plenty of citizens who mounted their personal soapboxes to declare how they would address "systemic racism" and that they would make a better world. *Systemic racism* is another amorphous term that will be addressed later in this book along with the self-righteous in all their piety telling the rest what has to be done: reinforcing the same statist policies that have been in place, only more so. White citizens carried placards and preprinted signs into black communities

---

[8]   Dictionary.com, accessed October 27, 2020.

that said "Black Lives Matter" and marched about, chanting slogans and, at times, hurling invectives at the police guarding their parade route or guarding the public and private property around the protests. Some of these selfsame white protesters would post their activities on their social media accounts with great pride. For some it became almost a competition to outdo their fellow demonstrators. "What would make my social media presence outshine others?" "How could I show the world that I am not complicit or responsible for any of the wrongs that have befallen the black community in the past or today?" "Perhaps if I drive down from Upstate New York with a few Molotov cocktails[9] and perhaps throw them into an idling police car in New York City?" Then that person can post on social media what a rebel he or she is. If the protester doesn't like the pronouns *he* or *she* in describing such person, then *they* might post on social media what a rebel they are.

The major media showed its political bias overtly, tending to report on the Black Lives Matter movement in a tilted way. For example, in trading relationships between nations, there is a concept of a regular trading partner, and then there are "most favored nation" trading partners. A most favored nation status may grant the other nation no or lower tariffs to import their goods into a country like the United States. It might be done to encourage an industry in the nation designated "most favored nation." It may be done for political expedience. In the event of the protests after the killing of George Floyd, the major media was not entirely objective. "Riots" became "unrest." Burning private businesses and government buildings became "peaceful protests." The image of a reporter saying on television, "Things down here are pretty peaceful," with a fire raging through a building in the background, was worth a thousand words on media bias and lack of objectivity.

The protests were not limited to Minneapolis but occurred throughout the United States and beyond. A phenomenon started

---

[9] A *Molotov cocktail* is a homemade firebomb that is usually constructed of a flammable liquid such as gasoline poured into a glass container with a fuse of cloth doused in gasoline. It is then lit and thrown. When it hits, the glass breaks, and the fire from the fuse then lights the gasoline that has now spread over the building, a car, or the people that the gasoline has splashed onto.

to occur where a professional protester would drive their van or car from one city or town to another and encourage further protests. They might say that they were providing water and medical aid to protesters, or perhaps they were fanning the flames of civil unrest. When stores and businesses in black communities were looted and burned, decades of blood, sweat, and tears went up in smoke for countless business owners, both black and white. When shops were burned, the jobs of countless African Americans and other Americans went up in smoke. But that did not concern the major media. Who was going to help rebuild these businesses that serve their black communities and provide jobs to their residents? At times the bias of the media got so bad that a white liberal could put on a "Black Lives Matter" T-shirt and go into a black community and vandalize, loot, and burn businesses and government buildings in the same community and consider themselves the vanguard of progress, to be lauded by the media. These protesters could then post their exploits on their social media to outdo their fellow white liberal friends. That is so wrong. Or how about a white woman telling a black woman in her fifties, who was wearing a "Black Lives Matter" T-shirt, that the black woman was not black enough to be wearing that T-shirt? What? Who encourages this delusional thinking?

We have heard much of the value of black lives, but which black lives are we to be concerned with? The Chicago Tragedy is also a story of black lives, yet it is to be ignored because these are primarily young black men from high-need communities who live in jurisdictions that have been governed by Democrats for forty or more years. In today's political climate, according to the major media and its fellow travelers leading American institutions, you may not defend men, you may not speak ill of the Democratic Party, and you may not discuss the high rate of death for young black men living in communities run by the same Democratic Party. Yes, our young men of color are losing their lives in Democrat strongholds. These Democrat machines effectively grind through our humanity of young men in the pursuit of machine politics, but the same statist approach of the last fifty years continues unabated. This is a violation of the civil rights of these young men. If you are a young man of color and you live in a city that has been run by Democrats for decades, then you have a significantly higher likelihood of dying a violent death than if you live in a city that has been run by Republicans for a significant amount of time. Period.

Chicago has had ten Democrat mayors and no Republican ones in eighty-four years.[10] Since 1947, Baltimore has had one Republican mayor and ten Democrat mayors. That means for sixty-four of sixty-eight years, it has been run by Democrats. Detroit has had eight Democrat mayors since 1962 and no Republican mayors.[11] That was fifty-three years. St. Louis has had nine Democrat mayors in sixty-four years and no Republican mayors. Los Angeles has had five Democrat mayors and one Republican in fifty-four years. The poster child for the Democrats may be Boston, which has had twelve Democrat mayors in eighty-five years and no Republicans.[12] So what is the life expectancy for young men of color? What is the leading cause of death for black youth between eighteen and twenty-six? An incidence rate for violent death and accidents at 57–72 percent far and away exceeds the next closest, suicide at 8.8 percent and heart disease at 8.3 percent, in 2015.[13]

When I ask friends or people who remark about our present political issues about the Chicago Tragedy, about one in four know automatically what I am talking about. For the others, it is a new concept. "Yes, in 2016 every day two young men of color died a violent death in Chicago." "Really?" It is unnerving. It is so unnerving to the Democratic National Committee that I can imagine when they send their weekly talking points out to the fifty Democrat state committees and the leading media outlets, such as *The Washington Post*, *The New York Times*, the *Los Angeles Times*, the *Miami Herald*, *The Boston Globe*, MSNBC, NBC, CBS, ABC, CNN, Hearst Media, etc., they always have a cautionary footnote at the bottom: "Do not, under any circumstances, discuss or refer to the Chicago Tragedy."

---

[10] Richard Franz, "Urban America Should Give Up on the Democrats," *Baltimore Sun*, July 2, 2015.

[11] Ibid.

[12] Ibid.

[13] United States Center for Disease Control, "Leading Causes of Death by Age Group, Black Males," Health Equity.

So the Democrat state committees and the major media try their best to avoid touching on the Chicago Tragedy. But if we used the measure offered by Senator Cory Booker, who ran for president, that "silence is complicity," then the DNC and all the major media outlets are complicit in their silence on the Chicago Tragedy! Is there an easy answer? No. But other Republican-run cities have markedly less homicide incidence rate for young men of color. And the policies later in this book are part of those plans and attitudes of "A Different Way: The Proper Way" to ameliorate this tragedy.

When I started work in New York City as a first-year associate in 1985, I first started commuting from my parents' home in Greenwich, and then I was able to find a living arrangement on the fifth floor of a town house on the Upper West Side. The quality of life in Democrat-run New York City was much less then than what it became by 2019. Squeegee men would "wash" your windows with unknown liquids when you stopped at a traffic light, for a "tip." Homeless people, many of whom have significant issues of substance abuse, broken families, and mental health concerns, were more prevalent then than today. Graffiti had a strong presence on subway cars, subway stations, and private and public buildings and signs. A narrow park near the Seventy-Second subway stop on Broadway was called Needle Park for the discarded hypodermic needles left there. It was best not to go too far above the reservoir in Central Park. A papier-mâché structure was built around Grant's Tomb on the Upper West Side to distract graffiti and vandalism of the tomb. You might not want to ride the subway too late at night or in certain neighborhoods. And there were certain neighborhoods you probably shouldn't go to at certain times of the day. The Fulton Fish Market was dominated by the Mafia. Mobsters occasionally shot Mafia leaders dead on the streets of New York. And the finances of the city were not good. Buildings that owners had abandoned in the five boroughs lay vacant, with the city taking them over. When the city owned them, then the city did not collect any tax on them. At least the city had a program for auctioning off vacant properties in the four boroughs and in northern Manhattan. The vacant residential houses in Manhattan were reserved for the corruption-enabling "requests for proposals." With the multimillion-dollar prices for apartments and town houses on Central Park today, it is hard to imagine that a slew of elegant town houses on West 110th Street were vacant and property of the city. The AIDS epidemic started to hit as well as the popularity of crack cocaine.

Now, New York City was the best city in the world again by the time the COVID-19 virus struck in the winter of 2020. What happened? Twenty years of commonsense Republican and Independent leadership. Former federal prosecutor Rudy Giuliani was the mayor from 1994 to 2001, and billionaire Michael Bloomberg was the mayor from 2002 to 2013. How lucky the city and its citizens were to have had these two mayors! First of all, let's consider the civil right of a young man to actually live. New York City's homicide peaked at 2,245 incidents in 1990 in the thick of Democrat progressive leadership and fiscal irresponsibility. The murder rate dropped precipitously under Mayor Giuliani. And after twenty years of commonsense Republican and Independent mayors, the murder rate went down to 3.4 homicides per 100,000 people by 2018, which was *below* the national average! So there does not need to be an assumption that a city has to be a more violent place than the suburbs or country. Can you imagine how the city could have been even better if the city council had been Republican led? Even more people would have been alive today, and the economy would have been even stronger.

The advances achieved under Mayors Giuliani and Bloomberg have been systematically rolled back by Democrat mayor Bill de Blasio and the woke city council. A bail reform passed by the city council and signed by Mayor de Blasio lessened or eliminated bail and created a merry-go-round for some itinerant criminals, who could be arrested in the morning, released on no or low bail in the afternoon, and rearrested that evening for another crime. With the protests against the police, and with perpetrators emboldened by lawlessness in other cities following the protests of the summer of 2020, the rate of shootings in New York City had spiked up compared to those of previous years. Buried on page A15 of *The New York Times* on September 2, 2020, was a story that shootings had doubled and murder was up by 50 percent.[14] Dean Meminger of Spectrum News reported that New York City was recording its largest murder rate increase in decades. In all of 2019, 319 people had been murdered in the five boroughs of New York City. By September, 321 people had been murdered in 2020. In the previous year, it had been 230 through September 14. That would be an additional 91 souls lost to murder in 2020. If the numbers were to continue through the end of 2020, then "the city would see the largest year-over-year jump in murders since at least 1990, when the number peaked at more than two-thousand and twenty."[15] According to the writer, city officials and community groups pointed to a number of factors that contributed to the increase in murder: criminal justice reforms, protests over police brutality (like those for George Floyd), gang violence, and job losses from the COVID-19 lockdown of the city.[16] Even the statistics of the police department of the city of New York did not paint a positive picture. In October 2020, they showed that the murder rate for 2020 up to that point was 43 percent higher than those of the previous two years and that murders had increased 32 percent compared to 2019.[17]

At the beginning of his mayoralty in 1994, Mayor Giuliani focused on quality-of-life issues. There was something called a "broken windows" policy. Basically, if you leave a window on a building broken, you may encourage ne'er-do-wells to break more windows on the building. Graffiti, or the vandalism of public and private property, would not be tolerated. The sale of spray cans was restricted to adults. We would not call it art when it defaces somebody else's property. There is no question that many of these taggers, a name for graffiti artists, were talented, and their work can be very creative and thought-provoking when it is installed on a space that the owner, city

---

[14]   Mihir Zaveri, "A Violent August in NYC: Shootings Double and Murder Is Up by 50%," *The New York Times*, accessed October 27, 2020.
[15]   Dean Meminger, "NYPD Stats Show 321 Murders So Far This Year—Trend Could Mark Largest Increase in Decades," Spectrum News NY1, accessed October 27, 2020.
[16]   Ibid.
[17]   Police Department of the City of New York, "CompStat: Report Covering the Week 10/12/2020–10/18/2020, Vol. 27, Num. 42," NYC.gov.

or private, has encouraged or arranged to be spray-painted or otherwise have a mural painted on it.

During Mayor Giuliani's renaissance of New York City, when a school-aged child was not in school during regular school hours, there was such a thing as a truant officer. Well, these are not just people from old-time movies—truant officers exist. When Mayor Giuliani came in, they started asking school-aged children who were not in school, "Who is your parent or guardian?" And then asking the parent or guardian, "Why isn't your child in school?" There were even penalties for not sending your child to school! Imagine that, encouraging children to go to school. *Going to school.* Terrible thing, that.

In police enforcement, they started to stop fare jumpers in the subway system who would jump over the turnstiles versus paying the fare. Small-level crimes were pursued. The theory was that if you stop the small stuff, then the individuals are less likely to do the big stuff. Stop them at infractions and misdemeanors versus waiting until the criminal is at the felony level. Stop the criminal before they use a gun or knife to rob another citizen of their belongings. Stop a rapist before he preys on a woman, young or old. Stop a burglar before he or she breaks into a home occupied by children and adults. There are two clear beneficiaries from this commonsense approach: the citizen, who would otherwise be subjected to a violent robbery, rape, murder, or property crime, and the individual, who was dissuaded from pursing bigger crimes because they had already learned that crime does not pay, to wit, their arrest for a public nuisance crime. This would mean more people staying alive. These are all quality-of-life issues. And the right to your own life is a civil right.

Unfortunately for New York City, Marxists and those who follow Marxist thought, or even those who are not aware that they are promoting Marxist-inspired proposals, are trying to push back on these quality-of-life issues and make the city ungovernable again. Marxists love that, as they wish to gain political power in times of upheaval and the upending of social norms. Part of the clouds on the horizon for New York City was a white-haired socialist occupying the mayoralty in 2020, Bill de Blasio. His policies encouraged homelessness. There were more squeegee men again. Graffiti increased. Mayor de Blasio's administration was deemed the biggest slumlords in the land, and they had to enter into a consent decree on how it would improve its massive public housing stock. As part of the settlement with the Department of Housing and Urban Development, the New York City Housing Authority had to agree to put $2.2 billion over the following ten years into their public housing stock for some four hundred thousand tenants, all the while the NYCHA would continue to receive $1.5 billion per year from the federal government. Where the $28–30 million weekly from the federal Housing and Urban Development Department to the New York Housing Authority go is anyone's guess. Apparently, not for improving the public housing stock. Perhaps it supports no-show jobs and public union jobs, where nobody can get fired; meanwhile, the public tenants have no hot water, erratic heat, nonworking elevators, peeling paint, leaking roofs, asbestos, etc. "Having a safe and nurturing environment is key to healing development."[18] Leading up to the settlement, HUD had "accused NYCHA of misleading HUD and the public about the extent of lead and other unsafe conditions."[19] Even in receiving $28–30 million a week plus the city's own funding and rental payments by tenants, HUD claimed that de Blasio's housing authority had widespread heating outages and "swaths of mold and the authority's attempts to mislead inspectors by hiding hazards with mock walls."[20]

But ever the skilled politician, the Democrats put through a bill thereafter that goes after private landlords. So it's okay if the city is a slumlord, but not a private entrepreneur. Of course, it is not okay for anybody to be a slumlord, but Mayor de Blasio's administration was falling short on its public housing, but they were deft politicians.

The Democrat mayor had also increased the public payroll with its generous health-care benefits, disability rules, retirement rules, and

[18] Sarina Trangle and Ivan Pereira, "NYCHA Settlement Gives HUD Bigger Role in Authority," quoting HUD Secretary Ben Carson, *AM New York Newsletter*, February 28, 2019, accessed October 27, 2020.
[19] Ibid.
[20] Ibid.

sick pay. Much of this new spending was helped by a strong city economy before the COVID-19 pandemic and the masses of new apartments built on former railway yards on the west side of Manhattan,
which generate not just property taxes but city income taxes as well
on all the new yuppies that moved into these apartments. That cal-
culus changed somewhat with the arrival of the COVID-19 pandemic in 2020 and the subsequent lockdown of the New York City
economy. Many younger residents moved up their relocation to the
suburbs and started to leave. Other well-to-do residents decamped
to their second or third homes in the country. The paltry reopening of restaurants strangled countless neighborhood businesses and
put them out of business. Restaurant jobs were reduced, and when a
restaurant closes, there go the jobs with it. Imagine that the bureaucrats allowed a limited reopening of restaurants at 25 percent capacity in 2020 but then mandated that they close at 10:00 p.m. If it is
okay to dine at 8:00 p.m., it is okay to dine at midnight or 1:00 a.m.
That would be up to the restaurant to decide and would open up
countless seats for businesses and workers to start rebuilding their
lives by earning more. But our betters[21] would not allow it. With
fewer people out and about, it created opportunities for criminals to
ply their trade, a further and unnecessary deterioration of the quality
of life in New York City.

Oh, and by the way, if you have worked long and hard and have
saved some money after all the taxes and fees that you have to pay to
live in New York City and New York State, Mayor de Blasio wanted
you to know this in his sixth State of the City Address in January
2019: "Brothers and sisters, there's plenty of money in the world.
There's plenty of money in this city. It's just in the wrong hands."
Spoken like a true socialist. So if you thought you were going to try
to create a legacy for your children by setting aside your hard-earned
money, Mayor de Blasio has other plans for your money. Welcome
to New York!

Lest you think that the only major city that has a low murder
rate is New York City, the city of Houston, which has had Democrat

---

[21] Our "betters" are those with higher educational degrees and greater net worth in assets.

mayors, had a rate of 11.7 murders per 100,000 residents, which is about double the national average, but better than those of other cities. Consider New York's impressive rate of 3.4 per 100,000 people in 2014. That is pretty noteworthy. When traveling around the country, if you mention that you live by or lived in New York City, you are sometimes met with concern about all that "crime" in New York and a big city. But New York has fewer murders per capita than the whole of the United States. It is possible. It can be done.[22]

Part of the problem with the Chicago Tragedy is that when a political party has had control of a city for so long, the party calls the shots and the citizen doesn't have as much of an input. Fortunately for Chicago, Lori Lightfoot became Mayor in 2019, and she came from outside the Democrat machine. Chicago has had a corrupt political leadership for decades starting back with the election of Anton Cermak in 1931. Imagine that during the 1928 primary election, shootings and bombings were used to frighten and eliminate opponents.[23] Mayor Cermak started a Democrat machine. According to Bob Crawford, a retired journalist who covered Chicago city politics, the Democrat machine was not "shy about using money, bribes or fake identities to get votes for Democrats."[24] Richard J. Daley, who was Chicago's mayor from 1955 to 1977, "mastered it" according to Mr. Crawford.

Tricks of the Chicago machine include the following:

- Electoral rolls that still had names of dead people on them, for others to vote for that name.
- Names from cemeteries used to fill out voter registration cards.
- No Republican volunteers at a polling place, so no eyes on the ballots.

---

[22] Not to be too ecstatic, as America's murder rate far exceeds that of other nations, such as Japan, Indonesia, Spain, Poland, Italy, South Korea, Germany, United Kingdom, Morocco, Saudi Arabia, Ghana, Canada, Malaysia, Egypt, and others.
[23] Kelly Bauer, "Chicago and the Rigged Elections? The History Is Even Crazier Than You've Heard," *DNAinfo*, October 19, 2016.
[24] Ibid.

- "Democrats would pretend to be Republicans and would volunteer, meaning there were actually two Democrats at polling places."
- Five dollars, a warm meal, and/or a free drink to vote the right way.
- If no Republicans to watch for suspicious activity, the Democrat precinct captain would vote for the people who hadn't come in, according to reporter Simpson.
- Ward committeemen going to nursing homes to help seniors mark absentee ballots by holding the voter's hand, according to Simpson.[25]

It is not healthy that one party rules one place for so long; that is why it is also a general proposition that a country does not want a family political dynasty, such as the Kennedys, Bushes, or Clintons. Once a machine is in power for too long, the chances for change are slim and democracy is undermined by the machine.

Some years ago, I remember reading an article about the corruption of Chicago politics that spoke of a middle-aged black man who was fed up with the politics in his neighborhood and thought he might be able to effect change. So he went down and registered his name to participate in a primary for public office. By the end of the day, the machine had gotten another citizen with the exact same name to register for the exact same primary. So two people with the exact same name on the ballot. And who wins? The machine. Who loses? The citizen.

The Chicago Tragedy exists primarily for young black men, who are its chief victims. The Chicago machine has also saddled its citizens with challenged finances. "According to a 2013 Pew report, 61 other US cities face similar difficulties, but Chicago's situation is one of the worst… If the gaping holes in Chicago's social and fiscal fabric…can't be fixed…then Chicago may end up serving as a cautionary tale about the grim political and economic fate awaiting

---

[25] Ibid.

other US cities that put off or wish away their problems."[26] "Moody's Investors Service estimated in a 2013 report that fixed costs, like pension contributions and debt service, could soon eat up more than half the city's operating budget, up from about 15 percent of the 2015 budget"[27] In a bit of cynicism by teachers working within the machine, "nationwide, 10 percent of all parents have their kids in private schools. In Chicago, 39 percent of public school teachers with school-age children have their kids in private school."[28] These hardworking teachers rely on the machine to pay their wages, but they don't trust their children to the school system that they work for and prefer to place their own children outside of the machine's school system.

I had read then-senator Barack Obama's book *The Audacity of Hope*. My understanding is that President Obama had worked as a community organizer in impoverished neighborhoods in Chicago before he worked as an attorney and later ran for office in Illinois. When he wrote *The Audacity of Hope*, he was one of two sitting US senators from Illinois. It is altogether fitting and expected that he would touch on the Chicago Tragedy, which was happening in the largest city in his state, citing that the top cause of death for young men of color was homicide. It was not as if he were a senator from a neighboring state; Chicago was right there in front of him. He did briefly mention the senseless violence between these young men generally, but he avoided the Chicago Tragedy specifically. I will surmise that there are two reasons for this. The first is to talk about the Chicago Tragedy in a city dominated by Democrats for decades in a state where he was one of the US senators does not look good when you look to lead the nation and the Democratic Party. The second reason is that if then-senator Obama, and later President Obama, were to discuss the Chicago Tragedy, it would have been focusing on the violence and death being suffered by primarily young black men. President Obama had a black father and a white mother. If

[26] Larry Elder, "Chicago: Economic Death Spiral after 84 Years of Democratic Control," Townhall, April 16, 2015.

[27] Ibid.

[28] Ibid.

President Obama had been perceived as a president mainly addressing issues confronting blacks, who comprised 12–13 percent of the US population, versus the issues concerning the other 87 percent of the population, then he might not have been seen as a president of all Americans. He might have been politically restricted on how much he could talk about this tragedy, but he is still a very powerful and wealthy man and can talk about the Chicago Tragedy today.

A big part of the solution has to do with the breakdown of the family and how the society, which is all of us, can build the family back up. How can a young man be convinced that a man takes care of his children just as a woman takes care of her children? There is no equivocation. Even as society has fallen short in the education system, the sequence for success is still there: graduate from high school and/or college, get a full-time job, get married, and then have children. For the opponents of family and of the success sequence, the latter is discussed at greater length later in this book.

Preliminarily, structural racism/statism needs to be reduced. The state needs to reduce the barriers it has erected for citizens to work in trades or on getting licenses as well as encourage entrepreneurialism. A citizen should not be criminalized, as the governments in most of our states have done, should he or she work in a trade for which he or she is not licensed. Imagine that! The statists want you to get a home improvement license in order to exercise the civil right of working with your hands and back to put food on your table and that of your children. We do not require a license to exercise our freedom of speech, press, assembly, or religion. Yet we require a license in many jurisdictions for work that requires no more than hand-eye coordination and a strong back to practice and earn a living: barber, beautician, framer, excavator, tiler, drywall hanger, taper, shingler, painter, carpenter, mason, landscaper, moving person, etc.

We cannot keep doing the same statist things and denying our citizens the civil right to earn their bread. Furthermore, the right to your own life is a civil right, just as much as speech, press, assembly, and other fundamental rights are. When a group of people is denied the right to their own life by having to suffer a disproportionately high rate of death by violence, society must discuss and address this issue. Society must be free to discuss it—free from the censorship of the dominant political party, free from the inhumanity of cancel cancer and its adherents and enforcers. A democracy demands and requires no less! We cannot arrive at the truth without a vibrant discussion of issues and ideas.

And the approach of Mayors Giuliani and Bloomberg was correct. Quality-of-life issues are important to bring stability to cities. Graffiti is not okay. Truancy is not okay. Broken windows are not okay. Squeegee men are not okay. Vagrancy is not okay. Fare jumping is not okay. A citizen cannot exercise his or her civil rights unless they are secure in their person and property. On the other side of addressing these quality-of-life issues that make life safer, whereby fewer people lose their lives, are the Marxist-inspired activists and their fellow travelers and useful idiots, who are no friends of the family of the mother, father, son, and daughter or mother and mother, son, and daughter or father and father, son, and daughter. These Marxian proponents will complain that the rights of the citizens are being violated and that citizens of color are being disproportionately affected by efforts to lessen vagrancy, graffiti, vandalism, fare jumping, truancy, assault, and panhandling, even if a disproportionate number of crime is being committed by citizens of color against other citizens of color. *The Communist Manifesto*, by Karl Marx and Friedrich Engels, published in 1848, is unequivocal in its antipathy to family. "The bourgeois family will vanish as a matter of course when its complement vanishes, and both will vanish with the vanishing of capital."[29] Marxists have no need for family, as Marx and Engels decried family as "the bourgeois claptrap about family and education, both the hallowed correlation of parent and child."[30] The mental, physical, and academic success of children who come from two-parent families consistently exceeds that of children who come from one-parent families. That is the data. That is the science. That is a condition to work toward and not away from. Critics of the approach to encourage family formation lament that due to poverty, we should

[29] Karl Marx and Friedrich Engels, *The Communist Manifesto*, (London: The Merlin Press, 1998), 17.
[30] Ibid.

not apply our "bourgeois" values on what is acceptable conduct. We should not judge. We do not need to have standards, we are told. Don't be judgmental, we are told. Having no standards is like proceeding without a plan. Without a plan, you will fail. Without a plan, society will fail. What are we supposed to be working toward with the massive Welfare-Industrial Complex that has been built up since the New Deal in the 1930s? Is it a hand up or a handout? We can recognize that as a society we have failed to give stronger public education choices to our young people from high-need communities for public charters and education vouchers to help pay the tuition at private K–12 schools. We have also failed to have a stronger economy with jobs for our young people from high-need communities. This makes it harder for young people in general, and these forgotten young African American men from high-need communities in particular, to work for their children.

And here is where the magic trick comes in. You may have heard that in centuries past, there was such a thing as debtors' prison. This was where a citizen might be sentenced to jail because the citizen had not paid back a debt. Debtors' prisons have long since been abolished, except in family court actions, where men and women are still jailed for failing to make payments of alimony or child support. An example of where debtors' prison might have been used is when a person with a $240,000 mortgage loan on their home is not able to keep up on their payments. In the meantime, the real estate value of the property supporting that mortgage loan has gone down. This happens in states like Connecticut, where the statists have been busy making promises to their special-interest friends to get elected, but the general citizenry cannot afford these unrealistic promises made by the statists, and then residents that are able to and have capital flee the state. As a result, house values have gone down in numerous communities. So the lender, who is owed the mortgage loan, sells the mortgagor's property in foreclosure and perhaps there is a $75,000 deficiency between what the house was sold for and how much the owner owes. In some cases, the lender might forgive that debt in a short sale, or perhaps the person files for bankruptcy protection. But one thing that will not happen is, the former homeowner will not be sent to prison for being unable to pay the $75,000 shortfall. They will not be going to jail.

On a bigger scale, a citizen may have created a business over many years, hired employees, purchased equipment, provided a service or sold products, but for whatever reason, their business doesn't make it. Perhaps the owner owes over $1 million to his or her creditors. Again, that businessperson would not be sent to jail unless fraud and deceit were involved in the failure of the business or in obtaining loans for the business. But there would be no debtors' prison.

Today, if a man has child support payment obligations to his child or children and goes to jail for a crime, those child support payments are still due and accrue while he is still in jail. It is harder to find a new job after you get out of prison, so it is harder to make up for the missed child support payments. Where the judgmental society that has standards of conduct would not necessarily place this man in prison for failing to pay money toward his child, the non-judgmental segment of society has no problem putting this man in jail for failing to pay child support toward his children. So the non-judgmental people will take your liberty, but the judgmental society does not take your liberty. So who is more ready to use the apparatus of the state to imprison someone for a civil wrong? We do not imprison someone who has fallen behind on their mortgage or car payments. Debtors' prisons existed once but have long since been abolished. Does imprisoning someone, usually a man, for failure to pay child support or alimony help young men of color from high-need communities embrace their role as a father?

There is no easy answer to this dilemma. Belatedly, we have come to recognize that fathers are important to the lives of their sons and daughters, just as mothers are. If a father is behind on child support payments, he may be concerned that when he visits his son or daughter, there may be a sheriff there ready to arrest him for failure to pay child support. How does this help the development of the next generation? How does this help tie the father to his own children? A man disconnected from his children is more likely to make bad choices than a man connected to his children. A man disconnected from his children is also more likely to fall into bad habits than one who is reminded of his obligation to his children and how special they are. Is this part of the Chicago Tragedy? Have these young men been forgotten, not only when they suffer a violent death at the hands of another man battling over gang-related issues or turf battles, but also when they try to do right and participate in the fullness of life and the union with another to raise their children? What structural barriers have the statists placed in their way? Isn't *structural statism* identical in many aspects to *structural racism*? Don't they overlap each other?

Where is the line between civil and criminal penalties? Should we discuss this use of state power by the proponents of "no judgment"?

During my time running for governor, my mentor, Dr. Boise Kimber, the interim pastor at Faith Tabernacle Missionary Baptist Church, an African American Baptist church in Stamford, Connecticut, suggested that I attend the annual National Association for the Advancement of Colored People (NAACP) dinner of the Stamford branch in 2017. So I did. The fee was modest, and it was held at the local Sheraton hotel. I recognized some people from Faith Tabernacle Missionary Baptist Church but otherwise talked with other attendees and at times discussed my campaign for governor. It came time for speeches, and one of the speeches was a standard speech employed by Democrats for decades: "Democrats are good. Republicans are bad. I promise to bring more government spending to your community, and I will not rest until the institution of family has been thoroughly wiped out in rural and urban poor communities."

In January 2020, I had been elected to the executive committee of the Stamford branch of the NAACP. It was a moderately productive year for me at the Stamford NAACP. In the winter, I had proposed that the NAACP hold a debate on the N-word to educate people, particularly young people, that the N-word is off-limits except in a teaching environment. I have heard the N-word numerous times in the lyrics of songs that are played on the radio, as well as its generous use by comedians. The official position of the national NAACP, as it should be, is that the N-word is off-limits and should be buried except in teaching settings. The idea was to have the debate with one moderator and four panelists. There would be two *for* the NAACP position that the word should not be used, and two *against* the position. We were able to find a cosponsor with the Black Student Union at the Stamford branch of the University of Connecticut. We were trying to find a black comedian and/or musician to be on the panel along with young and old citizens. Then the coronavirus came and the debate was canceled.

My next project was the use of the resolution mechanism of the NAACP to militate against recreational marijuana for our children and adolescents. The NAACP has a mechanism in its bylaws whereby any of its more than two thousand branches can adopt a resolution complete with "whereas" and "now therefore" clauses on issues relating to the mission of the NAACP, which is upholding the civil rights of African American and all citizens. I prepared a proposed resolution and wrote a sixteen-page memorandum against recreational marijuana use for our children and adolescents based on studies that showed higher anxiety and paranoia levels for consistent marijuana use by children. The ideation of suicide by young women who used marijuana regularly increased by an order of six times over similarly situated young women. The changing of the gray matter in the brains of adolescents was alarming, and also the many other negative effects of this "new big tobacco" that was trying to make money off addling our children and adolescents on this new drug. You don't want your children addicted to any drug, and you don't want your children addicted to recreational marijuana that the new big tobacco markets with strands called the Girl Scout cookie or delicious gummies and brownies of high-potency pot. The resolution against recreational marijuana for our children and adolescents was made more difficult as it was mailed out as if it were against recreational marijuana generally and not specifically against recreational marijuana use among children and adolescents. Nonetheless, by a very low vote count, the resolution against recreational marijuana use passed and was forwarded for consideration by the national office of the NAACP, which let it die alone in a folder somewhere.

About the same time, I started work on the concept for the National Slavery Memorial to be placed on the National Mall in

Washington, DC. I was a history major and have traveled to Europe and to the Far East a number of times, and it had come to my attention that the only major military or economic power in the world that had a memorial in its nation's capital to a historic wrong of the country was Germany. After East and West Germany were reunited in 1989 and 1990, as one nation, they later built, commemorated, and dedicated a memorial to the six million Jews murdered during the Holocaust under the National Socialism regime of Adolf Hitler before and during World War II. The Holocaust Memorial sits right in downtown Berlin, next to the US Embassy, and steps from the Brandenburg Gate, a symbol of a united Germany, as well as the Reichstag, which is Germany's capitol building. Even though it has a memorial to a national wrong right in the center of its capital, Germany is still standing.

It is altogether fitting that the United States have a National Slavery Memorial on the Washington Mall, within view of the national memorial for Lincoln, who was key to ending the original sin of slavery for our nation, and that built for Jefferson, who penned the Declaration of Independence. But the *Dred Scott v. Sandford* Supreme Court decision of 1857 stated that persons of African descent could not be and never were citizens of the United States, which meant that the children of President Thomas Jefferson and his slave Sally Hemings could never enjoy the rights that he had set forth in the Declaration of Independence. The Stamford NAACP approved forming an *ad hoc* committee to explore the viability of a National Slavery Memorial on the Washington Mall. And that was how I finally met Representative Himes. I had written him twice during my failed gubernatorial campaign in 2017, recommending a solution to the DACA dilemma of young illegal immigrants who were not guaranteed the ability to stay here. I also recommended "CheckAmerican" to him and our other congresspeople and US senators, whereby the category of "American" should be the first choice available on any government document that asks your race, creed, color, or ethnicity. Lastly, there was a modest proposal that soldiers have the full rights and privileges of citizenship by being allowed to drink alcohol after age eighteen. Neither Congressman Himes nor any of the other Connecticut congresspeople, or even US senators Richard Blumenthal and Chris Murphy, ever engaged me on any of these three issues.

At all events, Congressman Himes was very gracious to meet by Zoom with members of the Stamford NAACP and myself to discuss the National Slavery Memorial, NSM. By the time of our Zoom conference, the NSM had come to encompass three things: the NSM, the National Registry of Donors to the National Slavery Memorial, and aid to historically black colleges and universities. Graciously, Congressman Himes pledged his enthusiastic support of the NSM and informed us that both of Connecticut's two senators were also on board, Richard Blumenthal and Chris Murphy. That was an honor. For Congressman Himes to shepherd the NSM through Congress, it would be necessary for the national leadership of the NAACP to get on board and push it throughout the NAACP.

Naively, I thought this would come quickly. Our Stamford president, Guy Fortt, mailed a letter to our president, Derrick Johnson, in September, before the NAACP had its 111th annual convention, this time virtually. I was even honored to be voted as an alternate delegate to the convention, which was held in the middle of September. Ironically, my number was called for the Saturday session, where the many resolutions from local NAACPs were voted on. The resolution of the Stamford NAACP against recreational marijuana for our children and adolescents was not on the long list of resolutions to be voted on, however, as the resolutions committee has the discretion to modify and set aside any and all resolutions that come to headquarters. In addition, the NAACP had years before approved the legalization of recreational marijuana. Perhaps a resolution against recreational marijuana for our children and adolescents would be too controversial? As it turned out, resolutions were arranged into groups and voted on as a whole, so that might have been a problem.

Hopefully, the national NAACP embraces the NSM, the National Registry of Donors to the NSM, and aid to historically black colleges and universities, and that Congressman Himes will be able to shepherd all of it through Congress. But that was not to be as the NAACP National Resolutions Committee declined to forward the National Slavery Memorial resolution to that summer's national convention in July. This was in the same season that our nation recognized Juneteenth of June 19 as a national holiday when the slaves in the Texas territories were officially freed by the arrival of Union General Gordon Granger and his General Order No. 3 proclaiming the slaves free on June 19, 1865. Four days later the last Confederate General, Stand Watie, officially surrendered on June 23 to Union lieutenant colonel Asa C. Mathews at Doaksville, thereby freeing the remaining four thousand or more slaves owned by Cherokees, Seminole, and Creek Indians. Notwithstanding the opinion of the National Resolutions Committee, the NSM resolution is an excellent idea for our nation and will continue to be pushed forward. Perhaps it will be resubmitted the following year to the NAACP and/ or other organizations or legislators will sponsor it?

How can our nation move forward on the Chicago Tragedy? Can we discuss it? Or should other issues take precedence, to the exclusion of the Chicago Tragedy? One could be hopeful. According to US senator Murphy's website, his office held a workshop in New Haven in April 2017 on urban trauma. *Urban trauma* would be the instability that children face in an environment where one or both of their parents may not be present. Their own apartment or house or shelter may not be the same for any length of time. There may be substance abuse within their family group. There may be violence outside their doors and bystander shootings. The quality and quantity of food may be lacking. It is a tough environment to grow up in. The problem with the forum arranged by Senator Murphy's office to take place in a traditionally black neighborhood in New Haven was that there was not one black member of the panel to talk about urban trauma. Instead, it would be all nonblack people talking about urban trauma in the black community. Dr. Boise Kimber let the senator's office know that this was not acceptable. Arrangements were apparently made, according to Dr. Kimber, that Maysa Akbar, PhD, who had authored the book *Urban Trauma: A Legacy of Racism*, be put on the panel, and then a place was made for Dr. Kimber. The forum occurred, but Dr. Kimber stayed in the audience as a note of protest, and his chair with the other speakers stayed empty.

The anatomy of what has been called a "drive-by" is to get good photos and press that can be used to further a politician's re-election prospects. These photos and headlines can be emailed and mailed to supporters for contributions and votes. The cynical view is that just as Senator Murphy and his entourage arrived at the forum, someone told the driver to keep the motor running. "I won't be long," he said. "We just have to get some good photos and press material, and then we can leave." Did the forum by Senator Murphy focus on the damage done by the War on the Family, which is also known as the War on Poverty, or did the panel propose more of the same War on Poverty (War on the Family)? The absence of intact families hurts the emotional, physical, and mental development of children in urban and rural communities. Was that discussed? One of the most important things for a child is stability, and society should do what it can to foster family formation. In addition, it is important that our young people learn the essential values and morals required to realize their full potential as adults. Connecticut is fortunate, however, when it comes to the Chicago Tragedy, as it is not as violent as other American cities in Connecticut's major urban areas of Hartford, Bridgeport, New Haven, Stamford, New Britain, or New London, although it still happens, but on a smaller scale.

What gets much greater attention than the Chicago Tragedy in our nation is the illegal immigrant situation, and that of asylum seekers, rather than what is happening to our brothers and sisters in economically disadvantaged communities in urban and rural America. It is much more popular for the national media to wear their anguish for the plight of the illegal immigrants on their sleeve than it is for the major media to pause and reflect on either the War on the Family or the Chicago Tragedy. On July 13, 2019, in the town of Greenwich, a leftist organization, Indivisible Greenwich, had a vigil for migrants at the border. Cofounder Nerlyn Pierson was quoted by writer Ken Borsuk of the local paper *Greenwich Time* as saying, "We gather to raise awareness of the inhumane conditions at the border. We must speak of them regularly and not let this be normal." According to Mr. Borsuk, she "exhorted the crowd to speak out against the poor conditions and urged everyone to take action." The participants lit candles, flashlights, and their cell phones. According to Mr. Borsuk, there were signs that read, "Never again is now," "Don't look away," "No human being is illegal," and "Silence is violence." The last sign reminds me of Senator Cory Booker's statement that "silence is complicity." And that is the irony. Here these people truly believe that what is happening is wrong and the press fills our headlines with it. But in two days, three young men will have been murdered in Chicago. Any murder, either by drowning or starvation, is wrong. But the press and Indivisible Greenwich are conspicuously silent on the Chicago Tragedy. These young men and innocent bystanders are almost universally American citizens who were born in this country. Our country owes its duty to first care for Americans born in America. That is an obvious fact that the elite media ignores. Shall we encourage more illegal immigration so that these illegal migrants can undercut the wages of poor American citizens, thereby making the fulfillment of the American dream for these very same citizens more difficult?

Congressman Jim Himes was quoted at the same vigil as saying, "This has nothing to do with party. It doesn't have a lot to do with policy. We need to raise our voices and make sure that every mayor, every governor, every state senator, every state representative, every senator and the president of the United States knows we demand that we be a better people than we have been to these vulnerable people who have come here...because they appreciate this country, the opportunity it offers and most importantly, the decency of what it means to be an American." Congressman Himes was correct, but when are voices raised for the victims of the Chicago Tragedy, almost all of whom were universally young African American males? Why have we forgotten them? As American citizens, shouldn't we be paying more attention to them? What of the Napoleon judges who tie the hands of an elected administration to try to slow down the flow of migrants? Do we have the resources to care for our own poor American citizens in urban and rural areas? These Napoleon judges make their rulings extend beyond their jurisdictional areas and may have encouraged more migrants and illegal immigrants to come in the heat of the summer and to be exposed to human traffickers. That children were separated from their parents at the border was a mistake, but it was under court order that children could not be put in jail with adults. Normally, when you are arrested in the United States, they will call your spouse, partner, parents, grandparents, siblings to see whether they can take custody of the children that are with you. There is no such luxury at the border, however. Hard choices. Bad law. Who built the cages?

I do not doubt the sincerity of the people attending the vigil, but I ask why the same concern is not expressed for all the young men of color that die a violent death in Democrat-controlled cities. Is it because of the footnote in the DNC weekly talking points that there shall be no discussion of the Chicago Tragedy as it would reflect badly on entrenched Democrat progressive policies? If the Chicago Tragedy is avoided due to political considerations, then the protests on behalf of the illegal immigrants and migrants are a political act of favoring non-American citizens over American citizens. That is wrong. Every elected official in the United States at the federal, state, and local level is elected by 100 percent American citizens, at least in theory. If you don't agree that this order of priorities is wrong, then tell your constituents that in this circumstance you will prefer non-American citizens over American citizens and let the chips fall where they may. It is like our new attorney general in Connecticut, William Tong, who was styled by online newspaper *The Connecticut Mirror* as fighting President Trump on an average of three times a month, sometimes by joining other states against the president. As a black resident wrote in, perhaps William Tong should think twice as the son of an immigrant from Communist China. Does AG Tong feel that he should fight President Trump at every turn? When the president is trying to get jobs for all Americans? While the unemployment rate for blacks stood at 6 percent, nearly a historic low for blacks and also for Hispanics, should AG Tong be fighting the administration at every turn? Have we acquitted ourselves of our social contract to care for those born in this country? If not, then perhaps politicians like AG Tong should be a little more circumspect in the areas where they would fight the administration versus a Blunderbuss approach.

So to our elected representatives, isn't it important that we raise our voices and bring attention to the Chicago Tragedy in Chicago, Detroit, Philadelphia, St. Louis, Baltimore, etc.? The Chicago Tragedy is but one of the implicit pains of statism as designed and promoted by statists,[31] which statism will be expanded upon in Part 2. At least many of the migrants arriving on the United States border with Mexico have a mother, father, son, and/or daughter. That right there is a predictor that the children will be better off than many of our own young people in the cities and country who have only one or neither. So what can we do to strengthen family? What can we do to diminish the Chicago Tragedy and, ultimately, to eliminate it? There is a way, and that question became more poignant with the killing of African American George Floyd in Minneapolis, Minnesota, in May 2020 by a white police officer holding his knee on Mr. Floyd's neck for over nine minutes. There were protests and demonstrations across our country. The phrase "Black lives matter" became common-place among demonstrators and the press. It sprouted up in yards, on windows, and on articles of clothing. How could the tragedy of the death of George Floyd and other black Americans during an arrest, or the execution of a search warrant in the case of Breonna Taylor, shed light on the Chicago Tragedy, and can our nation's trajectory be changed? It can, as laid forth in the following one hundred questions after the killing of George Floyd and Breonna Taylor.

---

[31] A statist favors the state over the citizen. A statist will increase the size and power of the sate over the citizen, if given the chance. Examples of statists are Marxists, socialists, Democrats, communists, fascists, Maoists, Leninists, and Chavistas—to name a few. Fascism: "characterized by dictatorial power, forcible suppression of opposition, and strong regimentation of society and of the economy." https://en.wikipedia.org/wiki/Fascism - cite_note-3, citing *Merrian-Webster* Online, archived from the original on August 22, 2017, retrieved August 22, 2017.

Chapter 2

The Abortion Rate for Black Women

B EFORE PROCEEDING TO the one hundred questions, it would be fitting to shine a light on another tragedy, and that is the abortion rate for black women, which is at about four to five times more than that of white women, with the resultant annual abortion toll at around 360,000 black babies in 2011. This is an estimate given by citing data from the Guttmacher Institute.[32] For a 365-day year, that works out to almost 1,000 aborted black babies every day! That is a lot. Black women had abortions almost at five times the rate for white women in 2008.[33] The Guttmacher Institute, a generally pro-abortion entity, explained in its article "Abortion and Women of Color: The Bigger Picture" that these pregnancies are mostly unintended, with causes related to access and availability to contraceptives as well as their affordability. The article also pointed out that even if a method were available, it might not be used consistently, which naturally would lead to more unintended pregnancies.

---

[32] Walt Blackman, "Abortion: The Overlooked Tragedy for Black Americans," *Arizona Capitol Times*, February 25, 2020.
[33] Susan A. Cohen, "Abortion and Women of Color: The Bigger Picture," *Guttmacher Policy Review* vol. 2, issue 3, August 6, 2008.

By 2020, that rate had been reduced to about four times as many abortions as for white women.[34]

The quantified number of abortions for black women at around 360,000 is an estimate, as in 2020 five states did not report race-specific data. Those states were California, New York, Texas, Florida, and Illinois, which represent at least half of our nation's population.[35] Nonetheless, abortion at a rate of four times as much for black women as white women is a large number and is demographically consequential for the black community's future growth.

Certainly, improving the economic condition of blacks in America will help ameliorate this high rate of abortion, the economics of which this book addresses in subsequent chapters. But one can question why the rate is so high and the attention paid to it is little, similar to the Chicago Tragedy. In 2020, Arizona representative Walt Blackman pointed out "that 79 percent of Planned Parenthood's surgical abortion facilities were located within walking distance of minority communities."[36] He questioned whether this was targeting by Planned Parenthood, much like the tobacco industry had targeted young people with their advertising to get them hooked on tobacco products. Why Planned Parenthood places its facilities where it does can be explained by Planned Parenthood. At all events, the number of abortions performed in the United States has declined since the *Roe v. Wade* Supreme Court decision in 1973, with a high of 29.3 abortions per 1,000 women aged fifteen to forty-four in 1981, to a historic low of 19.4 in 2005.[37] The U.S. Supreme Court's decision on June 24, 2022 to overturn *Roe v. Wade in Dobbs v. Jackson Woman's Health Organization*, No. 19–1392, may or may not shed more light on how abortion disproportionately impacts the black community.

It is the wish across all political spectrums that a child have a long and healthy life ahead of them. In April 2016, President Barack

34 James Studnicki, John W. Fisher, and James L. Sherley, "Perceiving and Addressing the Pervasive Racial Disparity in Abortion," *Health Services Research and Managerial Epidemiology*, published online, August 18, 2020.
35 Ibid.
36 Blackman, "Abortion: The Overlooked Tragedy."
37 Cohen, "Abortion and Women of Color."

Obama's administration announced a Precision Medicine Initiative. Of the many partners in the initiative was the Bill & Melinda Gates Foundation. The foundation would hold an event later in the spring of 2016 to address the potential of big data and precision medicine to address biological, environmental, and social determinants of public health challenges, "particularly for society's most disadvantaged populations."[38] Why did the Obama administration and Bill & Melinda Gates Foundation deem this important? "Because of the critical importance of a *child's first 1,000 days after conception* [italics mine] in determining a healthy and productive life trajectory."[39] Whether intentional or unintentional, the language from the Bill & Melinda Gates Foundation cited the importance of the first one thousand days *after conception* of a *child's life trajectory*! Two hundred and seventy of those days are the child's days in the womb to birth at about nine months. Abortion is not part of life; it is the ending of life. There are debates between abortion proponents, who say that life does not begin in the womb, and abortion opponents, who say that life begins at conception and thereafter it is morally wrong to abort a baby in the womb. The acknowledgment of the Bill & Melinda Gates Foundation that the first one thousand days after conception are critical to a child's life trajectory unequivocally includes the nine months before birth. This is not to settle the tug-and-pull over the availability of abortion in the United States but rather to discuss the disproportionately large number of abortions within the black community. It is a number significantly larger than the Chicago Tragedy.

---

[38]   Office of the White House Press Secretary, "Fact Sheet: Obama Administration Announces Key Actions to Accelerate Precision Medicine Initiative," Obama White House Archives, published 2016, accessed January 11, 2021, cited in "Perceiving and Addressing the Pervasive Racial Disparity in Abortion."

[39]   Ibid.

PART 2

100 QUESTIONS AFTER THE KILLING OF GEORGE FLOYD AND BREONNA TAYLOR

With Policy Recommendations

Chapter 3

From Faith Tabernacle Baptist Church to the Stamford NAACP: Writing a Two-Pager on How White People Can Help End Structural Racism

OW DID I get to *100 Questions after the Killing of George Floyd and Breonna Taylor* in 2020? It was tasked to me by the president of Stamford's local NAACP branch, Guy Fortt, with whom I had become a member of the branch's executive committee only that previous winter. My membership in the NAACP came in a circuitous fashion. I had begun to attend an African American Baptist church in Stamford, Connecticut, some years before 2017, and the message of *life, love, liberty* in the weekly Sunday bulletin, for the sermon made a powerful impression on me. The positivity from each service was so uplifting I felt that the rest of our country was missing out on the positive message of Faith Tabernacle Missionary Baptist Church! While I had always been interested in politics and economics since junior high school, including the presidency of the Middlebury College Republicans, where I founded a newsletter for national and international issues that included a guest column for my brother and sister Democrats, I had not run for office at any other time. During my brief years in New York City as an attorney in the late 1980s, I had worked with the Freedom Republicans, an organization of black Republicans in Brooklyn, and together we had drafted enterprise zone legislation for the city of New York to help economically depressed areas of the city that had more black residents than other areas of the city. However, that enterprise zone legislation fell on deaf ears at the city council. There was only a brief inquiry from a lone Staten Island Republican on helping our less-fortunate city residents.

Reverend Tommie Jackson, the minister at Faith Tabernacle when I arrived, had coined the line "Life, love, liberty," which appeared in each Sunday bulletin. He, however, was eased out of the church after some twenty years of service, not too long after my arrival. Thereafter, Dr. Boise Kimber preached as the interim pastor every other week. The other Sundays were reserved for other African American preachers from Norwalk, Hartford, New Haven, Bridgeport, New York City, Newark, and the like. They all had the same positive message of life, love, liberty. While it was a disappointment to see Reverend Jackson move on, as he gave such outstanding sermons, it was a blessing in disguise because you could hear all these other preachers come through Faith and preach the same positive and healing messages without your having to drive throughout the tristate area to hear their message.

For those citizens of the United States that are not familiar with Connecticut, let me say it used to have a thriving economy. Fairfield County, its Gold Coast, is the county closest to New York City. Connecticut did not have an income tax prior to 1991 and was an attractive place to run a business, raise a family, and live in. After the institution of the state income tax, however, Connecticut went into a steady decline as compared to the growth rates of other states and the nation. In 1977, *The New York Times* reported that Connecticut had thirty-three headquarters of the top Fortune 500 companies. Chicago had been reported as having thirty-three in 1976 as well, which would have tied with Fairfield County as second behind New York City for Fortune 500 headquarters.[40] Not bad for suburbia. But that was then. By the spring of 2017, Connecticut was a laggard— she had not yet even regained the jobs lost in the Great Recession of 2008–2009 by the time the COVID-19 pandemic of 2020 struck.

---

[40] "Fortune's 500 and Connecticut," *The New York Times*, August 14, 1977.

The imposition of the income tax had done its damage, along with the long domination of state government by statists who had foisted the highest pay and benefits to public sector employees in the entire nation. Great for the public sector employees, but not so great for the financial health of a former economic tiger. This was coupled with the state's dismal fiscal condition due to the underfunded pensions and retiree health-care benefits promised to these selfsame public sector employees. The political leadership made great promises of riches to these public employees, cashiered their votes and political support for more terms in office, but intentionally underfunded their pensions while rolling the debt over onto the children of the public sector employees and all the other citizens of the state.

As a licensed Realtor and as a housebuilder, I had witnessed the stagnation of real estate values in Greenwich and in Connecticut along with the malaise of people leaving the state once their children had finished high school. People, talent, and capital were leaving the state. The state faced constant budget shortfalls, which were "fixed" by ever more taxes on people living their lives or trying to earn a living. Whether the taxes were on the sale of particular services or an increase in sales taxes or the shrinking of the list of "necessities and food" that no longer qualified as "necessities" for the statists in Hartford. Some taxes were called "revenues" and "invemnents." That is correct. The statists weren't taxing you; they were *investing* in the future of the citizens who might still happen to be around. These statists were comfortable that you couldn't actually take your real estate with you and the state could live off the property you left behind. Some studies had opined that if the incomes and capital that had left the state had not left for friendlier environments, Connecticut would not be seeing one- to two-billion-dollar shortfalls in its twenty-billion-dollar annual budgets. Well, Peggy Jorgenson, a star Realtor at Coldwell Banker, Greenwich, informed us in May 2017 at an office meeting that there would be a Realtor rally in Hartford to let the politicians know that they needed to do something to help the state. Peggy is a great salesperson. So good, in fact, that I decided to ride in the free bus complete with food provided to and from the rally and a lunch voucher for the rally with my fellow Realtors. There were over two thousand Realtors who showed up in Hartford that day on a beautiful park lawn with chairs and food tables. Republican and Democrat politicians addressed the Realtors. When another legislator would arrive to take a seat on the podium, all proceedings would stop for the moderators to announce to the crowd which "eminence" had just arrived. "Hooray!"

Over two thousand Realtors sat there that fine spring day to hear Democrat and Republican legislative leaders address the crowd, while Connecticut was slowly sinking, and not one leader spoke of any way out of the mess. It was as if there had been an agreement not to propose ideas contrary to the ideas of the other party. During the free lunch that followed, I asked Realtors from other towns such as Stratford whether they had heard any politician offer any way forward for our state. The answer was always the same: "No." The Realtors on the bus on the way back to Greenwich were of the same opinion. What a waste of time! Once at home, I ruminated on how dispiriting it was to be in a rudderless ship that had so many resources and potential. Connecticut sat outside of the best city in the world, New York City. Connecticut had the highest per capita income in the land, yet it was among the bottom five in fiscal health for the state government. It was either tied with Massachusetts or second in the nation with the highest-educated work populace, and there she was, drifting toward ruin, with the Hartford Chavistas at the helm. A *Chavista* is likened to the supporters of socialist Hugo Chavez, who, in the 1990s, took over in Venezuela, a country with the highest proven oil reserves in the world. He seized the wealth of individuals, including land and companies, and put his cronies in positions of power and expanded the power of the military. Now, Venezuela is a Cuban-controlled puppet, with Nicolas Maduro serving as president, at the pleasure of Cuba's internal security forces. Five million Venezuelans have fled this pauperized Cuban puppet state. Reportedly, 80 percent of the populace was malnourished by 2020 and had no access to health care, yet the Chavistas in Caracas, Venezuela, continued to claim that they represented the poor and the people, all while they had reduced the populace to begging for a simple bag of rice and beans to try to live another day.

The Chavistas in Hartford, Connecticut, likewise, are grinding Connecticut down under the weight and power of the state and sending citizens fleeing to other environs. The influx of New York residents during the coronavirus epidemic in 2020 was likely to be a temporary boost to the state's real estate and economy, even while the statists continue to retard the ability of the economy, schools, and houses of worship to fully reopen.

The Realtor rally in Hartford was so dispiriting I decided as an immigrant who is so grateful for this exceptional country that allows immigrants to pursue the American dream just like it does people born here, and also as a veteran lawyer from the US Army Reserve and father of three daughters, that I would run for governor of Connecticut on the positive message of "Live, love, liberty" from Faith Tabernacle Missionary Baptist Church! So as not to take the exact wording of Faith, I renamed it as "Gratitude, common humanity, and liberty." *Gratitude* is that we should be grateful for every day that we are given, as no day has been promised to us. *Common humanity* represents love, that we are all brothers and sisters, children of God. For the atheists among us, the other version is that 99.6 percent of our DNA is identical. All that we can see that is different is the 0.4 percent. Don't be a 0.4-percenter; embrace the 99.6 percent that we all share in common. The *liberty* part for Faith is different from the *liberty* set forth in our Declaration of Independence and in the Constitution. The *liberty* of my campaign was focused on the liberty of speech, press, assembly, religion, and the right to bear arms, the right to petition the government for redress of grievances, the right to one's own life, the right to work with one's hands and back to put food on one's plate and on the plate of one's children, the right against unreasonable searches and seizures, the right to due process and to be secure from the government seizing one's property, and the right to a speedy and fair trial, to a jury of one's peers, and to have an attorney to assist in one's defense, to prohibit excessive bail or fines, and to ensure no cruel and unusual punishments. By 2017, Connecticut had arrived at an imbalance and the state was no longer working for the citizen, but rather, the citizen was working for the state.

When I asked ace Realtor Peggy Jorgensen whether she would be willing to be the treasurer for my campaign, she informed me that she doesn't get involved in politics. "But you exhorted us all at the meeting to exercise our obligations as citizens and to get involved to help save our state!" The short answer was that sales is what she does! Touché.

As an attorney, I tend to be a little more focused on policy and preferred to write them down as small policy papers. It was also most important that, as I was a Republican, any policy had to be presentable to the African American and Hispanic communities. I asked for and received the help of interim pastor, Dr. Boise Kimber, to help me with my platform and articles. In fact, when I met him at the Sheraton hotel next to Faith Tabernacle Missionary Baptist Church in Stamford, Connecticut, I was impressed that the politician meeting him right after me was Bridgeport mayor Joe Ganim, who was also running for governor, but as a Democrat. I had come to the right place. Over the next nine to ten months, I would meet Dr. Kimber at his office or at a restaurant on Thursdays to go through my policy papers and my campaign. I had never run for office prior, and I didn't know what I didn't know until I started to actually run. And I really didn't know what I was doing, but I started to drive around to the weekly Republican Town Committee meetings all over the state to address the members, some of whom would be delegates at the state convention in May 2018. Dr. Kimber did push me to get a treasurer so that I could actually have the ability to receive donations. As a neophyte, I found that as no easy task. I was so grateful to Jacquelyn Smith, who had purchased one of the spec houses I had built and who had also been a College Republican, when she agreed to be my treasurer. I was so lucky! A treasurer is critical to a campaign but thankless at the same time.

I already had the website www.Check American.com, which I had created for the 2010 census. It is basically legislation and possibly an amendment to the United States Constitution that states that "whereas, there is no color for an American and we are a people whether we were born here or immigrated here; now therefore, let it be adopted that any United States /

state / local government form that requests that citizens identify their race, creed, color or ethnicity have as the first category 'American' to be put in an equal or more prominent position than the other categories." This is truly an individual's choice. If this legislation were to be adopted as an amendment to our Constitution, it would be the first day of postracial America.

Of the many articles that I wrote, I wrote on the floundering economy of Connecticut. There was a position paper on the DACA and DREAMer solutions addressing the over ten million illegal aliens in the United States, about two-thirds of whom were Hispanic and about one-third of whom were Asian. They either came illegally or overstayed their visas. It would basically allow for permission to stay for those who had been in the country for a number of years, to be determined by Congress, were law-abiding, and loved America. Since no immigrant should seek any special category or advantage for the privilege of living in this country, the categories of Hispanic and Asian American would be eliminated as minority categories. Having fewer categories translates to greater unity. The environmental policy worked out to environmental equity, which is that we will do whatever we can for the environment, provided it doesn't raise the cost of living for poor people. And the cost of living not just includes what you buy as food, clothing, and shelter but applies as well to your ability to earn a living and have a job. School choice for black, Hispanic, Asian, white, and other students from high-need communities was encouraged through public charter schools and vouchers to get students out of the school-to-prison pipeline run by public teacher unions. The Chicago Tragedy, discussed earlier in this book, was also touched upon.

The focus of the campaign was on improving real or substantial socio-economic disparities in Connecticut, including improving the ability to get jobs, learn trades, open businesses, and own real estate, equipment, trucks, and licenses. Prison sentencing reform along the lines of that championed by then-governor Malloy was also part of my platform. Videos were shot, social media content produced, and speeches made. But my campaign did not go anywhere. My hometown paper *The Greenwich Time* did a good job of canceling my campaign for a hometown boy who grew up in Greenwich, attended Greenwich public schools K–12, ran his law practice there for sixteen years, got married there, raised his children there, put them through the K-12 public school system there, ran his home construction business there all the way through the campaign, and was a Sunday school teacher at the founding church for Greenwich for seven years. Very effective. But Hearst Media is a pioneer of cancel cancer. There would be no stories. There would be no letters to the editor from my campaign published. A frequent observation of Greenwich residents years later: "You ran for governor? I didn't know." Job well done for the paper of record for Greenwich. If they don't publish it, then the campaign of "Gratitude, common humanity, and liberty," originating from the positive message of a black Baptist church in next-door Stamford, didn't exist and would not get any time in the sun. In their view, a voice should not be heard unless it promotes their statist narrative of rule by our betters.

By spring 2018, the Connecticut State chapter of the NAACP was sponsoring a gubernatorial debate in New Haven, Connecticut, in April. The debate would talk about the chances for prisoner re-entry into society. Questions would be posed by former inmates. At first, I opted for a candidate meet-and-greet in Westport but then realized that this debate was much more important and along the lines of my campaign platform. I ended up being the only Republican of the five candidates who appeared. The other four were Democrat candidates Ned Lamont, Susan Byciewicz, Guy Smith, and Joe Ganim. Candidate Lamont ended up being elected governor, and Ms. Byciewicz became the lieutenant governor, while Mayor Ganim continued to be the mayor of Bridgeport, the largest city in Connecticut. The debate was the highlight of my campaign as I was able to put forth the positive message of gratitude, common humanity, and liberty. I stressed that being an employee was not the only way to re-enter society, that the state puts unnecessary barriers in the way of citizens to learn trades and to become a business owner, the poster child being the requirement for one thousand hours of paid schooling to become a barber. Handshakes were exchanged, photos were taken, and backs were patted at the end of the debate.

Significantly, two men came up to me after the debate and had positive things to say about my stress on the entrepreneurial aspect of prisoner re-entry. I exchanged numbers with some, and one gentleman and I agreed that we would try to meet up. We did. He apparently had been in jail for killing two or more people while he was in his teens and still had some bullets in him. He had served his time and was now married, with at least one child, and was running a business in the automotive field along with gang counseling for the state. He was also a devout Muslim. During one of our meetings in Bridgeport, we even went to a local prayer center in stocking feet, as we took our shoes off at the entrance. I was honored that he would sit and talk with me. He stated that he was satisfied to be talking to a major party candidate running for governor. Together we put together a twelve-page policy sheet, "A Different Way: The Proper Way." This publication emphasized the importance of the individual to elevate themselves and the relevance of entrepreneurial efforts as well as the importance of family of mother, father, son, and daughter. Work should be decriminalized so that the citizen should not be subject to arrest for exercising their right to work with their hands and back to feed themselves and their family. Should the failure to pay child support be decriminalized so that more men might be with their children? The importance of faith and marriage to better outcomes for children of those unions was set forth. The potential for economic independence through long hours and low pay of owning your own business was proposed. That the War on the Family, conducted under the name of the War on Poverty, and whether the Welfare-Industrial Complex had any motivation or incentive to change its methods were posited. The only person who can elevate you is you.

I failed to get any delegates at the Connecticut Republican convention in May 2018. The Republican who ended up winning the nomination, Bob Stefanowski, did not participate in the delegate process himself and instead won a contested primary. My personal victory at the convention was to hear my name called from across the reception area of the hotel by none other than Scot Eisdale, the president of the Connecticut chapter of the NAACP, who had hosted the NAACP gubernatorial debate the prior month in New Haven! He called me Peter, and he even let me talk his ear off on policy until he had to go to his lunch meeting. That was very gracious of him.

I was already a member of the NAACP, as I had been at the Freedom Fund dinner in Stamford the previous fall, and the entrance fee included a one-year membership. In 2018, I started to attend the monthly meetings of the Stamford NAACP, which were low-key affairs. Then-president Jack Bryant was one of the early victims of the COVID-19 pandemic. Toward the end of 2018 or so, I even handed out "A Different Way: The Proper Way" to my fellow members of the NAACP. Treasurer Joyce Griffin asked me at one point thereafter whether I had any interest in joining the executive committee of the Stamford branch. To which I responded with an unequivocal yes! "It would be an honor!" I said. But that would have to wait until January 2020, as the Stamford branch stopped meeting in 2019 and was reconstituted by the NAACP state leadership in 2020. I was so happy to get voted onto the executive committee along with other members, but only after I stuck my foot in my mouth. Executive committee member David Jones had moderated part of the Freedom Fund dinner the previous fall, and when I addressed our incoming president, Guy Fortt, as David Jones while we were waiting for the green light to go to our meeting room, Guy observed, "I know that we all look alike," to inform me that he was Guy Fortt, to the universal laughter of the rest of the members there, at my expense. That was not the last chuckle at my expense. Early in 2020, I had wanted to get going right away on an idea I had for a debate on the N-word. There would be a moderator with four panelists, two for and two against using the word. The goal was to educate how the N-word should not be used except in a teaching environment. February is Black History Month, so the goal was to get it done right away in February. Fellow member Emma Goings pointed out that there was always "Juneteenth." "What is Juneteenth?" I asked. This again elicited numerous chuckles. "On June 19, 1865, federal troops freed the last slaves in Texas." Although Confederate Robert E. Lee had surrendered at Appomattox in April 1865 and the Emancipation Proclamation by President Lincoln had become effective on January

1, 1863, it took more than two years to free the slaves in Texas.[41] Even then, slavery continued to be practiced in Delaware and Kentucky, which, as border states, had not joined the Confederacy, and the slaves in Delaware and Kentucky had to wait for the passage of the Thirteenth Amendment to the US Constitution in December 1865 to be freed.[42] Although June 19 was relevant to the freeing of the slaves in Texas, it wasn't until June 23, 1865, that the last Confederate general, Stand Watie, surrendered. He was an American Indian and had led Cherokee troops in alliance with the Confederacy against the Union. American Indians owned slaves and even took them with them when they were resettled during the Trail of Tears from one territory to another.[43] General Watie signed a cease-fire agreement with a Union representative on June 23, 1865, in Doaksville in the Choctaw Nation, thereby freeing some four thousand slaves four days after the declaration by General Gordon Granger in Galveston, Texas, on June 19.[44] Author D. Amari Jackson put the number of slaves owned by the Cherokee at four thousand in 1860.[45] These awkward moments and lack of knowledge by me are mistakes that I have had to make to participate in a community that I am not normally part of. Stumbling is required to move forward and learn.

That American Indians owned slaves would come as a surprise to me but is part of our nation's history. This runs counter to the narrative of some leaders that there is some sort of natural alliance of "people of color," which can mean anyone but a white American. "American," however, is a better way than the politics of categories. Consider that half of Hispanics in Florida voted for President Donald Trump in the 2020 presidential election over Democrat Joe Biden. It is a slippery slope filled with many potholes to create policies that

---

[41] Juneteenth Organization & Supporters, "History of Juneteenth," juneteenth.com, accessed November 2, 2020.

[42] Wikipedia, s.v. "Juneteenth," accessed November 2, 2020.

[43] Tom Porter, "The Last Confederate Troops to Surrender in the Civil War Were Native American—Here's How They Ended Up Fighting for the South," Business Insider, June 23, 2019, accessed November 2, 2020.

[44] Wikipedia, s.v. "Stand Watie," accessed November 2, 2020.

[45] D. Amari Jackson, "Enslaved Black People: The Part of the Trail of Tears Narrative No One Told You About," Atlanta Black Star, March 17, 2018.

treat a group as a monolithic whole. Take the black community for example. I do not claim to have any view or knowledge of what life is like behind the veil of race in the United States, but it is fair to say that the black community is a diverse community. A majority of the black community is made up of descendants of blacks brought to the colonies, and later to the United States, as slaves. There are also blacks from the West Indies, also known as the Caribbean, who have immigrated to the United States from countries such as Haiti, Jamaica, the Dominican Republic, St. Lucia, and other nations, who had originally been brought to the Western Hemisphere in the transatlantic slave trade as slaves to work on sugar plantations and other plantations, who have also been raised under different national conditions before immigrating to the United States. Then there are black Africans who have and are immigrating to the United States from Africa in the twentieth and twenty-first centuries. While each of these three groups could be termed to be part of the black community, they all have their own individual identities, assumptions, and history. I respectfully submit that immigrants from the West Indies and Africa are not immigrating to the United States because they see it as a cauldron of racism but rather because they believe it will give their children and them a more secure and promising future as a land of opportunity.

When I mentioned to a doctor friend whom I had not seen for some time that I had been elected to the executive committee of the Stamford NAACP the previous January, she was surprised! "Did they know that you had voted for President Trump?" And that would be a typical response of one steeped in the political correctness of the time. My response was that I had shared "A Different Way: The Proper Way" with members at an NAACP meeting and I had regularly attended the NAACP meetings. An organization is not an organization if nobody shows up. During our conversation, my doctor friend had exhibited some wokeness by using the term *Latinx* numerous times as we talked about issues confronting the black and Hispanic communities. While *courant*, the focus on the words used and the virtue signaling that goes with using the latest politically correct term or terms fails to address the substantive issues of jobs, education, health, housing, and cost of living that one is talking about. It becomes an exercise in posturing versus focusing on the core issues for the amelioration of the condition of man. While a citizen is shamed by the intolerants if he, she, or they do not use the right pronoun or uses the pronoun that most of us are comfortable with, as 99 percent of all live births are the result of consensual heterosexual relations, the pursuit of the truth falls in the face of political correctness. The pursuit of truth should be the primary goal, far eclipsing other concepts of shaming and silencing voices and preventing citizens from participating in conversations about where our nation is and where we should be going.

Consider the discussion of the gender or nongender of words in the English language. While it may be deemed important by specific individuals, it is an anomaly of the English language that most of our nouns have no gender. We generally don't have genders for words in English that adjectives have to match with. We do, however, have genders of words in German, French, Spanish, and Russian, for example. In these languages, the adjectives that go with the noun are supposed to match the masculine, feminine, or neutral gender of the noun. In German, *woman* can be *das Fräulein*, *die Frau*, and *das Weib*. The first and third words are actually neutral nouns, which are neither masculine nor feminine. The middle one, *die Frau*, is a feminine noun. In German, *child* is *das Kind*, which is a neutral noun. In French, it is *un enfant*, which is a masculine noun. And the Russian word for *child*, *rebonuk*, is a masculine noun. In Russian, there are also three genders, masculine, feminine, and neuter. Adjectives must match the noun, and endings change whether it is in the nominative, accusative, genitive, or dative position. To demand that the gender of English change in order to conform to the political orthodoxy of the day is less about finding solutions and more about political correctness. Would one rework the entire languages of German, Spanish, French, and Russian to satisfy the Orwellian demands of our overlords? And the more politically correct a person is, the more intolerant they are. We should not encourage the intolerant!

By using *Latinx*, my doctor friend might have been flexing her progressive muscles but might also have shown that the use of the more common word *Latino* would mark the speaker as unenlightened, and therefore the message of the person is less worthy of consideration in the eyes of an intolerant. This is false. We must be able to speak to the issues to try to arrive at the truth. Where she was shocked that someone who might have voted for Trump was elected within the NAACP, she forgot that he pushed and signed the First Step Act and Second Chance Reauthorization Act of 2018, which made significant changes to federal sentencing laws as well as improvements to programs to reduce incidence of people going back to jail with comprehensive re-entry programs and to reduce the rate of substance addiction for people involved in the justice system.[46] Furthermore, she forgot that the rate of black and Hispanic unemployment had dropped to fifty-year lows for both groups and that the incomes of the bottom quintile were finally increasing faster than the top four quintiles after having lagged for years before the Trump administration. The COVID-19 pandemic set back many of these advances. A feat that was only possible with a very tight labor market that encouraged many people to re-enter the job market. Indeed, a rising tide lifts all boats.

Perhaps the question could be, Would someone be elected to the NAACP at the local level when that person supported more of the same statist policies of the War on Poverty, silence on the Chicago Tragedy, the denial of school choice, the criminalization of work, the denial of the right to work with your hands and back to feed yourself, and the increase in the cost of living, of housing, food, clothing, and shelter, through the imposition of ever more state burdens? Such policies have been ruinous for family formation and economic advancement for poor Americans in both rural and urban environments. It is time to question the statist setting that only the state can elevate the poor. When do we turn the page on a patronizing view of minority communities that minority communities cannot make it without special rules. What of Democrats who believe the minority vote is a birthright of white Democrats and they need only show up

---

[46] CSG Justice Center, "President Trump Signs First Step Act into Law, Reauthorizing Second Chance Act," CSGJusticeCenter.org, December 21, 2018.

every two or four years to collect on that birthright? And have you heard that if you are black and you don't vote for a white Democrat, then you are not black?[47]

The year 2020 progressed along with the advent of the COVID-19 pandemic, and the debate I was organizing for the NAACP in conjunction with the Black Student Union of Stamford UConn on the N-word was canceled. My resolution against recreational marijuana for our children and adolescents passed the local NAACP. Then I proposed the idea for a National Slavery Memorial on the Washington Mall in our nation's capital to our president, Guy Fortt, along with my fellow executive committee members. They approved the creation of an ad hoc committee to explore the possibility of the National Slavery Memorial under my leadership. Overlapping with the development of the National Slavery Memorial concept, African American George Floyd was killed in Minneapolis, Minnesota, when a white police officer kept his knee on Mr. Floyd's neck for over nine minutes, during which time Mr. Floyd said he was having a hard time breathing. National and international protests followed. Many of the protests were peaceful, but some descended into violence and looting. A few weeks later, my president, Guy Fortt, asked me, "I have heard from several of my Caucasian friends who have asked how can white ppl help [end] systemic racism? I would like you to respond with a two-pager. Can you explain?" My answer was a straightforward "Easily." But it would take more than two pages, as the problem was multifaceted and part of the problem was the amorphous term *systemic racism*, which travels around without any definition. Guy wanted the two-pager to be from my perspective as a white citizen. I then drafted what became *100 Questions after the Killing of George Floyd and Breonna Taylor*. I shared this with Guy, and he shared it with some other people. Keith was one of these individuals, and I am grateful for the feedback that Keith shared with me from others. A helpful suggestion was to split the one hundred questions up into

---

[47] Eric Bradner, Sarah Mucha, and Arlette Saenz, "Biden: 'If You Have a Problem Figuring Out Whether You're for Me or Trump, Then You Ain't Black,'" CNN, May 22, 2020, accessed November 2, 2020. This statement was made by Vice President Joe Biden during his 2020 campaign for president.

chapters and to insert policy recommendations. What follows are the one hundred questions that my Caucasian brothers and sisters should answer regarding what we should and could do after the killing of George Floyd to end structural racism. This is not meant as a recommendation to my brothers and sisters in the African American community as to what should or could be done, but maybe some of the points resonate?

Chapter 4

What is Structural Racism?

1. WHAT IS STRUCTURAL racism? It is important that you physically write down what you think *structural racism* is at the beginning of these questions to see whether there is any overlap in what will be reviewed below. *Structural racism* became a catchall phrase in the aftermath of the killing of George Floyd to indicate that a citizen was against something and they were not complicit in the system that allowed structural racism to exist. But asking someone what structural racism was could produce almost as many answers as when one hundred economists are asked the best way to grow the economy. For that reason, it would be helpful if the reader would jot down on a piece of paper or in their cell phone what they believe *structural racism* to be. The purpose is to see at the end of these one hundred questions exactly what *structural racism* is and what steps could be taken to eliminate it.

Chapter 5

Have you Intentionally or Unintentionally Abetted "Structural Racism" in Your Past Political Choices?

2. HAVE YOUR PAST political choices supported or enabled structural racism? Though pure of heart, can you entertain the possibility that your reflexive policy choices seemed logical and benevolent but ended up doing the opposite of what you intended? Will you continue to make the same political choices to support and enable structural racism? Many whites believe that they have not consciously abetted what could be characterized as structural racism and that if their past choices had abetted structural racism, they would not repeat the same mistake twice. Getting up on a soapbox to tell the world that you will fight to make a better world does not get us far if you merely double down on failed policies of the past, ambivalent to the unintended consequences of your choices. Can the citizen consider that what they supported before, although done with good intentions, may have abetted structural racism?

Chapter 6

The Self-Righteous and Politically Correct Mount their Soapboxes but Reinforce Structural Racism

3. Has the citizen scaled a soapbox and told the world what a wonderful person that person is and how that person is free of fault? If only everybody could be like the speaker! This citizen should consider that he or she may be a wonderful person, but their policy prescriptions have been ruinous to the African American community. Some in the African American community have been able to advance their educational and economic position in spite of these policy choices. Is it possible for the citizen to consider that their policy prescriptions do exactly the opposite of what the citizen professes the citizen would like to achieve or that it has retarded positive trends in education and economics for the African American community? What if you give more generous disability benefits and that discourages people from going back into the job market to find new work and participate in the economy? In the short term, disability benefits might pay more and might seem like a more humane way to treat someone, but if the disability benefit discourages the person from participating in the labor market or in pursuing a trade or business, then that person will be in the same place or, worse, twenty-five years hence. Upward mobility is only possible through individual action. Upward mobility cannot be

purchased with a monthly check that is unrelated to daily effort and skill. This does not even touch on the satisfaction that a human being derives for giving back to society in the form of work or other form of service to others.

4. Are you a chief executive officer of a corporation or public entity, and do you use that position to issue statements to accentuate your enlightenment and how you are going to lead your company and the nation to a better place? Can you accept that you haven't a clue and that you are likely to double down on the ruinous policies that you had supported in the past? This is focused not on how you have handled your business but in your political choices. That is the definition of insanity, doing the same thing over and over and expecting a different result. When the government policies and laws that a chief executive officer of a corporation or public entity has supported in the past may have strengthened structural racism, more of the same will not change the outcome, even when you promise more funding to do more of the same.

5. Do you accept that when you claim to be free of racism or sexism, you are merely stating that you are no more than any human being who hits their Reboot button to return to where they should be, just like when you reboot your cell phone or computer when it gets frozen with bad ideas? You are no better than those to whom you preach, and you have no more knowledge and insight than those to whom you preach. Would you consider reining in your condescension?

6. Are you willing to question your political preferences and choices of the past as we navigate a different way and the proper way forward to alleviate the obstacles that you have placed in the way of the poor in general and blacks in particular, to get ahead?

7. Are you an intolerant? Because if you are, you will not help us move forward as one nation. Do you automatically dismiss the arguments and positions of a politician once you hear their party affili-

ation? Are you willing to look at proposed policies from more than your own political party, or do you prefer to vilify a political party and anyone affiliated with that party? If an employee or executive of a company has contributed to the political campaign of a politician disfavored by the media, such as Donald Trump, should that person be fired? Should that end the matter? Is it important for you to punish a fellow citizen who supported a defeated politician beyond the ballot box? Is that a form of voter intimidation? Is that intolerance? Is it hubris to consider that you have discovered the truth and that all discussions on the topic must cease? We are all fallible. The purpose of the *rule of law* is that the citizen be sovereign and the government work for the citizens. Each citizen is entitled to have a voice and a vote. Should the citizen with whom you disagree be silenced so that he or she can no longer work to provide food and shelter for his or her family? Should they be economically ruined? That is not about unity but rather domination. That is not the message of love, that we are all sisters and brothers, children of God, or that we all share 99.6 percent of the same DNA. Love your neighbor as yourself. Even after you have an argument, she is still your sister. He is still your brother. Stop to consider that sometimes you can be wrong. Step back from your intolerance.

8. Do you know that the more politically correct a person is, the more intolerant that person becomes? Any poll that asks the question, "Do you agree that the more politically correct a person is, the more intolerant they are?" confirms the intolerance of the politically correct. The traditional view of political correctness is that its proponents are trying to be nice to people and to avoid offending their fellow citizens. There is also the view that the politically correct are trying to protect the underserved and marginalized in society, and that is certainly a meritorious endeavor. The problem, however, arises when the character and motives of those who do not fall in line with the political correctness *du jour* are characterized as mean or insensitive on a good day but racist, misogynist, sexist, homophobic, anti-LGBTQ, etc. on any other day. Just writing these negative epithets risks condemnation if they were not written in the form approved

by the intolerants. Some of the politically correct are well-meaning citizens who wish to do no harm. Others, however, use political correctness to intimidate their political opponents without ever having to debate the underlying political issues of economics, race, health care, affordable housing, immigration, schooling, or international relations. Political correctness is a tool used to intimidate without the need for discussion. Political correctness is also closely allied with identity politics, where our nation is broken down into subsets of citizens and even noncitizens. There are the basic categories of women and men, and some promote the use of *womyn* instead of *woman*, as the former does not contain the noun *man* in it. There are the basic categories of black, white, yellow, and brown. There are straight and gay categories, and there are those who object to the concept that there are only two genders, that of man and woman, and instead there's a multiple of genders or no gender at all. Identity politics breaks us down into categories to the extent that you are no longer a person or human being but a category. When I see you, I am supposed to put you into a category, and the category that I place you in affects whether I should listen to you or ignore you. Issues on economics, education, housing, and health care end up being viewed through a prism of categories.

If it can be argued that a particular group or category has experienced worse economics, education, or health outcomes, then the system is accused of being systemically wrong to some degree. Arguments that other factors contribute to a statistical variation are brushed aside as they do not support the preferred explanation of "structural" inequities. The COVID-19 coronavirus spread through the United States and the rest of the world in 2020. African Americans were dying at a rate higher than those of non-African Americans. Some of the reasons for it was that there were often multigenerational households, with younger generations living with older generations. The COVID-19 coronavirus was significantly deadlier to senior citizens than to young people by a factor of six hundred to one thousand times. Many African Americans had work in service industries, which required interaction with other citizens, like work in the nature of stores, restaurants, shipping, and other similar occupations.

This greater exposure was then brought home to the grandparents. African Americans may have been more readily turned away from emergency care at the hospital as their symptoms worsened than other citizens'. Jack Bryant, past president of the Stamford NAACP, passed away from COVID-19 in the early days of the pandemic in 2020, after he had been turned away or discharged from the hospital numerous times before they agreed to take him in, after which he died. A legitimate question has been raised whether the health outcomes of African Americans could have been better with different policies in place. That is a worthy inquiry.

But if an inquiry focuses on a group disfavored by the politically correct, then it is more likely to be waved off or ignored. As a white male, I have noticed that white males are routinely dismissed by certain segments of the political spectrum. Many of the ills of the world are the fault of white males, as a group of men and as whites. That would be two categories. Usually, the ills of the world are not blamed on black, Hispanic, or Asian males. Instead, it is white males as a class. Examples of sexist tirades against white men from the internet are not even needed as this default is pretty well established. As a white male, I find it inaccurate, as the sins of my fathers are not mine. Each individual is just that, an individual, a free agent. As a home builder, I take pride in all the fine homes that we built or renovated. You are not allowed to refer to the roads, bridges, cars, trucks, buildings, airplanes, schools, hospitals, trains designed and built by men to point out that men are not all bad or destructive. They can and have built many useful and beautiful things. During the COVID-19 crisis, we heard of the disparate impact of the COVID-19 pandemic to different categories of citizens, but there is one that was plainly available that was not discussed by the dominant institutions of the press or the politicians of the United States, that about twice as many men were dying of COVID-19 as women in Europe.[48] According to the New York State Department of Health, 60 percent of people who

---

[48] John Ng, Kishan Bakrania, Chris Falkous, and Richard Russell. "COVID-19 Mortality Rates by Age and Gender: Why Is the Disease Killing More Men Than Women?" Reinsurance Group of America, July 10, 2020, accessed November 4, 2020.

died from COVID-19 were male. "The European Centre for Disease Prevention and Control (ECDC) reported that the male-to-female ratio for COVID-19 deaths across the EU was 2:1."[49] The death rate in Great Britain for men was twice that for women. This news of a two-to-one death ratio of men to women might surprise some people. That is a significant difference in death rates. If two women had been dying of COVID-19 for every man dying, then that would have been a recurrent theme on the news and by politicians. Since men are a disfavored category of the politically correct, the high death rate for men did not qualify as news for the media or subject for debate by politicians. That would not be the politically correct thing to do.

Another group that is disfavored by the media and the politically correct are young black men. That is the Chicago Tragedy of scores of young black men dying a violent death in our cities every day to the collective silence of our nation. For the politically correct, the deaths that should and do merit attention are those handful that involve the police shooting an unarmed black citizen or a black citizen dying in the custody of the police. All of which would merit our attention, as it is a confrontation between citizen and the state, which is different from the conflict among these young African American males that claim the lives of young black men as well as innocent bystanders, young and old. Identity politics is not applied in the case of the Chicago Tragedy by the politically correct. Instead, the Chicago Tragedy is conveniently swept under the rug.

It may come as a surprise to the champions of political correctness and identity politics that many of your fellow citizens see you as the most intolerant. You should not take solace in your intolerant political correctness. Your fellow citizens see you for what you are: intolerant! Perhaps some of you don't care as you use political correctness and identity politics as a cudgel against your opponents to amass more power.

9. Have you witnessed the politically correct vilify, condemn, hound, and silence voices and ideas not aligned with their received wisdom and beliefs? There is the tactic of "doxing" someone. In that

---

49   Ibid.

case, personal and private information about a person is published and disseminated, usually on the internet, with the idea that fellow intolerants will harass that individual. They might show up at their place of work to embarrass them or to try to get them fired. Perhaps people demonstrate outside of the person's home or apartment, where their spouse and children also live, to make the life of the entire family uncomfortable. Maybe graffiti is spray-painted at the person's home or place of business. Doxing has nothing to do with promoting discussion and dialogue, but rather intimidation. Congresswoman Maxine Waters went so far in June 2020 to ask people to confront people who were in the Trump administration cabinet in going about their daily lives. "They're not going to be able to go to a restaurant, they're not going to be able to stop at a gas station, they're not going to be able to shop at a department store, the people are going to turn on them, they're going to protest, they're going to absolutely harass them."[50] That is outside the bounds of respectful debate.

Does Representative Waters believe that she knows the truth and that debate should stop? Was she recommending that an administration official who believes in school choice for black, white, Hispanic, Asian, and other children from high-need backgrounds be hounded at a department store? School choice means more public charter schools and vouchers so that children from poor backgrounds can have more than one choice of where to go to school. They thereby have an opportunity to leave the school-to-prison pipeline. But perhaps Representative Waters opposes school choice and eliminating waiting lists for these children to get into public charter schools? Did Representative Waters believe that a cabinet official who believes in and works for not just record low unemployment in our nation in general but also record low unemployment in the African American and Hispanic American communities specifically should be harassed when pumping gas into their car? Should an administration official be molested because they believe and work toward a strong economy that re-employs ex-cons at a much higher rate than previously

---

50   Julia Manchester, "Maxine Waters Calls on People to Confront Trump Officials in Public Spaces," *The Hill*, June 24, 2018, accessed November 4, 2020.

achieved, as opposed to the politicians' catchall phrase that they support *job training*? If you haven't noticed, a real job is worth much more than job training for a nonexistent job. That is what you relegate ex-cons and the least to when you have a weak economy, job training with the mirage of a job on other side. Did Representative Waters encourage the harassment of an administration official who is trying to decriminalize work so that the citizen can exercise his or her civil right to work with their hands and back to put food on their plate without worrying that the state will arrest them for working without a license? Should an administrative official who is trying to lower the cost of living for the poor through fewer regulations and delays for businesses to open and operate so that they can deliver products and job opportunities at a higher rate be targeted? Is a cabinet officer who opposes addicting our children and adolescents on marijuana supposed to be harassed at the dry cleaners? Adolescence goes to age twenty-five, and the adolescent brain does not stop developing until age twenty-five, yet there are many minions for the "new big tobacco" of marijuana to push to get our children addicted despite the science that marijuana is replete with carcinogens and alters the development of a young person's gray matter in the brain while also increasing anxiety, paranoia, suicide attempts, and also sixfold increases in suicide ideation for young women. But following the science on the proven harm of recreational marijuana to our children and young adults twenty-five years old and younger may merit public vilification if the intolerance counseled by Representative Waters were followed. And the list goes on. The efficacy of the War on Poverty as presently waged in our country is not an open-and-shut case. The policies supported by Representative Waters are not necessarily achieving the goals that they were intended to achieve. As such, it is not wrong to discuss or implement policies that may be more effective than the policies of the War on the Family, also known as the War on Poverty. Both sides are trying to arrive at the same end, but by different means.

There is also the "cancel cancer," also known by the more popular expression "cancel culture," where someone is ostracized in their social or professional circles online and in social media. The effort can involve stopping people from listening to their music or enjoying their work, to remove the person's public platform and power.[51] By their trying to boycott this person, they are denying them the attention or customers that he or she needs to earn a living.[52] This cancel cancer has been related to "safetyism" on college campuses, where young students are afraid to say anything that they might be called out for. The student cannot take risks in what is supposed to be a learning environment. Therefore, you do not want to ask questions or express unpopular ideas, for fear of being ostracized for expressing "wrong, oppressive or inappropriate opinions."[53] And you thought that college was supposed to be a learning experience with academic freedom. You would be wrong under the assault of the politically correct. By the same token, our society is under assault by the politically correct to stifle debate and to stifle diversity of opinion. Are you one of those intolerants? Do you give shelter or make excuses for this intolerance? How long until they come for you?

10. Why do intolerants terrorize their opponents? Is it because they fear the competition of ideas and the pursuit of truth versus pursing their political dogma? Young people must cower on and off campus for fear that the internet mob may come for them. Consider the challenges of being an adolescent or young person today. First, there is the whole process of adolescence and growing up. The young person has to become their own person and navigate their way through middle school, high school, and beyond. Those of a much older generation did not have to deal with Facebook pages, Instagram, TikTok, etc. We did not have to say how many followers we got. We did not have to say home many "likes" our internet posts received. We did not have to be concerned with people unfriending us on a social media site. "Why did you unfriend me?" "Oh, you went off social media for a break?" "Okay, I get that." In addition to not being the cool kid in the class or not even having many likes, now

---

[51]   Wikipedia, s.v. "cancel culture," accessed November 4, 2020.
[52]   Ibid.
[53]   Ibid.

young people can be cyberbullied for lack of likes, uncool posts, or even the machinations of someone jealous or competitive with them, launched from anonymous sources. What if the "mean girls" decide to pick on you on the internet? Young people commit suicide from cyberbullying. Now you add to that the intolerance of the intolerants. If a young person makes a "mistake" of posting or reposting the wrong thing, there could be hell to pay as the intolerants heap scorn and derision on this poor soul and mobilize perfect strangers to heap even more bile and invective on this poor young person. When you see a peer cyberbullied, shamed, doxed, or otherwise terrorized by the sanctimonious on the internet, you will think twice about the freedom to say anything or ask anything. It is much safer to keep your head down and conform to the political orthodoxies of the day.

How do you think China is keeping control of her citizens? China is dutifully monitoring the social media accounts, emails, and texts of all her citizens. They do not even have access to websites outside of China, for fear that unapproved ideas or stories counter to the orthodoxy of the Chinese Communist Party might gain visibility. Those who step out of line in China have their accounts swiftly shut down, with the person even receiving cautionary advice of not straying too far from the state's version of reality. It is no different for our young people. If they step out of line, they can be crushed. What adult, let alone a child, is able to withstand bullying and being ostracized by their peers? And it does not stop with our young people, as the politically correct will cyberbully adults and bring flocks of intolerants down on the citizen who has stepped, knowingly or unknowingly, out of the lane prescribed by the politically correct. The intolerance fostered and practiced by Marxists, by their fellow travelers, and by useful idiots on America's campuses has now been exported to the general populace and to life in large corporations today.

The intolerants are in and outside of government. The intolerants do not have to use the apparatus of the government to silence those with whom they disagree; they can go outside of the government and draft willing actors in the private sector, such as professors, teachers, editors, reporters, business chief executive officers, scientists, trade unionists, and environmentalists, to demand that a voice be silenced. There is no need for a bureaucrat to silence the citizen with government tools when they can get other private citizens to do it for them. This is the intolerance of the intolerants. They may not have come for you yet, but it is only a matter of time before they come for you.

The incidences of intolerance at colleges of diverse views and opinions abound. In 2017, Charles Murray, a conservative writer, was accosted while trying to speak at Middlebury College. They forced Mr. Murray and his host and moderator to flee the discussion room and try to seek shelter elsewhere at the college to conduct the talk by video feed. It was all well and good with the administration and president of Middlebury College, in my opinion, that Mr. Murray was manhandled and silenced as he was a white male, but then when the intolerants manhandled Professor Allison Stanger and yanked her hair and neck, which sent her to the hospital and merited a neck brace, then it was not okay, because now a woman had been manhandled. Such is the way and logic of the intolerants. You should not consider yourself immune for when the mob turns on you.

Chapter 7

Humility, Compassion, Forgiveness, and Redemption are Necessary in Addressing Structural Racism as a United Nation and Saving Democracy

11. WHAT WOULD THE opposite of the intolerance of the politically correct look like? What is the antidote to the poison of identity politics and political correctness? How do we get away from doxing, cyberbullying, cancel cancer, safetyism, and voter intimidation? Humility, compassion, and forgiveness are the opposites of the intolerance of the intolerants. The concept of redemption works in concert with humility, compassion, and forgiveness. To engage in a civil dialogue, to maintain our civil institutions, to maintain the love of our neighbors as our brothers and sisters, to allow a civil discourse to try to find the truth, to have a diversity of opinions, to allow a diversity of people to engage in discussion, and to protect our freedoms of speech, press, assembly, religion; to petition the government for redress of grievances; and other rights guaranteed to us under the Declaration of Independence, the Constitution, and the Bill of Rights, we need the counterweight of humility, compassion, forgiveness, and redemption.

To have humility is to recognize that we are all human and as such we are fallible human beings. As fallible human beings, we make mistakes, intentional and unintentional. To hold a person to the standard of perfection is an inhumane standard, as no living being is perfect. There was only one who was perfect. To go into the past or present of a citizen to find fault with an utterance, a photo, or a political position so as to disqualify that individual today from the civic duty of participating in our democracy is unreasonable and unfair. To pretend that no human has stumbled or can stumble is inhumane. It also depends on the view of the person judging their brother or sister. The individual, or the collection of individuals, deputizing themselves as the gatekeepers of who may and may not participate in public discourse is practicing tyranny to terrorize their sisters and brothers into silence. That is not a democratic, but instead dictatorial, impulse of bullies and dictators.

Compassion is a human trait that calls for consideration of the position of other human beings. They may not look like you, they may not come from the same socioeconomic class as you, they may not have the education that you have, and they may not wear the same clothes that you do, but they are human, just like the rest of us. Each individual is entitled to a level of dignity. "But for the grace of God, there go I" is a summation of compassion. Through the good fortune of place, parents, or work, you may be in a better position than other citizens, but that does not mean that they are any less worthy. The other citizen may not have come to the same political position as you, but that does not mean you can harangue and economically ruin them because they do not toe your political orthodoxies. The other citizen has a right to participate, as do you, without fear of economic and social ruin. Those are the tactics of the intolerants.

Forgiveness is not an easy quality to embrace, but it is in our genes as a nation. Many citizens embrace forgiveness, in part because we know that we may seek it somewhere down the road ourselves. We all make mistakes. At some point we will all ask for forgiveness for a slight or injury suffered by another, intended or unintended. If we are not willing to grant forgiveness today, then forgiveness may not be available when the time comes in the future that we need it.

To believe in redemption is to believe in the power of all individuals to follow the right path to a productive life in harmony with their brothers and sisters. Where a convicted criminal must serve out the sentence imposed upon them, once that sentence is served and/or the fine is paid, that citizen is able to rejoin society and go about pursuing the American dream as they see fit. By the same token, if you have determined that someone has said something or did something today or in the past that you disagree with, is it not possible for that individual to have a voice today or to recognize that wrong and move on as an equal member of society? Redemption allows all citizens to participate in our civic life.

Humility, compassion, forgiveness, and redemption are the antithesis for the intolerance of the politically correct, who bring social ostracism and economic harm to those the politically correct have deemed unworthy. They are the prosecutor, judge, jury, and executioner, all dressed up as one. We should adopt humility, compassion, forgiveness, and redemption as the keys to a return to civil society with less political rancor.

Do you have those qualities, or do you find them antiquated?

12. Do you believe in redemption and the rehabilitation of a human being? For example, can a convicted prisoner become a full member of society after serving their term of punishment? If you believe that, will you help this former prisoner re-enter society? Are you willing to accept that your past political choices increased the barriers for him or her to make a living or to put food on their plate? After the killing of George Floyd, will you continue to maintain and build up these barriers, or will you work to eliminate barriers to the ex-con's return to working and participating as a full-fledged citizen? Hopefully, the answer is yes.

13. Do you accept that a human being is imperfect? How could you not if you have reached adulthood? We all make mistakes, and we will continue to make mistakes until we no longer have the daily gift of life. Who counsels ostracizing someone who made a mistake for the rest of their lives? Will you accept and welcome similar treatment of you when you inevitably step outside the ever-changing terrain of political correctness? The purpose of political correctness is not the amelioration of the human condition or to encourage unity; the purpose of political correctness is power and control. We cannot

wear political correctness. We cannot eat political correctness. It will not shelter us from the rain, sun, wind, or cold. Political correctness will not clothe us, nor will it provide us with medical care. Political correctness will not entertain us with the arts, movies, dance, or whatever other pastime you enjoy. No, political correctness is to intimidate you into submission. If you do not go along with political correctness, you will be vilified as racist, sexist, nativist, xenophobic, anti-LGBTQ, etc. There will be no end to the list of terribles that you can be accused of as you are kept in a state of suspended animation, always wondering what the new taboos are and where you should not tread lest you be accused of being less than human. This has been done on our college campuses and has now been expanded beyond to the entire country.

Middlebury College is a great example. In 1980, when Ronald Reagan was elected president, there was not one professor that my fellow, like-minded students thought would have voted for him. The day after the election, the campus was somber and depressed, although it surely did not compare to the hypersensitivity in 2016 when Donald Trump won the presidency, with students excused from attending class if they were grieving or stressed out. For all the Democrat and left professors at Middlebury College in 1980, they saw it as quite nice that everyone thought like they did. It is so much easier when nobody questions your political inclinations and choices. What's a little difference of opinion? By making social and academic life for conservatives and libertarians difficult, they were less likely to even be allowed to teach, let alone express their opinion. These professors, and by extension the administrators, must have marveled at the "monolithic thought" universe that they had created at Middlebury! No professor or administrator would openly support candidate Ronald Reagan! If only everyone thought like me. But now these selfsame professors and administrators are self-censoring their speech and writing, lest they be accused of being any among the list of horribles that were hurled at conservative and libertarian professors then.

Today, there are many mainstream Democrats that are captives within their own party. Speak up for our country and the *rule of law* and risk being called a racist or white supremacist. Maybe a progressive or socialist will be drafted to primary that politician in the next election cycle. It is conjecture, but there are numerous Democrats who do not agree with the anti-American and anti-*rule-of-law* animus of elements within their party but are too afraid to speak up, lest they be pushed out of the party and accused of being a racist. In lower Fairfield County, Connecticut, in a state senate district that included all of Greenwich, a well-to-do town, plus northern Stamford and New Canaan, the Democrat candidate Alex Kasser called the United States "white supremacist" and still narrowly won re-election. That is crazy talk! While our nation had an imperfect beginning in 1776, it is not a white supremacist nation. If it were, why are Hispanics, Asians, Africans, Indians, Pakistanis, Syrians clamoring to get in and pursue the American dream? Because the United States is an exceptional nation of many peoples and the epicenter of democracy, as the *rule of law* was invented here with the Declaration of Independence in 1776, the drafting of the Constitution in 1787, and the protection of our Bill of Rights! Those who trade in the negative version of America as a failed experiment peddle in ignorance of the history of man as they intentionally ignore the significance of the most important advancement in the political history of man, the founding and perseverance of the United States of America, the greatest experiment in democracy the world has ever known!

The politically correct allow no room for imperfection as they move the requirement of "wokeness" regularly to exert control. Do you support their antidemocratic methods intentionally or unintentionally?

It is salient that you recognize that imperfect human beings have value, as do imperfect nations. Both can improve.

14. Why are American universities and colleges now the epicenter of intolerance and political correctness? College is supposed to be a time for learning and being exposed to new ideas, as opposed to political indoctrination. Instead, American universities are increasingly monolithic in their thinking of what is acceptable to be discussed versus the pursuit of the truth. Are you familiar with

the Killing Fields of Cambodia, utilized from 1975 to 1979, when the Marxist Khmer Rouge (*rouge* is "red" in French) systematically killed around two million or more people out of about eight million Cambodians. The academy[54] has purposefully tried to eliminate any accurate reference to the Killing Fields in the education of our youth, just as they fail to teach the basic civics lessons on why the *rule of law*, the Declaration of Independence, the Constitution, and the Bill of Rights are singularly significant in history, not just to the United States, but to the entire world. Before the United States, there was no *rule of law* in any land anywhere in the world where the citizen was sovereign.

During the time the Killing Fields in Cambodia were employed, if you wore glasses, that meant you could read and you might have been exposed to ideas that the Marxist Khmer Rouge did not approve of, which would lead to them killing you. If you spoke a foreign language, such as French, the Khmer Rouge would kill you as you might have been exposed to ideas that the Khmer Rouge did not approve of. Many of these killings were accomplished by putting a plastic bag over the head of the poor soul that they were executing, with their hands and legs tied so that they could not get the bag off, and the victim would then suffocate. Plastic bags were cheaper than bullets for the Khmer Rouge. But our young people, our children, our fellow citizens are not supposed to know of this as it casts a bad light on the allies of the progressives and socialists in our land, since socialism, where the state owns the means of production and the dictatorship of the proletariat is part of the political process espoused by Karl Marx. That dictatorship would rule by the "consciousness of the proletariat." That basically means that selected individuals at the top could divine from their own minds what was best for the country and not actually bother asking the people through fair elections for the consent of the governed.

In a similarly intolerant manner to the tactics of the Khmer Rouge, like-minded teachers, professors, students, and their fellow

---

[54] The *academy* are American colleges and universities, as well as the administrators in our high schools and middle schools, who are responsible for teaching our children.

travelers have used terror to silence students on American campuses who have ideas that these intolerant teachers, professors, and students do not agree with. These same intolerant teachers, professors, and students have also used terror to silence professors that they did not agree with. And again, these intolerant teachers, professors, and students have likewise used terror to silence administrators that they did not agree with. And now this intolerant mob is coming for anyone outside of the academy[55] with whom they do not agree. They have a plastic bag with your name on it. It is only a matter of when they will come for you and not whether they will come for you. Why do you continue to support their intolerance on and off campus? Why should the United States taxpayer give a dime to these intolerants in the nature of tuition and grants? That should stop for any college, university, or other teaching institution that trades in intolerance and does not teach the significance of the *rule of law.* Any private institution that does not ask or receive any public monies can teach whatever they wish, but they cannot ask for money from the public fisc if the college or university practices intolerance.

The academy has gotten so bad that for decades they have tried to bury and ignore the name of Adolf Hitler's political party. It is generally accepted by academicians on the left and right that Adolf Hitler, his Nazi Party, and the murder of more than six million Jews and others during the Holocaust were an evil enterprise. The intolerants, however, don't want our students, you or our brother and sister citizens, to know what political party Adolf Hitler led! Try to find the name in a history book and a discussion of its significance. Adolf Hitler's political party was the National Socialist German Workers' Party. That is correct. It was a socialist workers' party, complete with progressive rates of taxation, with more taxes for the well-to-do and championing of the worker, with annual Workers of the Year awards, complete with worker retreats on the Baltic and in the Alps! But this besmirches the political platforms and exhortations toward more government control of the left. What dishonesty to bury the name of Adolf Hitler's party, the National Socialist German Workers' Party!

---

[55]   Our colleges and universities.

But our country apparently allows it, as we do nothing to correct the record.

15. What should be done about the intolerance taught and enforced by the academy, our colleges and universities? The intolerants who inhabit the academy as professors, administrators, and students fail to exhibit the humane qualities of humility, compassion, forgiveness, or redemption. Surely, it is the right of private institutions to teach what they wish, but a state institution must uphold the Constitution of the United States as well as the constitution of that individual state. Our nation cannot abide by this intolerance. While it may be the right of Yale University to teach and enforce intolerance, we, the citizens, do not have to financially support the intolerance of Yale University. When Yale fails to hire professors, male or female, that do not adhere to the political orthodoxy of the left, that is Yale's right. But when Yale allows other students, professors, and administrators to pursue students, professors, and administrators who diverge from the enforced political orthodoxy of the school, they are intolerant and are not supporting the mission of higher education to explore ideas and ask questions. If Yale wishes to wallow in its narrow view of the world and that they have long since discovered the truth, that is their right. When in 2016 one of Yale's famous graduates, Hillary Clinton, called half of candidate Donald Trump's supporters as "racist, sexist, homophobic, and xenophobic," that just about sums up the lack of tolerance of the academy and the "betters" of our brother and sister citizens. This became known as a "basket of deplorables." What she said was no accident. It was part of a speech at a fundraising event for her run to be president and to lead the United States. She basically used the well-worn tactic of the intolerants on campus to call one-quarter of our nation racist, sexist, homophobic, and xenophobic. While this clearly made her feel good about herself and certainly pleased her crowd, it is a typical example of intolerance. Is that the intolerance that you subscribe to? If yes, will you continue in your intolerance after the killing of George Floyd? You have never met one-quarter of the nation, yet you put yourself above them. This does not help build a better future together.

Therefore, there should be no more government assistance in the form of loans, grants, and subsidies to intolerant institutions within the academy. The standard for intolerance is straightforward. Our comedians are our conscience. They examine the human condition and our relationship with one another insightfully and in honest ways. It is their honesty and our embarrassment at their accuracy that makes us laugh. Sometimes we laugh at our own expense, and sometimes we laugh at someone else's expense. Comedians Dave Chappelle, Kevin Hart, Jerry Seinfeld, Chris Rock, Jim Gaffigan, and Gabriel "Fluffy" Iglesias are our conscience. Their social commentary is spot-on. Please take a moment to look at their audiences. Their audiences are us, and they are willing to laugh at themselves and others, but not in a malicious way.

Consider if the people who attend these comedy shows were asked to conceive and design a government for their brother and sister citizens? As these audience members are willing to laugh at risqué humor at the expense of others that make light of our humanity, the governments that they would design would be eminently more humane, forgiving, and compassionate than a government invented by the professors and administrators of Yale University. These intolerant mobs that have taken over the academy and who are streaming into our everyday life would impose their political correctness and political orthodoxies in an Orwellian[56] nightmare. People would have to believe and utter certain phrases or be shunned. They would have to socialize and work in preconceived ways.

On the other hand, if you had to take the first one hundred people out of the phone book, these would be your brothers, sisters, neighbors, employers, and employees and would represent the man or woman in the street. In designing a government, they would respect the citizen and the citizen's life as well as the fallibility of people. Their design would allow the citizen to live his or her life and to pursue their happiness as the citizen saw fit.

---

[56] Orwellian: "characteristic of the writings of George Orwell, especially with reference to his dystopian account of a future totalitarian state in *Nineteen Eight-Four*" (*Oxford Dictionaries*, accessed November 5, 2020); "doublespeak, propaganda, curfews and petty state control of daily life," *Merriam-Webster*, quoting Clayton Jones.

The faculty of Yale University, with its scolds, would most likely conjure up a politically correct government hell for you and your family. It would be the definition of a totalitarian state, with these professors as the final arbiter of your worth as an individual. Ask a young person a joke today that verges on politically incorrect and you will see a young person terrified of reacting the wrong way! If a young person is called out for saying the wrong thing or laughing at an off-color joke, that young person is at great risk for being canceled by the politically correct mob. The intolerants have shown that they would not be sated by a simple "I'm sorry." No, the intolerant mob of the politically correct would demand much more. Expulsion, financial penalties, and online bullying. And this mob would follow this young person for the rest of his or her life. We need to protect our young people from this intolerant mob, from these bullies, and save our Constitution at the same time. If comedians Dave Chapelle, Kevin Hart, Jerry Seinfeld, Chris Rock, Jim Gaffigan, and Gabriel "Fluffy" Iglesias cannot tell their shtick at a college campus without being harassed and vilified, then that campus is intolerant and should cease to receive any public monies for loans, grants, or subsidies. Only at the point at which the administration of that campus has created a tolerant environment where the conscience of our nation, our comedians, can appear and allow them to do their regular act, and where students, professors, and administrators can discuss the issues of the day, or academics, without fear of recrimination and canceling, can a resumption of loans, grants, or subsidies, be considered for such institutions. If Yale University cannot run a campus tolerant of all people, genders, and views, then they should live off their billion-dollar endowments as can Harvard University. Federal or state subsidization of student loans, student grants, and research grants would go to institutions with a commitment toward the free exchange of ideas and the protection of a diversity of thought on campus.

The forces behind this methodical intolerance at our colleges and universities, and now in our country as a whole, are the college-educated, affluent white elite, their fellow travelers, and useful idiots. In the name of tolerance, they are cleansing our institutions of people who do not share their political views. Their primary tool is intimidation, silencing, and canceling. There is public humiliation. There is public shaming. The unenlightened are fired. They don't even make an exception for our comedians or their audiences. There is little sign that these intolerants will stop until all dissenting voices are vanquished. Yale, Stanford and Harvard Universities have massive endowments and wealthy alumni. All will do just fine without any government loans, grants, or subsidies. These government loans, grants, and subsidies can be used to support institutions among the academy with academic freedom and devoid of cancel cancer.

16. Is it okay to silence someone that you don't agree with? In the past, have you joined in efforts to silence a speaker, or were you silent while the mob silenced a speaker? Are you complicit in this intimidation? Will you stand by in the future if academic and political discussion is silenced by the intolerants? Failure to do so puts your own freedoms at risk for eventual elimination. If you don't allow other opinions and ideas, how long will your ideas be allowed time in the sun? How will we arrive at the truth?

17. Do you hate people who are prejudiced? That might sound like an easy question to answer, but it is a trick question. To say that you hate people who are prejudiced is to say that you don't like yourself, since you have prejudged a prejudiced person before you have even met them. *Prejudice* is defined as "a judgment or opinion formed before the facts are known; preconceived idea, favorable or, more usually, unfavorable" or "a judgment or opinion held in disregard of fact or opinions."[57] As human beings, we are all prejudiced, even if we might say that we are not. We are not supposed to be, but human beings will prejudge other human beings based on their own past experiences and surroundings. This, again, is a reminder to not be so fast to categorize others in your like and dislike columns.

---

[57] *Webster's New World Dictionary of the American Language* (Cleveland: The World Publishing Company, 1964), s.v. "prejudice."

Chapter 8

Statism: The State or the Citizen?
Shall the State or the Citizen
Be Sovereign?

18.   D O YOU BELIEVE in the aggrandizement of the power of the state and the diminution of the power and rights of the citizen? In civics classes in the United States some decades ago, we were taught that in a democracy, the citizen was the highest level of authority and that politicians had to work for the citizen and the government was there for the health, safety, and well-being of the citizens. Fast-forward to today and the government, whether it be federal, state, or local, has taken on more powers for itself and touches ever more parts of our lives. Some citizens recoil at the growth of government, and others see the growth of government as good and as a counterbalance to large business or labor interests. Some see the government as a tool to improve the lives of the citizenry. When the government starts to consume ever more resources in the way of taxes, fees, surcharges, and license fees, that may give pause to one's embrace of the government. Then there are restrictions on when and how big we can build our apartments and houses. There are more regulations on how and when you can open a business or what is required when you have employees. One small fee or regulation on top of another small fee or regulation individually might be palatable, but the cumulative effect of all these small taxes,

fees, regulations, and permitting can make a citizen feel as though they are working for the government as opposed to for their family and themselves.

The people working for the government are referred to as public servants. They are not literally servants, but rather, they are supposed to be there to help the citizen accomplish what the citizen wants to do for a house, business, or recreation. There are others, however, who, like how the government has the power to tax, which is the power to destroy but also the power to regulate and tell businesses and individuals what to do. A *statist* is one who will pick the state over the citizen. That is opposite of what the Declaration of Independence stands for. The Declaration of Independence sets forth that "Governments are instituted among Men, deriving their just Powers from the Consent of the Governed, that whenever any Form of Government becomes destructive of these Ends, it is the Right of the People to alter or to abolish it, and to institute new Government."

An example of the government working for the people is the call for accountability by the police to the general citizenry after the killing of George Floyd. People objected to a person, acting under the authority of state law, choking the air out of Mr. Floyd by placing a knee on Mr. Floyd's neck for more than nine minutes. Yet it is highly likely that your past votes and policy preferences have made accountability for such an act off-limits. Laws that were passed by pro-statist legislatures as well as the collective bargaining agreements enacted under such legislation protect bad officers or bullies in police departments from accountability to the general citizen. Those who escape accountability are the few bad apples that give a bad name to other peace officers in the force. Even the Stamford Police Association, for example, supported "transparency and accountability in policing" after the killing of George Floyd. But will you continue to vest power in the statists, who prevent accountability by the police to the citizen? This comes back to the consent of the governed. The state is to serve the citizen and not the other way around. At any time, did you consider amending the laws that you had approved in the past to prevent accountability? Are you willing to "undo" your past support for binding arbitration of public union contracts that vitiate the responsibility of the people's representative, the legislature, to do right by the citizenry and put it into the hands of unelected officials, in the form of a labor arbitrator? Instead, would you support an elected representative to see to it that the police are given the resources to do their work and, at the same time, ensure that the public can examine and discipline the few officers who abuse citizens? Then you may have to change the politicians that you routinely vote for and step down from your personal soapbox.

19. Do you support "no-knock" warrants, which allow the state to break your door down without knocking while you are sleeping inside your home? Would a judge signing such a warrant be true to our constitutional right against improper searches and seizures by approving a no-knock warrant? The Fifth Amendment to our Constitution assures us that we shall not be deprived of our right to life, liberty, or property without due process of law. This was extended to the states by the Fourteenth Amendment, which was enacted after the Civil War. EMT Breonna Taylor was shot dead during the alleged execution of a no-knock warrant while police were investigating for drug-related crimes in the spring of 2020, and this unfortunate event gained greater attention after the killing of George Floyd. Could the government have achieved the objectives of their search by waiting until the target of the warrant, the boyfriend of Breonna Taylor, left the apartment and then searching him and the apartment? Perhaps no-knock warrants can be greatly reduced? The Louisville, Kentucky, police in the Breonna Taylor case did say that they knocked before going in, but if you are sleeping, you may not hear the announcement that the police is coming in, but you may be stirred by someone breaking down your front door. Ask questions later. Certainly, the judge and the police in that case would have done it differently had they the luxury to do it again, which they don't, as Ms. Taylor was killed.

20. When there is a competition between the citizen and the state and the law is not clear on whether the state or the citizen has the right, who should win, the citizen or the state? Most gambling

casinos have the rule that nobody wins in a tie between the house and the gambler. This makes sense, as the house makes the rules. The house would lose money if the customer won in a tie. In blackjack, the gambler has to go first, and if they go over twenty-one, they lose before the house even has to choose cards. The house wins in the long run. But the relationship between the state and the citizen is not a competition. In fact, the state is supposed to be working for the citizen. Article 1, Section 2 of the Connecticut Constitution states that all free governments are instituted for the benefit of the citizen. That makes sense that the purpose of the revolution was to have the government serve the people and not the other way around. That is to restate the words from the Declaration of Independence that the government derives "their just Powers from the Consent of the Governed."

The citizen did not give the power to the state to win in ties between the citizen and the government, but that has not stopped statists from insisting that the government wins in ties. They use such language as a "statutory scheme," would compel such a result, or "you can't make exceptions for one person, otherwise you would be making exceptions for everyone." "The officer in government who has been charged with carrying out this statutory scheme has interpreted the statute this way, so we must give deference to the department charged with enforcing the statute." This is all garbage. If the statutory language does not on its face favor the government's position, that ends the inquiry and the government loses. "The powers not delegated to the United States by the Constitution, nor prohibited by it to the States, are reserved to the States respectively, or to the people."[58] All this is done to "secure the Blessings of Liberty to ourselves and our Posterity."[59]

Our constitutional government was never designed for the general welfare of the state or that blessings of liberty would be ascribed to the state. The state does not enjoy liberties. The state is supposed to be there first and foremost to uphold the liberties of American

---

[58] Tenth Amendment to the United States Constitution.
[59] Preamble to the United States Constitution.

citizens. The state does have a duty to have a strong military defense against all foreign foes that would seek to subjugate and destroy us. Domestically, the state is supposed to uphold and defend our liberties and not take them. Therefore, the concept that the statists have developed to give the government a win when statutory language is not clear and unequivocally in favor of the government does violence to our constitutional system. At the point in time that there is an ambiguity, the state should lose. When there is a tie between the state and the citizen in the interpretation of the law regarding a criminal statute or to acquire a permit to work or to obtain a license to practice a craft, the citizen should win that tie ten times out of ten. The tie should go to the citizen, for whom the government has been founded. Or do you support the power of the state to win when there is a tie regarding the rights and liberties of the citizen? If you supported the state in the past, would you still support that today in judges who favor the state over the citizen?

You may have professed concern over the killing of George Floyd and have vowed to rectify "structural racism" as a consequence; will you turn a new page that, when it comes to a conflict or competition between the state, you will support the citizen? The issues of transparency and accountability are directly related to the ability of the city of Milwaukee to examine what happened on May 25, 2020, to George Floyd and whether changes need to be made. The due process rights of anyone charged with a crime must be honored under the Fifth and Fourteenth Amendments, and all citizens are innocent until proven guilty in a court of law as opposed to the verdict of the mob.

If you have vowed to make changes as a white person to make the system fairer, are you willing to reduce the power of the state and the power of the public servants in the state to avoid transparency and to avoid accountability? Or is that a bridge too far? Are you willing to undo parts of collective bargaining agreements that hinder transparency and accountability? If you are not willing to enable transparency and accountability, then say so now and we can end the discussion at the same time that you step down from your soapbox.

21. Would we be better off if the state adhered to our Constitution, the Bill of Rights (the first ten amendments), and the subsequent seventeen amendments? That is what the NAACP has stated it is trying to accomplish, to live the Constitution. They wish to see all the rights and privileges set forth in the Declaration of Independent and in the Constitution and Bill of Rights be real for all American citizens. The concept of America is that all citizens, black, brown, yellow, or white, be vested with every right that inheres in American citizenship. Our schools may or may not teach the significance of the Constitution to world history generally, but to Americans specifically, the Constitution and the Bill of Rights of the first ten amendments are a human endeavor long in the making. It had been in the making as soon as women and men stood on this earth. Early on, people were not postulating, "I think, therefore I am," or other such lines of thought. It was survival. The only sure thing in life was hunger, and disease, war, and death. You had to make the best of your short time on earth, maybe twenty-five to thirty years if you made it out of infancy without dying. Who had the luxury to think about man or woman as a citizen?

To be a citizen is to be "a member a state or nation, especially one with a republican form of government, who owes allegiance to it by birth or naturalization and is entitled to full civil rights: as, this British subject is now an American citizen."[60]

Who had the time to think that a lowly human being, pressed into service for his town, region, or tribe to provide for and defend its people, could actually have a claim to something called rights? It was not in the interest of kings, queens, khans, tribal leaders or, headmen or headwomen to let their subjects think that they had much say in anything. You do what the leader says. The Greeks and Romans were critical to developing the thinking and laws that would lead to the development of the *rule of law*, first in the United States in 1776, and then elsewhere in the world thereafter. Nonetheless, you can go back to the Code of Hammurabi all the way back to 1754

---

[60]   *Webster's New World Dictionary*, college ed. (Cleveland: The World Publishing Company, 1964), s.v. "citizen."

BC to where present-day Iraq is. It is said that the Babylonian king Hammurabi had 251 laws written out that even included a presumption of innocence for the citizen and that the accused could even give evidence in his or her trial. This was not the only code from the area or the time. Some of the Code of Hammurabi was found chiseled into a large stone. This stone is now at the Louvre Museum in Paris, France. While the Chinese civilization had existed for thousands of years, the *rule of law* did not develop there. The creation of a *rule-of-law* nation is an extraordinary event, even if the academy prefers not to teach about it but rather focus on the perceived injustices of the most incredible nation that was ever created on the face of the Earth, without which the darker impulses of man would run amok in the guise of dictatorships of the proletariat, such as China, North Korea, and Cuba, or authoritarian countries, such as Russia, Iran, and Saudi Arabia. The coterie of *rule-of-law* nations around the world would be hard-pressed to promote the liberal democratic model in the face of these authoritarian and totalitarian regimes in the absence of the power and moral authority of the United States.

That is why our Constitution is important not just in creating a better society in America but also to the political health of the world. It is only fitting and proper that the citizenry exercise their right to petition the government for redress of grievances, that transparency and accountability be respected. But if the statists continue to hold sway in your state or town and you continue to vote statists into office, then there will be plenty of talk of transparency and accountability, but no transparency and accountability will actually occur. That is your choice. The lessons and laws of the Constitution are so important. If we were in a constitutional balance where the state worked for the citizen, the issues of transparency and accountability would not even come up because the laws and regulations would have been set up to serve the citizen and not to favor the friends of the statists to shield public employees from the public's eyes and accountability to the public. But it is out of balance. What will you do to rebalance our system to adhere to our Constitution?

This is not limited to just looking at the relationship between our police and the society, but it goes into the relationship between the state and the citizen. The right to work and the right to earn your living with your hands and back should be unfettered from interference by the state. It will be argued below that beyond some licensed professions such as those of plumbers, electricians, and heating contractors, there are numerous professions that require a license that shouldn't, but if they do, the fee to acquire the license should be miniscule. The citizen should not have to ask the state for permission to exercise the fundamental civil right to earn a living. We do not ask a citizen to have a license to exercise their freedom of speech, press, assembly, or religion. The state should be very circumspect when demanding fees and licensing for a citizen to earn their bread. We must work to eat. We must drink water, eat food, and breathe air to live. To interfere in the right to work is to interfere with a civil right. Yet we have enacted laws and elect politicians to restrict our right to earn our living again and again. Will you continue to support such policies? Does it matter to you that blacks have about one-eighth of the net worth of whites in America (see Appendix C: Table 2. "Family median and mean net worth, by selected characteristics of families, 2016 and 2019 surveys")?[61] A lower average age only explains a small part of that shocking chasm. By requiring these fees and, in some cases, unnecessary licenses, you make it harder for people who have less money to participate and to earn their daily bread. Will you continue to unnecessarily burden all workers? The state must stand aside and allow the citizen to exercise his or her rights under the Constitution.

22. If we are to resurrect our civil rights, do you believe in the rights to speech, press, assembly, religion, bear arms, be free from arbitrary searches and seizures, and the due process of law and property rights?

---

[61]   Board of Governors of the Federal Reserve System, "Changes in U.S. Family Finances from 2016–2019: Evidence from the Survey of Consumer Finances," Vol. 106, No. 5, September 2020, Table 2. Family median and mean net worth, by selected characteristics of families, 2016 and 2019 surveys, p. 11.

23. Is the right to your own life a civil right? This right is usually not listed under constitutional rights but is a basic civil right, without which you cannot exercise any other. The *rule of law*, whereby the citizen is sovereign and not a king, queen, czar, khan, or dictator, is what gives value to the citizen's life. If it were a *rule-of-man* government, then the citizens' desires and rights are secondary to those of the leader of the *rule-of-man* government. The glory of the leaders is more important that the simple citizen. If a king, queen, khan, dictator, or tribal leader orders the death of a citizen, who can stop it? By definition, without the *rule of law* to protect the sovereign, who is the citizen, the king, queen, or dictator can do whatever they want, to whomever they want. There is no check or balance to stop the leader.

If you cannot enforce or protect your rights, you have no rights. In China, for example, the state can decide to charge, try, and execute a citizen in one month's time. Nobody can defend you against the state there. And without the right to your own life, there are no civil rights in China. Civil rights lawyers in China are routinely harassed by the government and even imprisoned. The killing of George Floyd with Officer Chauvin holding his knee of Mr. Floyd's neck for nine minutes, forty-six seconds in Minneapolis on May 25, 2020, brought about nationwide and worldwide protests. The killing of Breonna Taylor, which was not recorded on video, has also elicited greater attention to the taking of a citizen's life, and in this case a black citizen's life, a violation of the most basic civil right, the right to your own life. Will it make you question your assumptions about the relationship between the state and the citizen?

Chapter 9

The Civil Right to Earn a Living, Denied by Our Politicians and Judges

24. THE TERM *STRUCTURAL racism* received frequent mention in protests, in newspapers, on television, and on social media platforms, but there is no generally agreed definition of what *structural racism* is. It is argued here that structural racism overlaps greatly with structural statism, which are the obstacles that the statists put in the way of the citizen to go to school, live in a house or apartment, get and hold a job, work, pay for necessities, etc. It is the hurdles, burdens, and barriers that the state puts in your way for you to earn your keep, put a roof over your family's head, and pursue happiness as you see fit. If you support a proactive, strong government, chances are, you have fortified structural statism/racism to make it more difficult for your fellow citizens in general, and blacks in particular, to earn his or her living. The significant uptick in wages and earnings for the lowest quintile of workers during the Trump administration only started to happen with lower rates of unemployment at about 3.5 percent and a fifty-year record low on unemployment for blacks and Hispanics. Increased regulation and taxation does not bring the country to 3.5 percent unemployment; a strong economy does. Is it more important to increase taxes and regulations or to get to even lower levels of unemployment through a strong economy for all our citizens?

25. If you want to help the African American community, why do you criminalize work? Perhaps that is news to you. Will you continue to favor criminalizing work?

26. Why do you make an African American, white, Hispanic, Asian American, or other citizen apply and pay for a license to work with their hands and back just to earn a living? Many states require some sort of home improvement license for one to work at someone's home. These statutes are put in place with good intentions, but that is the temptation with laws, that you think you can do better by your citizens and make a better society by passing more laws. That is a fallacy. Every law that we pass takes one more power away from the citizen. Clearly, we do not want a citizen to be a reckless driver, and we wish to curb that with laws, or that somebody be a public nuisance by polluting our community. But when we restrict times of business, minimum requirements to practice a trade or profession, licensing requirements to conduct a business, or permitting to build or improve something, we are interfering with the desire of a citizen to improve themselves or their community. This does not mean the citizen or business should be allowed to do whatever they want, but rather to be cognizant of the dampening effect of each and every rule and regulation. If one were to stack the statutes of your state in 1960 against those in 2020, on a pile next to each other, the 2020 stack would clearly exceed the other. We had cars, houses, planes, trains, roads, schools, sports teams, civic organizations then just as we do today. Clearly, we have become more knowledgeable in protecting our environment and making our buildings less vulnerable to fire, but for all these rules and regulations, how much better is our life today that in 1960?

The increased standard of living of citizens in their income, the size of their homes and apartments, the rate and number of car ownership, the amount of clothes and variety of food consumed, the prevalence of dining out and ordering in are significantly more today. The quality of our medical care has consistently improved, along with our life expectancy, through better housing, nutrition, and medicine. The frequency and the comfort of our vacations are greater.

The vast majority of the improvements in our quality of life has been achieved not by local, state, and federal governments passing laws but rather by the private economy producing more for our citizens. Certainly, having good roads, railroads, buses, and airports contributes to our productivity, but productivity is something the economy does. Research and development supported by the government and technologies that came from our program to land on the moon and explore space were expenditures of money. These programs were not about expanding the size of our statute books but, rather, expanding the size of our knowledge.

Look at education, where we spent twice as many inflation-adjusted dollars on K–12 education in 2020 as we did in 1960, but we are not getting twice as much education for the public dollar! Are our students twice as well prepared in English, math, and other subjects today as they were in 1960, when they graduated from high school? Or barely staying even? Our increased prosperity can be represented by air-conditioning in a house or place of business, which went from being a luxury to a necessity. It has certainly made living in Southern states and in the Southwest more manageable, if a respite from high temperatures can be found in an air-conditioned home. This the economy made possible. In our automobiles, we now have air-conditioning, electric windows, door locks, cruise control, and electric seats almost as standard features when they would have been a luxury in 1960. Adding to the thickness of our statutes books does not increase our economy and our prosperity which goes with it, both of which are relevant to the quality of life for the least among us! A rising tide raises all boats! When an economy is sluggish, the poor have the most difficult time to make ends meet.

The state of Connecticut, for example, has one of the five poorest fiscal health conditions of the fifty states, yet the politicians in both the Republican and Democratic Parties will fill your mailboxes with fliers and send you emails to tout the many bills that they have passed or proposed at the statehouse, thereby reducing our freedom every year by a few more laws, but nothing has happened to appreciably change the state's slower economy and ailing finances. Are you still supporting politicians who wish to increase the size of our statute books without increasing our economy for the benefit of the poor, who are disproportionately from impoverished communities? Will all those rules that you would like to impose diminish structural statism or exacerbate it? If the past is any indication, more statutes will increase structural statism, which disproportionately makes life harder for blacks specifically and for all of us generally. That is structural racism. Are you happy now?

27. When you list off the freedoms in our federal Constitution, you can probably list the salient freedoms of speech, press, assembly, religion, the right to bear arms, a fair trial, not having to give evidence against yourself, the presumption of innocence, and the right to petition the government for redress of grievances. The Declaration of Independence says, "All Men are created equal, that they are endowed by their Creator with certain unalienable Rights, that among these are Life, Liberty, and the Pursuit of Happiness."[62] As we try to live these words, who would contest that the right to feed yourself and your family by working with your hands and back is a civil right? Is that not among the most basic right of any man or woman? How can you enjoy or pursue any of your other human rights if the state prevents you from earning your bread, or if you try to earn your bread, the state arrests you?

It is a basic right to struggle to feed and clothe your children, yet why do you support politicians who fetter that right with ever more licensing requirements and certifications? The requirement of the state to get some licenses is an infringement on that civil right. Consider that the Home Improvement Contractor Act in Connecticut requires a person to have a home improvement license to work on another person's home. This could be as simple as mowing the lawn or painting a fence. Failure to have such a license can be grounds for the state to arrest you, although that is rarely ever resorted to. This work should be decriminalized. We do not require a license to speak, exercise our religion, or assemble to meet with like-minded people. Nor is there a fee to petition the government for

---

[62]   United States Declaration of Independence, 1776.

redress of grievances. Licensing could be eliminated in some trades, and the requirements for obtaining a license in other trades could be reduced to balance the inalienable right to earn your living against the state's legitimate interest in public health and safety. It is understandable that an electrician and plumber needs a license, as well as an attorney and doctor, but the requirements for those licenses could be examined to see whether all of them are required in the main or whether it has been carefully crafted to require only the minimum. For example, to become an attorney generally requires three years of law school, whereafter the student customarily takes a state bar exam and a national bar exam from a private testing company. If you can pass the two exams and your background check on your character passes, then the citizen can become an attorney. The requirement of three years of law school is not relevant to passing the bar exams, nor to the quality of your character. Two years of law school can prepare a student for both the state and national bar exams and will sufficiently train the student in ethics. That would eliminate one-third of the tuition, board, and lost time for law students to pursue a trade or profession to put food on their plate. The third year of law school is to help law schools have more students paying them tuition. It also limits the number of newly minted attorneys and the competition for work among existing attorneys. This simple change can open the practice of law to more citizens who could not otherwise afford the time and effort of three years' worth of classes, which can take much longer if you are working full-time and going to law school at night. One less year of classes could make the difference.

Doctors also need to be well trained, but are their residency requirements strictly related to what it takes to be a doctor? After grinding out four years of undergraduate work and then going to medical school for four years, doctors then have to do a residency at a hospital, with a doctor, or with a medical organization to learn what it means to practice medicine. After having taken on the significant financial burden of tuition for undergraduate and graduate work, doctors must then do a residency based on what specialty the doctor would like to pursue. That can mean very long hours with moderate pay. Primary care physicians like family doctors can be the shortest at three years, while surgical residency for something like brain surgery would be among the longest at about six years.[63] When it comes time for you to have your brain operated on, you will probably favor the one with many years of training. Then there is the consideration that the younger doctors may be trained on the newest methods or research. These are all choices between the physician and patient. At the same time, however, the interest of the profession to limit competition and for large hospitals to help their bottom line with hardworking, newly minted doctors for long hours with modest pay might introduce interests that wish to require residencies that are longer than necessary. The hospital's financial well-being might be based on this residency model. But is it what the Constitution requires for those seeking to become a doctor? If it exceeds the minimum, then it violates our Constitution. Determining what that minimum is is the discussion that the citizenry should have before adding ever more requirements. How does one address a dearth of doctors serving rural areas or staffing at public hospitals in urban areas with many high-need patients? Does the lessening of minimums for licensing help open the profession to more doctors, and does it help rural and urban hospitals serve their patients?

Doctors, lawyers, electricians, plumbers, heating contractors—those are professions that need licensing. Too many things could go wrong if the practitioners don't meet specific minimums. What those minimums are should be up for discussion to see whether people with fewer resources are able to enter those trades or professions. What is not so difficult is to consider the absurdity of licenses for a painter, landscaper, roofer, shingler, or carpenter. That is but a sampling of trades that should be without licenses. Nobody is happy if they get a bad painter or carpenter. That is why there have been things like the Better Business Bureau. Only people with good recommendations and a good record could be a member. That might have been an easier way to check on someone's qualifications. The best reference is from someone you know that used him or her. That

---

63 "Medical Residency Timeline & Length (2020–2021)," MedEdits.com, accessed November 9, 2020.

is why word-of-mouth recommendations are so important in the business world. It becomes a personal recommendation by someone you know socially or at work. Some states, like Connecticut, have a Home Improvement Contractor Act. The idea is that anybody who works on someone's home must be licensed, and in 2020, the state of Connecticut was charging $220 for the privilege of being a home improvement contractor. That does not sound like a lot to many, but it is a fee on exercising a constitutional right. Blacks have one-eighth of the net worth of whites in the United States. Some might call this $220 fee structural racism, but instead, it is structural statism, as the statists make it more difficult for all citizens to pursue the American dream, regardless of color. Why should a citizen have to have a license just to move plants at someone's house or to install and/or paint a fence for them?

There is a second element to the statutory scheme in Connecticut, and it's that if you use a registered home improvement contractor and they do a bad job and the contractor does not come back to make the job right, the state has a Guaranty Fund to help pay the homeowner some of the money back. This is all nice and well, but this should run voluntarily. If a contractor wants to be in the state program, he or she can pay into that program and be a licensed home improvement contractor, which would come with a backup with the money in the fund. But if the citizen does not want to be part of this list of licensed home improvement contractors, it is the constitutional right of the citizen to opt out and work without such designation. It is incumbent on the citizen to check references of someone they are seeking to hire and to be careful in the rate at which they pay out money to contractors before the work is complete. The problem that a citizen has with a person who works on their home should not infringe on the constitutional right of his or her fellow citizens to work with their hands and back to put food on their plate. Any statutory promise by the statists that fraud and poor workmanship would be eliminated is a mirage. With or without the licensing, there will be good work and bad work this year and next year. The concepts of fraud and poor workmanship are not eliminated by the stroke of a pen. We continue to be human beings, and we will continue to be imperfect. That cannot be removed by legislation. Efforts to make life risk-free are a mirage or require so many rules and enforcement mechanisms that our economy and our rights suffer.

28. Why is it that statists have few qualms about layering up requirements that a person must satisfy before he or she can work to earn their living? Consider the absurdity in Connecticut that a person who wants to be a hairstylist or barber must pay for and attend one thousand hours of barber school! That is half a year of classes! And the citizen must pay for those one thousand hours of class and training! When black Americans have one-eighth the assets of white Americans, it is structurally harder for blacks to afford to pay for and attend six months of classes, and yet the state requires it. Licensing requirements should be stripped down to their bare minimum so as not to interfere with a citizen's civil right to earn a living. A barber's/hairstylist's class could be reduced to one week to emphasize hygiene of hands, breath, and equipment. It is between the barber/hairstylist and the customer to decide what a quality haircut is.

Who is to say that one thousand hours of classes would make a person a good hairstylist/barber? Some have better hand-eye coordination than others. Some do not require as much training. Some may be good right off the bat and only need a few hours of training. But with the precision of a shotgun, everybody is required to do one thousand hours, with the full support of the barber/hairstylist schools. This one-thousand-hour requirement is "the goose that laid the golden egg" for the training schools. Existing barbers and hairstylists are probably satisfied with the hours required to become a barber/hairstylist, as it limits competition. And they had to do it, or more. Basically, if anyone can become a hairstylist/barber after a week of school, there could be an explosion of hairstylists/barbers, and that would likely force the price of a haircut down. It has been written that the cost to cut a woman's hair is more than the cost to cut a man's hair. If there were a plethora of hairstylists, then it is likely that these prices would go down. If the cost of a haircut or hairstyle goes down, there are likely to be more people who would get a haircut or hairstyle. Overall, more money might be spent on haircuts and hairstyles. That means more business for the state. It is not for society to favor one group over another but rather to create equality of opportunity. Structural statism, however, makes it more difficult for all citizens.

The entire Home Improvement Contractor Act should be turned from compulsory to voluntary overnight. If a consumer wants to hire only a person or company in a database in Hartford or in your state capital and to potentially participate in a fund that helps to compensate for lousy work by registered home improvement contractors, then let the consumer choose that option. But there is no reason to interfere with a citizen's right to work. No citizen should need a license to cut your grass, paint your house, fix your screen door, or clean out your garage.

This change from a compulsory to a voluntary Home Improvement Contractor Act would decriminalize work. This would make it more likely that a person from a poorer background would consider learning the trades without risk of arrest or higher monetary barriers for working with their hands and backs. You can try it without risk of penalties or paying a fee to the state and filling out paperwork. The consumer would get more available labor to choose from. One of the shortcomings in the construction trades at present is a shortage of workers. While we need to increase the quantity and quality of our housing stock and to improve the efficiencies of the heating, insulation, and air-conditioning in our homes, we need workers to do that. Some green advocates for the environment talk about hiring scores of workers to "weatherize" our homes to make them more energy efficient. One can discuss the merits of subsidizing such work, but at the end of the day, you need workers to do that. You cannot just one day say that society will make its homes more efficient without enough tradespeople who can actually do the work. To draft people with little experience in the hand-eye coordination of manual labor in the construction trades and expect them to do good work is a recipe for disaster. The public would not get value for their dollar. Politicians would again claim that they are doing well for society while they burn yet more of the public's dollars.

Trades are an honorable and timeworn method to put food on the plate. Be careful in your political choices that you do not burden this right.

29. Why do you fetter the right to earn a living with excess rules, regulations, permit fees, licensing fees, and educational requirements? How many special interests are you trying to placate and feed versus the interest of the general citizen? In the previous numbered paragraph, the countervailing interests to the right of the citizen to earn their living with their hands and back were touched upon. There are people plying these trades today who would rather see less than more competition. There are the law schools, medical schools, barber/beautician schools that want more students and for a longer period of study, to increase the tuitions paid to help their school's bottom line. There are hospitals and medical insurers who rely on the cheap labor of newly minted doctors who need depressed wages, for interns to make their numbers work. How is the citizen gaining through more state control? Conceivably, those citizens with greater resources are willing to burden the rest of society with higher costs so that the former can lead a neater, more predictable life. The doctors, lawyers, barbers, home improvement contractors will have received greater training. They will all be on lists maintained by the government. Those not on the government lists may not legally participate in the economy governed by those lists. Now, the citizen who supports more requirements won't have to do his or her due diligence in getting a carpenter, because the person they choose has passed the requirements of the state, which implies competence. Life is not as neat as that, and in trying to make life neat and with impeccable paperwork, it becomes more difficult, and thereby more expensive, for the average citizen to pursue a profession licensed by the state. Will you continue to support that construct, or are you willing to entertain rolling back some of the requirements?

30. While you consider your allegiance to the regulatory state, why do you make it harder for African Americans to travel the well-worn path to owning machinery, equipment, commercial real estate,

licenses, leases, and businesses? Many of the Hispanic Americans who have immigrated to the United States over the past few decades are traveling a well-worn path to economic independence: the free enterprise system. Some of these immigrants are starting their own businesses, from food preparation to automobile repair to landscaping, to make ends meet. First, it starts with purchasing a lawn mower or ladder, then a blower, perhaps a trailer for a portable food stand, then edgers and chain saws, and perhaps a truck. As the business continues to meet the requirements of customers, next a place to keep all these things or trailers is needed, so the person rents some storage yard or shares commercial space with another business to defray the costs. First, it is a corner of the property. They are not the main tenants, as they may not even have sufficient creditworthiness for a landlord to consider them lease-worthy. With the increased equipment, storage, and vehicles, the businessperson's business is able to serve its customers reliably and seek out more. Perhaps they add some more full-time and part-time employees. That allows for taking on even more business. After all, the owner only has seven days in the week to work, and twenty-four hours in the day, and they are using that to the maximum that their health will allow. If an eighth day could be added, these businesspeople would surely accept it as either an opportunity to get more work done or to finally get some rest. After years of burning the candle at both ends and paying rent for some space, this small business has a record of paying their share of the rent, so an owner of a small neglected lot or building may be willing to rent to this businessperson. Now, he or she has his or her own place to store their equipment or vehicles at, or maybe it is used to prep or perform work for the customer, like a car repair shop. After some more years of their constantly going to work, adding some more equipment or employees to the business, and paying the rent on time, a bank sees the record of timely payments and offers to extend a mortgage for the person to buy that piece of commercial real estate or one at a different location. A mortgage is granted, and more equipment and business are added. All the while, employment opportunities for others in the same community are created, and these employees also start to learn trades. After twenty-five or thirty years, the businessperson starts to think about retirement, and it can be that this erstwhile employee has now paid off the mortgage on the commercial property or two that they own. This commercial property could be sold as a nest egg for that person's retirement, or perhaps the owner rents it out and uses the rental income to support their retirement. This businessperson and his or her family will not be looking solely to their social security or 401(k) retirement fund for their retirement.

This is a step-by-step process of building wealth and independence. It is called economic independence through long hours and low pay. The reason it is low pay is that the entrepreneur reinvests their earnings into better and more equipment. Or perhaps into more employees? This means that the entrepreneur skips vacations and time off but is trying to build a better life for him- or herself and for their children. They are trying to build a legacy. Statists, on the other hand, set up structural barriers for citizens to learn a trade for every dollar more that they require in fees and in licensing requirements. The barriers should be lowered for all.

Consider that the average plumber earns as much as the average attorney, yet an attorney must complete the equivalent of four years of undergraduate college and then three years of law school. The plumber can go to a trade school at night but does not need seven years of college education to end up in the same place. As previously mentioned, law school could be reduced to two years, as law students are more than qualified to pass the bar exam after two years of law school. Right there is a 33 percent reduction in the cost of going to law school. And that represents not just one year of tuition but one year of your life as well. Why don't the statists allow it? Could it be that the special interests that benefit from extra law school get statists to keep the requirement there through donations? In the end, the statists pump more money out of those who want a law degree and to set them further into student debt, which further delays their purchase of their first condominium or house, as well as delay family formation. Although the amelioration of the social contract is the stated goal of statists, their primary goal is power—the power to tell people what to do, what business can or cannot be conducted, who can provide services to the citizens, and who will or will not receive a permit or license to build something or to earn their living. The citizens need to understand that to succeed, the citizen must lie prostrate before the administrative state, its minions, and their betters, who direct the administrative state.

31. What about where you work or the business that you run? Do you unnecessarily add other requirements and degree requirements to jobs that do not require them? While you are doing a stellar job in your position, you did not necessarily have the educational requirements and work experience for your job that it now demands. It is unfair to require higher education and work experience for a job than is actually necessary. This disproportionately affects African Americans, who generally have fewer economic resources to pursue educational degrees than the average American. By requiring a degree for a job that does not absolutely require it, you are adding to structural statism by disproportionately reducing available job opportunities for blacks and others from economically disadvantaged communities. Some might call this structural racism, but it is indecipherable from structural statism when practiced by the state.

While statists have already attempted to eliminate the first rung on the ladder of success by creating structural barriers to get your foot on that first rung, you cannot expect someone to already be on rung 3 when you have made it structurally more difficult to even get to rung 1. And that poor citizen, who is disproportionately black, may finally reach that first rung at a later age in life because of the barriers that you have placed in his or her way with educational or job experience prerequisites.

Chapter 10

The Denial of School Choice to High-Needs African Americans and Other Students

32. WHY DO YOU deny school choice to African Americans, Hispanics, whites, Asian Americans, and other students from high-need communities by insisting their children stay in schools run by public unions, even if these communities want different choices? Children and young people from economically challenged communities should have the ability to choose from more than just one educational option, the local public school, but those choices are severely limited in a state like Connecticut, for example. The two largest teachers' unions, the National Education Association and the American Federation of Teachers, have banded together and are working diligently and strategically against public charter schools and vouchers for children from high-need communities. They have even quixotically drafted the national leadership of the National Association for the Advancement of Colored People (NAACP) for a moratorium on the expansion of more public charter schools for children from high-need communities, who tend to be disproportionately black. That is the power of the statists!

Some of the arguments manufactured against public charters in the last decade are related to economic self-dealing by some charters themselves or that the public charter schools cherry-pick the best students. The idea of cherry-picking your students is fallacious, as some charter schools are picked by lottery. It is hard to cherry-pick when you are picking names out of a hat. The charge of economic self-dealing is a nonstarter if local parents and guardians still want to send their children to the local public charter school, since the parents and guardians are choosing what they believe to be in the best interest of their children. That is where the inquiry should end, as nobody knows their children better than their parents or guardians. It is not for our betters, the statists, you, or me to deny the choice of the parents and guardians for a public charter.

33. In Connecticut, about 9,000–10,000 students, primarily African American and Hispanic, attend public charter schools, which represent around 2 percent of the K–12 Connecticut student body. Another 7,000 primarily African American and Hispanic students have been on waiting lists for public charter schools because public unions and their political allies, whom you steadfastly support, stand like George Wallace in the schoolhouse door and say that African American, white, Hispanic, Asian, and other children from high-need communities may not enter a public charter school as they work diligently against the expansion of charter school seats. Connecticut has 1,332 public schools, with 523,363 students, by comparison. Having 24 public charter schools is a pittance compared to 1,332 public schools! Are you like our betters, who think they are so smart and clairvoyant as to deny these parents and guardians their choice? The statists don't know these children like their parents and guardians do. Would you make a different choice for your own children if you were offered the choice of a public charter school or vouchers for a private school versus a local public school that was consistently failing the math and English standardized tests of your state? Will you continue to deny these children school choice in the aftermath of the killing of George Floyd?

The answer is very simple. The National Education Association and the American Federation of Teachers, the two largest unions for our public school teachers, rely on union dues to live and to promote the agenda of their members and of the NEA and AFT themselves.

These are priorities 1 and 2 for the NEA and AFT by law. Children only come in third, after the first two priorities, where children should come in first. The NEA and AFT are allied with statists, who want to expand the scope and footprint of things run by the state. Yes, a public charter school is a "state" school, but they are usually not under the heel of the AFT, NEA, or their affiliates. Connecticut public charter schools, for example, tend to be run differently than our local public school and are usually not unionized, although there are some unionized public charters schools as well. When a student goes to a public charter school, the funding generally follows the student. If, for example, 20 percent of the parents of children in a local public school opted to send their children to public charter schools in their community, then it is possible that the local public school could see a reduction in the number of teachers needed in the school that the students left and a commensurate contraction of the number of dues-paying members of the NEA and AFT. This diminishes their ability to fund and support politicians who vote against school choice for high-need students in the African American, Hispanic, white, Asian, and other communities.

Will you continue to be in that number of those who oppose school choice for children of high-need communities? Why is it that some of the finest public schools with the highest scores in New York State and Connecticut are public charter schools? Because they work. Will the press continue to favor the status quo ante and militate against school choice? Will the press continue to cancel the performance of public charter schools by not writing about it?

As an example, Connecticut gave $11,250 per year per public charter school student in 2019, while per student expenditures in public schools, urban, suburban, or rural, approached $16,000 or more. The per-student amount had been increased from $11,000. Purposefully keeping the funding of public charters schools at $11,250, which is at least $4,000 below what it costs cities in Connecticut to educate a student, is purposefully defunding public charter schools that serve primarily African American and Hispanic American students in Connecticut. Teachers, supplies, janitors, heat and building maintenance continue to go up each year, but the funding by the state does not. Would you support the defunding of these public charter schools that serve primarily students from high-need communities? If not, then why do you elect politicians who vote against the expansion and increased funding of public charter schools year in and year out? Why do you support defunding public charter schools that serve primarily African American students?

34. Supreme Court justice Sonia Sotomayor is a hearty proponent of the Blessed Sacrament School in the Bronx, from kindergarten through eighth grade.[64] This was close to the Bronxdale Houses public housing complex, where she lived. The Blessed Sacrament School was a Catholic private school. According to writer Greg Kandra, for people who were a member of the Blessed Sacrament Parish, the annual tuition was $2,900 at that time. After Blessed Sacrament, Justice Sotomayor continued on with her education to receive her undergraduate degree at Princeton University and her law degree at Yale University. This is not the everyday person's trajectory, but vouchers can give poor students options that they would not otherwise have, and it is cheaper than paying for that student in a regular public school. Vouchers do not typically cover a student's entire tuition at a religious or private school; rather, they make it more affordable. A religious school might give a scholarship to a student, and the student's family might contribute the balance of the tuition. Anything to get the young person a little better chance. So why oppose it? Why not allow a student to opt out of the school-to-prison pipeline?

If you want to pursue a different course after the killing of George Floyd, do you still oppose vouchers for poor black, Hispanic, white, Asian, and other students to help with the tuition of private secular schools and religious schools, such as a local Catholic school? It is invigorating for Justice Sotomayor to have traveled to the top of the legal profession from public housing to being a justice on the United States Supreme Court. The opportunity for a child to go to something other than the local neighborhood school should be avail-

---

[64] Greg Kandra, "Roots: Visiting Sotomayor's Catholic Grade School," Beliefnet.

able to children from high-need communities. Vouchers would be based on the financial resources, or lack thereof, of the parents or guardians. Well-to-do parents are able to afford more options for their children ranging from their local public school to private day schools or boarding schools. Although public schools in high-need communities might have some commercial real estate in their property base to help pay for their schools, the rest of the tax roll is usually significantly less than in better-off communities. State governments will channel money from affluent and not-so-affluent communities back into high-need communities through taxation. Nonetheless, fewer parents and guardians in high-need communities have the financial wherewithal to send their children to something other than the local public school. For that reason, vouchers can help bridge the gap. A $6,000 voucher per year is not going to cover the full cost of a year at a Catholic, Protestant, or other religious school or at a private school but would be used in conjunction with money from the parents and guardians or other family members and possible grants or tuition aid from the private school itself to enable their child to attend. Yet this educational choice troubles some people because a private school could be a religious school, like the one Justice Sotomayor attended.

35. Of those opposed to school choice, some are bigots who dislike anything having to do with religion. Is that you? Others will say that the state should not give any money to a religious school. But this is cutting off our nose to spite our face. The religious schools give higher results in math, English, and post-secondary school studies. Would it be okay to give vouchers for high-need students to attend a nonreligious school? Would you deny another student the road to success that Justice Sotomayor traveled? The First Amendment to the Constitution is for the free exercise of religion; it does not prohibit the exercise of religion. It is not freedom *from* religion. Are you against giving vouchers to African American students so that they can attend a Catholic school, where their parents and/or guardians believe the children may receive a better education than the one offered by the local public school?

When a parent or guardian has decided that their child would be better off using a voucher to go to a private school or to attend a public charter school, the inquiry should end there. The opponents of school choice have created numerous arguments against vouchers and public charter schools. They say the state should not give money to a religious organization. But it is the parents and not the state choosing where the voucher is spent. In addition, religious organizations already receive money to help feed and care for the poor in terms of soup kitchens, shelters for battered women and homeless families, or adoption services. The opponents of school choice will say that some schools are not financially transparent or they are hiring relatives to work there. Giving children from high-need environments a choice other than the local neighborhood school is said to take students away from that neighborhood school. That is correct. And when enough students go elsewhere, then the funding for that school diminishes and some teachers and/or staff are let go to adjust to the existing school population. This is a process that has been happening throughout the United States and not just in failing urban districts. In rural communities, young families may have moved away from a farming community for a different future or may have left island life on the coast of Maine for opportunities on the mainland. A factory closes, and many people lose their jobs. People leave the area. There is a constant ebb and flow of people to and from communities and to and from schools. It is the parents and guardians who determine this ebb and flow, as it should be.

There is nothing sacrosanct in how many children go to a particular school. When parents and guardians pull their children out, it is not done intentionally to hurt students or schools left behind. But if parents and guardians move their children in and out of school systems, that is their choice, and that choice should remain with them. In the case of New York City, where charter schools are often co-located in the same building, a charter could slowly increase its enrollment and the traditional school might lose some enrollment, with the teaching staff adjusted to reflect such a shift. But it is untenable to the NEA, the AFT, and the opponents of school choice that public union positions and dues payers to the NEA and AFT be reduced, even if that is the choice of the citizenry.

36. Do you fancy yourself better than the parents and guardians of African American and Hispanic students? The opponents of school choice use various rationales to argue against school choice for these parents and guardians. But once they have made the choice, it is no longer time for the opponents to question the choice of the parents and guardians. These parents and guardians are with their children all the time. They know their children. You do not. You cannot prejudge their children and decide that they should not have the opportunity to attend a public charter or private school with the help of a voucher. The state cannot know the individual circumstances of each family better than the parents and guardians themselves. We allow the state to remove children from abusive households, where the physical and mental well-being of children is at stake. We have trained social workers who monitor many families to see how they are getting on and where resources might be available for them. At no time should society challenge a parent or guardian for the educational choices they are making to opt into a public charter school or for a voucher to send their child to a private school. There are rules for truancy, that if a child is consistently not showing up for school, a society wants to know why the parents and guardians are not getting their child to school. You cannot leave your children to be raised in ignorance. Even the decision of a drug dealer or inmate of a prison to send that person's child to a public charter school or to take advantage of a voucher program should not be questioned. As hard as it could be to imagine a drug dealer or inmate having the same concerns for their children as you do or would for your children, accept that they can and do. Could they set a better example to their children? Yes. But that does not mean that they do not want to improve the future conditions for their children.

The opponents of school choice do not have a right to second-guess the preferences of parents and guardians for their children just because it does not serve the interests of the statists. The whole tactic of the NEA and AFT to leave the expansion and creation to "locally controlled educational authorities" is a cynical political ploy to stop the growth of more public charter schools or vouchers. A local public school has so many champions beyond the many good teachers in the school. There are all the parents and guardians of the children in the school who are told that funding for their school will be cut if a local charter is instituted. After-school programs will be terminated. Class sizes will be increased as teacher positions are cut and they have to consolidate the remaining classes with fewer teachers. The local community also has its parent-teacher association, PTA. The PTA is the strongest arm to do the bidding of the NEA and AFT to "save our schools." Nobody wants to disagree with the teachers and administrators for our local school. Many people in the community went to that school. They played for the Tigers or the Cardinals team. "We can't let that be taken away by a new charter school!"

And a new charter school has few stakeholders in the local community other than a few outnumbered parents and guardians who want school choice. The new charter school does not have any teachers or administrators in the local community to speak for the new charter school, while speaker after speaker from the PTA as well as administrators and teachers go down the list of "horribles" as to what school choice could mean to their school. It's not a fair fight, adults against children. Will you continue to oppose school choice?

When parents and guardians have decided to send their children to a public charter school or to supplement a voucher and send their kids to a private school, why do you oppose that? You must step out of the school door entrance and allow our children to pass through these school doors as they please. To stand steadfastly in the schoolhouse door is to stand in solidarity with George Wallace. On June 11, 1963, Democrat George Wallace, governor of Alabama, stood at the door of the Foster Auditorium at the University of Alabama to deny entry to two African American students, Vivian Malone and James Hood.[65] Governor Wallace had promised at his inaugural address,

---

[65] Wikipedia, s.v. "Stand in the Schoolhouse Door," accessed November 10, 2020.

"Segregation now, segregation tomorrow, segregation forever."[66] Will you continue to stand in solidarity with Governor George Wallace and oppose school choice for African American, Hispanic, white, Asian, and other children from high-need families? Despite your impressive credentials and curriculum vitae, you are not qualified to choose for these children. It is up to their parents and guardians.

37. Have the killings of George Floyd and Breonna Taylor shown that the two largest teachers' unions, the National Education Association (NEA) and the American Federation of Teachers (AFT), are a king with no clothes as they gleefully work against public charter schools for African American, Hispanic, white, Asian, and other students from high-need environments and, as required by law, promote first their teachers, then their own unions themselves, and third, our children? And while they may have no clothes, they have plenty of muscle to intimidate and vilify any opponent of their aggrandizement along with the state? Who will speak up for the interests of our children, black and white, if the NEA and AFT, with the local parent-teacher associations as their lackeys promote the agenda of the NEA and AFT against school choice?

Consider the headlines in 2020 after the coronavirus shut down schools and news outlets decried the disparate impact of stay-at-home schooling for black and Hispanic students. Students from poorer socioeconomic backgrounds did not have the laptop or the internet connection, or even a quiet space, required to participate in online learning that their better-off peers did. There were stories that black and Hispanic students were falling further behind with remote learning during the COVID-19 pandemic. And that is wrong. Countries such as Holland, Sweden, Germany, China, and Australia had reopened their schools. Australia is on the other side of the world, so their summer break is during our winter. There is data that COVID-19 is much less lethal to children than adults. There is risk, and the risk-averse media will tell the story of this and that young person who died from COVID-19. In previous years, they

---

[66]   Ibid.

did not tell stories of young people, middle-aged people, or senior citizens who died of the seasonal flu, and tens of thousands do die each year of the flu. In the summer of 2020, the teachers' unions in the United States weighed in against reopening in the fall as there was too much risk. They were correct that there were more risks for the entire staff of teachers, administrators, janitors, kitchen workers, etc. But how were these other countries able to put the interest of their children first and we were not able to?

It went so far that some states prevented private schools from opening, even though they wanted to. Whereas a public school can always reopen, as the state will give it money, a private school needs students and tuition to stay open. Cynically, the public unions were happy if private schools were put under stress, as perhaps they would go out of business and their children would return to their public school. The Education Department of the state of Oregon got so artful that although they allowed school districts with seventy-five or fewer kids to open in counties with fewer people, a Catholic school with less than seventy-five students was not allowed to open. To allow these alternatives to open threatened to divert funding for the public schools, as the funding would follow the child. That is all too cynical.

Our children should not stay home. It was and is damaging to their psyche and educational development. Those students who suffered most under closed schools were African American and Hispanic students from economically disadvantaged communities. A statist cannot lament the technology gap for African American and Hispanic students on the one hand with remote teaching and then refuse to open schools on the other hand. That is politically astute to lament the technology gap at the same time that you make a long list of demands to keep schools closed or to teach by remote learning or smaller in-person learning. The press will sell both stories and not make the connection that more risk should be taken to prevent a lost generation of students who miss out on one or more years of schooling.

It is fully understandable that a teacher did not want to return under the COVID-19 conditions in 2020. Due to COVID-19, it might be that classroom teaching may no longer be in the cards for some teachers due to their own health makeup or the health makeup of the people they share a household with. These teachers should have made that choice and see if there was a way for them to teach remotely. But the emphasis should have been on teachers who could teach in person. Isn't that putting our children first? That would have seemed to be the fair thing to do for our children.

38. Why do you support "rubber rooms," where incompetent teachers and public union employees go to spend the day to collect a day of pay, sick days, health benefits, disability pay, pensions, and personal days, because that person is not a good teacher or employee and cannot be efficiently fired? The word *accountability* was used after the killing of George Floyd and Breonna Taylor. It was focused on the police, who are sworn to protect and serve. It turned out that sometimes it is difficult to eliminate problem police officers. Upon closer examination, it was noted that some rogue officers, who appeared to be more involved in violating the civil rights of citizens, kept on working. Their collective bargaining contracts had several layers of procedural protections for these officers. While most officers are dutifully putting their uniforms on every day and risking their lives so that we, the citizen, may be secure in our person and property, some officers have abused their position as peace officers. Then, when it appears that the public cannot learn of the misconduct or effectively remove such officer, accountability comes into question. *Accountability* was a popular word in the summer of 2020. But have the legislative efforts that were passed increased accountability, or are they another public relations ploy that left the collective bargaining agreements intact?

Accountability also applies to our teachers. Our dedicated and inspirational teachers have a key role in educating our young, who are our future. Shouldn't the public have an ability to look over and weed out bad teachers? Certainly, a teacher who has been charged with abuse of a student or students can be removed. Nobody wants bad teachers teaching our children. Even the NEA and AFT don't want bad teachers teaching our children, but they also don't want to fire them. Instead, the NEA and AFT do what they are required by their fiduciary duty to do, which is to defend their members and keep them employed at all costs. Any effort to remove a teacher faces administrative steps of confidential personnel records, letters of warning or reprimand, hearing, and appeals, which make it difficult to remove such teacher. And if the teacher is removed, then there may still be lawsuits to turn over their termination.

For that reason, the NEA and AFT have created "rubber rooms." Technically, they have not officially created these rubber rooms, as it is administrators who work for a municipality who create rubber rooms, but rubber rooms are a response to the effective representation of teachers by the NEA and AFT. That there is even a concept of a rubber room goes against constitutional government of government by the people and for the people. There were no moving speeches or pamphlets written when our constitutions were adopted to emphasize that a government worker should still be employed and paid out of the public purse, even if that employee were unsuited for their job. This is wasting the people's money. Should you personally know an employee of a municipality who is being terminated, that is sad, as nobody likes to see a friend lose their job. But running the government for the people is required to be done efficiently and impartially to the benefit of the general citizen. Nonetheless, it is likely that you will do little to chip away at the many collective bargaining agreements in place that have extensive procedural protections for government employees, whether they be rouge police officers or ineffective teachers. That is the emptiness of your vows on the ramparts after the killing of George Floyd, that you would change things for the better and demand accountability.

Chapter 11

The Definition of Good Government as the Happiness of the Citizen

39. **D**O YOU BELIEVE in the principle that there is such a thing as good government? If you were moved enough to pay attention to the protests and issues raised after the killing of George Floyd, then perhaps you asked the question whether what happened was wrong, how it happened, and how that can be prevented in the future, not just in Milwaukee, but anywhere in the United States. On its surface, this was an employee of the state, a police officer, who held his knee on the neck of a citizen, who objected that he could not breathe with a knee on his neck. Other state employees, also police officers, controlled the area and disregarded objections by other citizens that Mr. Floyd could not breathe. In creating our government, the citizens have granted certain powers to the state to transact the business of government on behalf of the citizenry. The government is theoretically working for the people. At the point that the government is no longer working for the people but is putting the interests of state actors above the legitimate concerns of the people is when you have a government out of control.

Consider that we have an Army, Navy, and Air Force. These will soon be joined by a Space Force. The officers who direct these military branches are all soldiers, sailors, and Air Force personnel. At the top of each branch sit generals and admirals and the chairman of the

Joint Chiefs of Staff. But this is not the top of the military chain of command. Each branch of service reports to a secretary of the Army, Navy, or Air Force, for example. The secretary is most likely to be a veteran, but the position of secretary is a civilian post. They show up in a jacket and tie and not in a uniform. At the top is the president of the United States of America. That person is in a civilian position, and he or she is ultimately the first servant of the people. The black box with nuclear codes to launch intercontinental nuclear weapons at the foes of the United States is carried by a person, and he or she follows the president wherever he or she goes. The black box does not follow a military officer or the head of the Joint Chiefs of Staff. By the same token, the ultimate authority of our government are the people. The ultimate authority over state and local governments are the people. When an employee of the state kills a citizen under color of authority of the state, such as a police officer in the case of Mr. Floyd, then special scrutiny is paid to that act. The killing of one citizen by another citizen is tragic but receives a lower level of scrutiny, as the power of the state is not involved. The examination of how the power of the state is implemented is all part of striving for good government.

James Madison defined *good government* as two things when he was writing in support of adopting our Constitution after 1787. "A good government implies two things: first, fidelity to the object of government, which is the happiness of the people; secondly, a knowledge of the means by which that object can be best attained."[67] It is the happiness of the people that is paramount and not the happiness of the people working for the government. When one speaks of the "people," this refers to the general class of citizen *qua* citizen and not a specific class of citizens. In other words, when the government takes a legislative action or executive action, it is supposed to be acting for the benefit of the general citizenry. When a system is set up whereby binding arbitration agreements that set forth the employment terms for public employees are dictated by unelected officials or entered

---

[67] James Madison, "No. 62: Madison," in *The Federalist Papers* (New York: New American Library, 1961), 380.

into by officials who are beholden not to the will of the people but rather to the will of the people who got him or her elected, there can be a disconnect between what is enacted and what would be good government.

Transparency and accountability are two elements of good government. The citizenry should know what the government is doing and who is doing it. If a government official or branch is exceeding the authority granted to it or is running roughshod over the citizenry, then there needs to be accountability for such rouge branch or employees. That was part of the protests after the killing of George Floyd and other unarmed African Americans: transparency and accountability. It was a demand for good government that puts the happiness of the citizen at the top and how to best help a citizen achieve that happiness. Knowing the record of the few bad apples in a police department is part of good government. Seeking to hold a few bad apples in a police department accountable is part of good government. But perhaps you will continue to elect statist politicians who put the power of the state over the citizen above the interests of the general citizen. If that is the case, then it is time for you to step off your soapbox and stop talking as though you want to make government more accountable to the people. For all your "wokeness," you are still supporting the power of the state over the citizen, a dismal outcome. You may be a statist, after all.

At no time does good government authorize the legislative and executive branches to enact legislation benefitting one group of citizens that exceeds those available to the general citizenry. In other words, as soon as one group of citizens is to receive more than their fellow ordinary citizens have, that act is unconstitutional and corrupt. This is not focused on transfer-of-wealth payments that are done through welfare payments, rent subsidies, or free health care, as that is a balancing done under the social contract; rather, this imbalance refers to the preference of state employees over employees in the private sector, which is the vast majority of people. How does that happen? How is good government perverted? It is perverted when the factions that favor the state workers are constantly maneuvering and strategizing to maximize the pay, benefits, pensions, and protections for the state workers while the general citizen is engaged in the daily effort to earn their daily living and conduct their own lives.

Higher pay, pension, health care, and other employment benefits, including job security, for working for the state versus working the same job in the private economy are signs of corruption, where the powerful receive benefits that are not available to the general citizen. But that doesn't bother you. Money does not grow on trees. States must balance their budgets. How is it fair, for example, that the health insurance plans for government workers outstrip that of the general populace? It is not, but your past and future votes assure that that imbalance persists in favor of the public sector over the private sector.

Chapter 12

Less-than-Average Schooling Offered, but Flawless Paperwork Required to Earn a Living under the Heel of the Statists

40. WHY DO YOU protect the well-to-do from having to pay for work and materials provided by workers unless the tradesman or tradeswoman has flawless paperwork and disclosures? With good intentions, consumer protection laws were enacted to protect the citizen from the unsavory business tactics of some businesses. When people take out first or second mortgages, they have a three-day right of rescission to cancel the loan after it is completed. The idea is that after reflection, there may have been some terms or fees slipped into the transaction that had not been previously disclosed or the person had not fully appreciated. This might be in response to shady business practices. So the consumer can then opt to get out of the transaction and get their money back or their fees back. There are other disclosure requirements that mean well. Consider the law of Connecticut for Home Improvement Contracts. There, a written contract should have all changes and modifications; contract signing date, start date, finish date, and the date by which the consumer can cancel the transaction; a separate notice of right to cancel document, and both must sign

and date the contract.[68] These good intentions, however, have not gone unpunished.

Traditionally, consumer protection rules like this are done to protect the consumer from pressure sales, fine print, and usurious rates. At the federal level, there is a three-day right of recession for loans and mortgages on your home.[69] The idea is that if a slick lender or mortgage salesperson gets a homeowner or a senior citizen to sign some papers under duress or without the person having time to examine the papers and fees that go with it, that homeowner or senior citizen has three days to read what they signed, ask friends and family for their advice, and before the three days are up, they can cancel the deal and owe nothing.

These protections at the federal and state level are nice and were enacted in response to abuses of the consumer by sharp operators. The protection against shoddy workmanship or contractors who take a deposit, do one day's work, and then never return is understandable. These protections are nice in a perfect world, but we do not live in a perfect world. Even with these protections, shady contractors can still deliver the paperwork, take a deposit, do one day's work, and then never show up again. All the statutes in the world are not going to eliminate shady operators. The consumer is left back where he or she started. The best protection was and still remains the same: due diligence. The consumer needs to check out the reputation of the contractor for doing quality work on time and within the budget. The consumer is not excused from taking the contractor's word in lieu of checking out references and the work of the contractor. But how do these additional statutory requirements for detailed contracts in addition to the requirement for a worker to have a license to exercise what is a civil right, to work with your hands and back to earn a living, affect the citizen worker?

It is not an exaggeration to say that the public school monopoly has failed to provide educational choice in poor urban and rural

---

[68] Connecticut State Department of Consumer Protection, "Consumers-Home Improvement Contracts," CT.gov, accessed November 11, 2020.
[69] 15 USC. sec. 1635, "Right of rescission as to certain transactions."

communities, and these students are generally limited to the one local neighborhood school. This is an oversimplification, as the defenders of the public school monopoly will point to magnet and trade schools within the public school monopoly, where alternatives are offered. The public school monopoly will also always lament that there is not enough funding, but funding, though relevant, does not always correlate to performance. Students from public charter schools and religious day schools far outperform their public school peers with students from the same high-need communities with fewer dollars. Should you be sitting in a relatively well-off community with an adequately funded public schools system, this will all sound Greek to you, since there is no big problem where you live, or at least that is what the PTA reports to you. But it should not surprise the reader that some students from poor urban and rural schools may be behind in their English, math, writing, and other academic areas versus students in the reader's own community. Yet the state is expecting all these students to have flawless paperwork once they get into the working world, and particularly in the trades, in order to get paid! What?

We fail the student on the front end and then deny the worker his or her wages for work and materials on the back end when their papers are not in order. If the worker or contractor does not have a signed contract that contains the elements required by the statute, then the courts will not enforce that contact in a statist's paradise like Connecticut. The court will pretend that they are doing their duty of applying the laws of the state to the contract. If the contract does not have the minimum elements, then the worker can't even win a dime, regardless of the benefit conferred on the homeowner. Even the legal concept of *quantum meruit*, where at the end of the day the customer did receive something of value for which they should pay, is blocked by the statists' demands for perfection. And the judges just stand there and pretend that they must follow the statute as opposed to reaching for the constitutional right to earn a living with your hands and back, which right may not be unreasonably fettered by the state. A person must be paid for the labor they provide. The beneficiary cannot hide behind the tricks of the crafty and say the paperwork was not in order. So the property owner gets to sit behind the facade of consumer protection and keep the labor and materials provided by the laborer, who may not have had the same educational choices as the homeowner when growing up. And yet you will continue to support such an unjust system. After all, if we just pass a few more laws, we can make everything perfect, or at least that is what our Republican and Democrat politicians tell us. They remind us of their law-passing prowess during each election cycle with informative mailers and Facebook posts. But have the principles of our Declaration of Independence, Constitution, and Bill of Rights been upheld or diminished by these politicians?

41. There is a constitutional right to work and earn a living with your hands and back. And it has the same value as your freedom of speech, assembly, and religion. Arguably, the right to work with your hands and back to earn a living and to feed your family is above these other rights. Without the ability to feed oneself, the citizen is not at liberty to enjoy any other freedoms or rights, as the citizen will die. A similar principle is applied to the need for a citizen to be secure in their person and property in order to exercise their other freedoms. If the government, or if a group of citizens, threatens to take away a citizen's business, property, or house in the event the citizen wanted to speak his or her mind or follow that person's conscience and exercise their religion, that citizen's rights would be significantly chilled to the point they might hesitate or avoid exercising their constitutional rights. If a citizen is left destitute because the government punitively withdraws their liquor license, medical license, law license, electrician's license, or permit to do work or says there is a health code violation, because the citizen objected to the government's position, the government is unlikely to hear from that citizen for very long, as the citizen flounders in unemployment. When a citizen is reduced to just trying to eke out food and shelter for himself or herself, there is little time or energy left to petition the government for redress of grievances. It was said that during the 2020 coronavirus shutdown in New York State, an upstate bar challenged the governor's rules. Lo and behold, the proprietor had its liquor license pulled. Unrelated, but a bar called Chuggers in New Rochelle, New York, was shut

down in January 2019 for not paying its real estate taxes. Apparently, there had been a shooting outside the bar about a month before. "This property has been seized for nonpayment of taxes, and is now in the possession of the State of New York."[70] According to an article, the amount of outstanding taxes was $9,552.31. That does not seem like a lot of money for an ongoing business that hires bartenders, servers, and cooks that also pay taxes to the city, county, and state to be put out of business for.

Or consider Grace Community Church, which was trying to restart its church services during the 2020 COVID-19 pandemic in Los Angeles. The church had attempted to have services indoors but was hit with a preliminary injunction in September 2020 to stop having indoor services. Prior thereto, the county of Los Angeles had already fined the church $1,000 for misplacing signs regarding coronavirus guidelines. And that was after the county of Los Angeles terminated a five-decade lease to a parking lot behind the church after the church brought a lawsuit against them challenging the prohibition of in-person worship.[71] On the one hand, it is okay for the government to ask for an injunction to keep things as they stand at that time so that the church could not have in-person services, but that did not apply to leaving five decades of parking lot leases in place. The county went directly to a punitive assault on the church versus letting the process work its way out. The ability of the state to take your civil rights when you challenge the government by wanting to exercise your civil rights has a chilling effect on others from enforcing their rights or questioning the actions of the government. It is a well-worn tactic of dictators to take away the sustenance and shelter of its opponents so that they drop to their knees and seek nothing more than rice and beans to eat, or they flee the country. The impact is the same. The opponents of the state are silenced.

What ability does the citizen have to insist on the civil right to work with their hands and back if the courts do not recognize it? Will

---

[70] Christopher J. Eberhart, "State Shuts Down New Rochelle Bar for Outstanding Tax Payments," Lohud.com, January 8, 2019, accessed November 11, 2020.

[71] Graham Piro, "County Evicts Church behind Coronavirus Lawsuit from Its Parking Lot," Washington Free Beacon, August 31, 2020, accessed November 11, 2020.

you continue to elect into office statists that deny this right? Will you deny the ability of workers to be paid for their work because their paperwork is not perfect? Must the citizen jump over state-mandated hurdles in order to earn their living in a trade as basic as carpentry? Jesus was said to be a carpenter. Would he need a license from the state to work with his hands? Would Jesus be denied his ability to be paid because he did not have the right paperwork? While it is true that those with a lesser education or a weaker ability with the English language can and do get other family members or friends to prepare and interpret contracts and legal forms for them, that does not mean it should be a requirement to recover payment for goods and services provided. How well a citizen learned in the public school monopoly should not affect his or her ability to work or to get paid. That is an unfair impingement on a person's right to earn a living.

42. If you insist on denying the workingman and working-woman his or her pay because the proper paperwork was not submitted or a licensing fee was not paid to exercise a human right, will you also insist that their work be criminalized? Perhaps it is not punitive enough to deny these workers recourse to the courts to get paid. Perhaps you revel in your power and comfort and you would like them to be arrested. Is that because you want things neat and perfect and on lists and disregard that life for the poor may not be as neat and perfect as you imagine life to be? In Connecticut, the state can arrest you for doing home improvement contractor work without a home improvement contractor's license. Arrests happen rarely, and they are more likely to happen to itinerantly bad workers. Nonetheless, why have you supported a system that has the power to arrest a man or woman for painting a homeowner's screen door or planting a vege-table garden for the homeowner? One does not know when the state will use its many powers against the citizen to silence the individual, to punish the individual, and/or to make an example of the individual? But you have granted those powers to the state. Shouldn't the right to work with your hands and back in the trades be decriminalized so that you cannot be arrested for exercising this civil right? Will you change your support and vote to decriminalize work?

43. And while you live in relative comfort, which you have earned, you might have asked what you can do differently after the killing of George Floyd. Perhaps you can back off from your obsessive-compulsive behavior to have everything on neat lists with neat credentials and thereby deny avenues for African Americans, whites, Hispanics, Asian Americans, and others to put food on their plate, to learn trades, and to become owners of businesses and equipment? More importantly, will you stop intimidating men and women, young and old, from trying to earn a living by stripping away the levels of paperwork and training required just to try a vocation? Your penchant for more rules versus less rules dissuades people from even trying the first time. Economists have a measure of what the impact of a rule or tax might be on conduct. The standard is not on what you would do if the tax or regulation were put on you, but rather what one hundred businesspeople would do when faced with a new tax or regulation. Out of that one hundred, how many would still build the new house, open a new restaurant, continue running their restaurant, open a car service center, or expand a beauty salon and so on? Will one hundred out of one hundred still do it, or will only ninety-eight do it, or heaven forbid, will only ninety out of one hundred people do it? The latter would represent a 10 percent decline in economic activity. That is significant!

Personally, you might be at a point where you would be of the last fifty to try that new business or stay in your business with ever more taxes and regulations. But your choice is only one of millions that affect our economy daily. When expressing concern that you would like to make this a better country for African Americans, appreciate that it is important to increase the numbers of licenses, permits, degrees, equipment, trucks, machinery, commercial real estate, software, and residential real estate that is owned within the African American community. This is accelerated by a strong economy. When discussing taxes and regulations, the question should not be, "How many people out of one hundred will stop pursuing an economic opportunity?" Instead, the question should be, "What policy, tax incentives, and/or deregulation should we pursue so that more than the one hundred people show up for a particular trade or business than were there before the policy change?" We don't want just the one hundred running an auto repair shop or a dry cleaner; we want one hundred and five people pursuing that opportunity. That is what a growing economy is about. How do you get more people to engage and participate as an employee or as an entrepreneur? Because if you are not in it, you cannot win it! That means that nobody gets into the middle class or higher by receiving a government check for not working. You only get into the middle class if you work. You have to be in it to win it!

Why should a person of color want to engage in the paperwork due the state if it can be avoided? It requires time and money. Every requirement that is saddled on top is another reason not to. Ninety-nine might still do it, but that one person dissuaded is a loss. And if an African American has one-eighth the net worth of a white American, then the statists' demand for money, training, and time makes it less likely that an African American has the resources to even try. Remove the barriers. Eliminate the fees beyond what is absolutely necessary for all Americans to exercise their right to work and feed themselves. Question whether each burden placed on our right to work substantially improves the quality of life for our society. Is it right to marginalize those who begin life with fewer economic resources and continuously increase the requirements to earn a living? The politicians should be examining what the minimum burden that should be placed on the citizen is.

It is the curse of word processing and laser printers that statists are emboldened to cut and paste requirements from one job onto another project and say, "Oh, these are nifty requirements for a permit or license in the Miller file. I will just cut and paste those requirements into the Armstead file." Or "I see a neighboring state has further feathered the bed of its vested interests who are in bed with the politicians and increased the regulatory requirements for such-and-such business. I'll just cut and paste those requirements for our state and demonstrate to people what a diligent state worker/legislator/lobbyist I am and make it more difficult for all residents of the state to potentially earn a living and/or make their cost of living higher through increased compliance costs for business." Bureaucrats should go back to their permitting processes from twenty years ago and look critically at the many added paragraphs in permits today and ask if it is absolutely required. Cutting and pasting new requirements from one permit to another is a broken model and does not fit the definition of good government, as it is not for the happiness of the citizen.

At the risk of trying the reader's patience even further, I will give a stark contrast of what was sufficient for drainage in building single-family homes twenty-five years or so ago in Connecticut compared to what it has become. Twenty-five years ago, at the end of building a house, landscaping, and driveways, the owner had to submit a certification from a licensed professional engineer that the property basically did not dump water on its neighbor differently than what had been the case before the project had been commenced. Thus, you could not shoot the water coming down your new driveway into your neighbor's yard. And this requirement was found, of all places, in the plumbing code. And it worked. Now it is a matter of submitting plans to show where the water goes today with computer modeling showing what it is anticipated for a one-inch rainfall and what might happen in a one-hundred-year rainstorm. Then the property is supposed to hold the first inch of rain on the property, and this comes with extensive modeling and calculations that only engineers can understand. The result is that in towns like Greenwich, $55,000 in professional fees and drainage structures can be buried into the ground, never to be seen again, and that depresses the number of projects pursued. That depresses the number of projects permitted, which depresses the permit fees to the municipality, which depresses the number of closings and conveyance taxes to the municipality and to the state, and it definitely depresses the number of jobs in the trades that are needed as well as the economic activity of supplying the materials to build these houses. This depressed economic activity stresses the finances of cities, towns, and state, as they have fewer resources to carry on the business of government, but it also leads to fewer job opportunities in building, trucking, warehouse work, lumber yards, vehicle sales and maintenance, and other trades related to home construction, and this means fewer economic opportunities for all residents of the state, including but not limited to African Americans. But you don't care.

Chapter 13

Making Life More Expensive for the Poor and Shutting Off Avenues of Advancement

44. IF YOU PROFESS a desire to make life better for blacks in America, why do you make life more expensive, generally, and thereby disproportionately make life more expensive for African Americans? Do you assuage yourself in saying that you support transfer-of-wealth programs such as food stamps and social welfare programs in general as a justification? Are you not aware that the only person who can elevate you is you? If you are sitting on the ground and I go over to pick you up and put you on your feet, that can be a good thing. But if after I leave, you sit down again, there is nothing I can do for you to elevate you. "Only you can elevate you!"

The purpose of social welfare programs is part of the social contract to provide a safety net for when people fall on hard times, which many of us do from time to time. That is why there are private charitable organizations and government programs for housing, food, health care, and job training. There is a difference between a hand up and a handout. A *hand up* is meant to be aid to get one situated in life or to make it through a rough patch. A *handout* is thought of as a recurring payment that never ends, which means the person never made it beyond dependence on government programs, which is a result that is supposed to be avoided.

The various supports given by private and public entities are not meant to be a permanent way of life. National Public Radio (NPR), however, can document white families in rural Ohio, for example, that have been on government assistance for four generations. Grandmother, mother, and children living in the same household, which builds a monthly budget on available programs. The mother telling her son of about eight to act stupid for the interview with a social worker and specialist so that he can be diagnosed as mentally disabled so that the family can receive a few more dollars per month in disability payments. So what are his chances when his mother tells him that he is stupid and disabled and he should act that way to the outside world so that she can get a few more dollars to make the budget work? This is what the Welfare-Industrial Complex has reduced many of our citizens to. What are the chances for this boy later in life?

As regards the African American community, there is a sensitivity to avoid having any special designation applied to their child as disabled with some sort of learning disability. The point is to avoid a label on your child, as one does not want this label to follow him or her through school, as it may diminish his or her chances.

How do we change the dysfunction of the modern welfare state that encourages citizens to adapt and bend to the rules set forth by the Welfare-Industrial Complex and thereby keep themselves dependent on it? It was shown during the 2016–2020 time frame that when disability requirements were increased to make it harder to qualify, more people entered the labor force and got jobs. A job or business is the only way that a person could hope to be economically independent fifteen years hence. If a citizen stays on disability, then there is no chance that they can become economically independent. That brings to mind the state employees who retire and claim a disability. A determination of a full or partial disability increases their retirement pay because their ability to work is reduced. In some police departments, over 50 percent of police officers retire with a disability to supplement their retirement pay. What of the state worker who retires on a disability and is out fishing every week or on the golf course? They will avoid doing certain types of work so as to avoid upsetting their disability payments. This almost assures that they will not advance their economic position due to the benefits of their disability payment, which is counterproductive for them and society. People will have a better chance in life if they are actively engaged in employment versus on the sidelines. What is decried as "cruel" or "inhumane" can actually be better in the long run for the person than the cruel and inhumane "compassion" of the government dole.

45. Why do you support tolls to make it more expensive for the working poor to get to work? In the state of Connecticut, there were many politicians enthusiastic to put up tolls on highways so that poor people would have to pay even more money just to get to work. These same politicians have made no accounting for why Connecticut's administrative cost per mile of road is a multiple of *nine* times of the national *average* and not just 10 or 20 percent higher than the national average. No, Connecticut administrative costs per mile were *nine times* the national average per mile![72] The statists will come to the aid of the state and reorder those numbers to show that the state is actually on a par with its neighbors, but worry not, and while you are at it, institute tolls without a reduction in costs at the Department of Transportation. Why is that okay? These same politicians do not answer how they have raided transportation funds from the federal government and gas taxes again and again to pay for general budget items. These same politicians have not explained why they continually shift items out of the general budget and put these items into "transportation," where it had not previously been some ten years before. More smoke and mirrors to keep the Ponzi scheme going. Instead of asking for corrections. you seek to charge a poor person another six dollars per day just to go to work. That worker is already paying gas taxes that are diverted away from the very roads that poor person is driving on.

---

[72] Lawrence Rizzolo, "Memo Re. HB No. 7280, an Act Concerning Support for Transportation Infrastructure," to transportation committee, CT.gov.

46. Why do you require the poor to give $7,500 for rich people to live a green lifestyle so they can buy a $135,000 Tesla electric automobile? Climate change is real. Climate change deserves our attention and efforts. But why do you put the burden on the poor? Shouldn't the standard be environmental equity, whereby we will do whatever we can for the environment, so long as it does not raise the cost of living for poor people? Shouldn't that be the standard, environmental equity? *Environmental equity* is separate and apart from the Paris Climate Accord, which allows countries like China and India to increase their pollution through 2030 without any enforcement mechanisms to lessen the rate that they increasingly pollute and together are building the eighth continent of plastic waste in the Pacific Ocean![73] Since blacks have significantly fewer economic resources than whites and other Americans, why do you ask blacks to subsidize the green lifestyles of the well-to-do to buy $135,000 electric cars? A millionaire does not need $7,500 to buy an electric car. When opting to follow a green initiative, shouldn't we ask how much this is disproportionately affecting African Americans in raising their cost of living and their ability to have a job and earn a salary? Since the poor are not lining the pockets of politicians with political donations, they don't have a seat at the table. They are at the table, but only as props, so that the statists can remain in power. Whether the condition of the poor is improved matters not to the statists. The statists will visit the poor from time to time to shoot video and get material for social·media posts to show their "compassion," then return every two or four years for votes in return for more Welfare-Industrial Complex programs.

Since the poor were not in the corporate boardrooms of Silicon Valley and its internet billionaires, they had no input in the scheme to make poor people subsidize the green lifestyles of the rich. Anybody who can afford an $85,000 car is well-off and may qualify as a millionaire. The green special interests and their millionaire friends got together with politicians and decreed that the federal government

---

[73] Prior to 2020, China was putting twenty-eight times as much plastic waste into the oceans as the United States, but China's progressive and statist allies in the West say nothing.

would give a $7,500 credit to a purchaser of an electric car, with the rationale that electric car technology needs to be developed to hopefully lower carbon emissions into our environment. But to give a $7,500 credit to a millionaire seems like an oxymoron when they could buy an $85,000 Tesla versus a cheaper Nissan Leaf at under $40,000. But it gets worse—even if you loaded up your $85,000 Tesla with options and milked the price up to $135,000, you still received the $7,500-per-car credit. Perhaps that meant that we were paying for a $7,500 option for nice, comfortable leather seating. So good to know the government dollar is going to a necessary expense. Nice to know that we have helped millionaires load up their car with options. Poor people cannot afford these Teslas. Middle-class Americans cannot afford these $85,000 Teslas.

To make matters worse, the "green" millionaires and their politicians decreed that the companies that make cars that poor people might actually be able to afford at $1,000 down and $199 per month would have to give billions more dollars to Tesla for the electric cars that General Motors, Ford, Nissan, and Toyota didn't build. GM, Ford, Toyota, and Nissan could buy "carbon-emission credits" from Tesla for electric cars that GM, Ford, Toyota, and Nissan didn't build and thereby further subsidize the automaker for millionaires. This naturally makes the cars that poor people might be able to afford on payments even more expensive.

At the same time, you should consider that the wealthy are generally carbon pigs. They are carbon pigs because their apartments and homes are generally larger than those of the poor and require more energy to heat, cool, and keep lit. In addition, these carbon pigs sometimes have more than one house. They also have a staff, and they also drive cars with large motors, or at least the people who maintain their many homes or deliver their take-out food drive cars. This is not to say that the lifestyle of the rich is not useful. It is very useful. The rich and well-to-do provide countless job opportunities for home repair, childcare, landscaping, restaurants, automobiles, clothing, resorts, and the list goes on. It is great that they have multiple homes that need to be maintained and that they pay property taxes to multiple jurisdictions, although their children generally only go to one school system, so their property taxes help subsidized the education of children in another jurisdiction. America needs the jobs that these carbon-pig millionaires and well-to-do citizens create. We want as many of them as we can get. Let's just not confuse them with green lifestyles and subsidize their consumption habits.

There is a cynicism, however, to some of the political positions of this millionaire and well-to-do class. They tend to like the presence of illegal immigrants from Central and South America and from Asia to take care of their children, clean their houses, prepare and serve their restaurant meals, wash and polish their cars, carry their golf bags, give them pedicures and manicures, cut their grass, and so forth. These illegal immigrants make the lives of the rich and well-to-do fabulous. The only problem is that illegal immigrants tend to depress the labor costs for all these jobs, which negatively affects African Americans who were born and raised here. An illegal immigrant is likely to work for less and under tougher conditions, as that is still far preferable to going back to the country that they came from. These lower wages do not help African Americans.

The ultimate hypocrisy for electric cars is that if an electric car is truly green, then there should be no air-conditioning, electric windows, or electric seats in the car, because they all require electricity to work and that shortens the travel range of the electric car. That energy could be used for other purposes to reduce carbon emissions. Hard to imagine, but cars in the 1960s and 1970 had manual seats, crank windows, and no air-conditioning, and we still lived and worked in the same places. These green hypocrites also jet around the country and world and require ever more exotic vacations with ever more services to satisfy their everyday desires, while they demand the subsidy for their car. To ask the poor to subsidize the carbon-intense lifestyle of the rich and well-to-do is unfair. If you own a Tesla, instead of that smug look of contentment and superiority, why not return the $7,500 by donating it to the local branch of the NAACP closest to you or give it to the nearest General Motors, Nissan, Ford, or Toyota dealership, as they actually sell cars that the poor might be able to afford? And don't forget to lose that smug look on your face, as this was a really bad deal for the poor that has disproportionately affected African Americans.

Climate change is real, but at what rate it is proceeding and how much one nation, like the United States, can do about it when China and India are belching soot into the air and plastic and chemical pollution into the ocean at stupendous rates is questionable. For political purposes, it is not polite to point at the prodigious pollution being produced by China with her 1.4 billion people and India with 1.35 billion. That is almost 40 percent of the Earth's population! To ask the United States to take extreme measures to increase the cost of its electricity, home heating oil, propane, gasoline, airplane flights, for example, in order to reduce consumption of these things is to make life harder for our poor.

There is something called the Green New Deal that claims to address climate change and economic inequality.[74] Instead, it promises to raise the cost of living of Americans, which would be particularly onerous for the poor. Witness the efficacy of the Tesla electric car subsidy that does absolutely nothing for the poor but increases their cost of living through higher-priced cars from GM, Ford, Toyota, and Nissan, not to mention that Tesla owners pay no gasoline taxes to maintain the roads. There should be an Electric Car Equity Act to have electric car owners pay a fee to replace the gas taxes that they do not pay to use the roads and bridges that the less-affluent pay for every day when they buy gas.

The Green New Deal seeks to have net-zero carbon emissions for the United States by 2050 by "meeting 100 percent of the power demand of the United States through clean, renewable, and zero-emission energy sources." Around 40 to 60 percent reductions from the carbon emission levels of 2010 would be achieved by 2030. Somehow, there would be massive growth in clean manufacturing and removing pollution and greenhouse gas emissions from manufacturing and industry as much as is technologically feasible during these time frames. To take out as much pollution as technologically feasible means that expensive technologies would be employed, because that

---

[74]   Wikipedia, s.v. "Green New Deal," accessed November 11, 2020.

qualifies as "technologically feasible." Expanding renewable energy manufacturing sounds good, but what if it is more expensive than existing technologies that will increase costs and prices? Working with farmers and ranchers to remove pollution and greenhouse gas emissions from the agricultural sector would be aimed in part at the flatulence of all the cows and hogs that are raised and end up on our dining room table.

Curiously, the Green New Deal flouts "a more sustainable food system that ensures universal access to healthy foods." That is ironic, because after the killing of George Floyd, in numerous American cities looters were let to run rampant and destroy food stores and even large retailers that were part of the solution to eliminate food deserts of poor-quality food selection in high-need African American communities. So if looters were "protesting," then why was it okay to create food deserts and take us further away from universal access to healthy foods? The Green New Deal wants to overhaul the transportation system "to remove pollution and greenhouse gas emissions from the transportation sector as much as technologically feasible" through investment in zero-emission vehicle infrastructure. This means cars, trucks, planes, and trains that don't create carbon emissions. Even if a car runs on electricity, it is not a zero-emission vehicle, as the electricity has to come from somewhere. At present, that is from coal, natural gas, atomic power, petroleum, wind power, and solar power. The latter two make a small percentage of a reliable electrical supply. Certainly, an increase in atomic power is the best hope for a reliable zero-emission power source. Wind and sun are not reliable and need backups from other sources. Having electricity come from renewable sources is desirable and admirable, but an eye must be kept on the cost and reliability. Environmental equity states that we shall do whatever we can for the environment, provided it does not raise the cost of living for poor people. In shifting to cleaner ways to do things, the questions must always be asked whether it is raising the cost of living for poor people. Is their heating bill going up? Is their electricity bill going up? Is their natural gas or propane bill going up? Is the cost of rent going up? Will fewer houses and apartments be built, and will those that are built be more expensive because of the extras added into them, thereby putting them further out of reach for the poor, thereby exacerbating the unavailability of affordable housing, which increases the cost of housing through supply and demand? While politicians and our betters burnish their social standing with references to the Green New Deal or to *sustainable* practices and simultaneously lament the shortage of affordable housing for the poor and middle class, they double down on the drivers of unaffordable housing.

In February 2021, the US Census put the average cost of a new single family home at $394,300. The cost of government regulations made up 23.8 percent of that cost at $93,870.[75] While this may not be alarming to our betters as they usually live in more expensive areas than $394,300 for a new house, $93,870 is very real to the poor and middle class of America. The National Association of Home Builders survey of builders and land developers in 2021 broke the regulatory costs down to $41,330 during development and $52,540 during the construction of the house. This applies to building your own new house on your own lot: $52,540, which is neither roofing, siding, plumbing, kitchen, laundry, nor bedrooms, just the cost of government regulation during the construction process. You will bury this $52,540 in regulatory costs in your backyard, never to be seen again. This does not mean that there should be no regulation but rather regulation has gone too far and is the primary culprit of our affordable housing shortage, another implicit pain of statism. The Green New Deal will make housing even less affordable and available. Soon, the regulatory cost will blast through $100,000 per new construction house. And the statists put the American dream even further out of reach for the citizen.

The Green New Deal merely seeks to layer up ever more obstacles and costs to delivering affordable housing. The manner in which costs are imposed go beyond the obvious time-is-money delay. There are increased development costs through additional requirements, reports, and commentary that can add six months to the lot approval

---

[75] Paul Emrath, PhD, "Government Regulation in the Price of a New Home: 2021," Economics and Housing Policy, National Association of Home Builders, May 5, 2021.

time. Then there are the hard costs paid to surveyors and engineers for field tests, studies, and engineering models for government agencies—federal, state, and local. Actual fees to government agencies are paid with ever more fees tucked in to satisfy yet another pet project of a politician for their reelection campaign. Then there is the land that is forcibly left unbuilt that had been buildable under existing rules, but with the friction of getting an approval today versus years down the road after litigation, land is given to the local government or to a neighborhood group to be left unbuilt. Setback requirements from property lines are sometimes adjusted beyond the ordinary to make development of driveways, septic systems, wells, garages, and houses more difficult. And this is only for the creation of buildable lots. Then there are the even more onerous burdens on actually building a house for someone to live in. Just the changes in the various state and local building codes between 2011 and 2021, which will be referred to below, adds around 10 percent to the construction costs. These building code changes have zero appreciable benefit for a citizen to sleep in a bedroom, cook on a stove, eat a Thanskgiving dinner with family and friends, park a car in the garage, do one's homework, or complete work at an in-home office. Not one difference. Yet our betters and statists impose this upon us as they game the system for themselves. Some communities will even have minimal architectural design factors, such as no vinyl siding, for example, to make a house less affordable. And then there is the pure cost of delay for ever-more percolation tests as-built measurements and construction inspections that never used to exist for houses that are still standing 150 years later. How can the statist justify his or her existence but by the imposition of greater control and oversight by the state? And what have we gotten? Unaffordable housing. Lack of housing. This is the implicit pain of statism!

The Green New Deal is merely assuaging the guilt of our betters for their prodigious consumption habits and significant carbon footprints. It is not about improving our environment as about mollifying the environmental conscience of our betters who will not take a vow of poverty to reduce their consumption habits in housing, transportation, food, leisure, exercise, vacations, clothes, etc. Nor would

I want them to as they create needed jobs for all Americans in their consumption habits. Rather, our betters want the poor and middle class to subsidize their electric cars, charging stations for electric cars, enable them to sell electricity off their solar panels back to the grid, whether needed or not. The hypocrisy of schools of environmental studies, which are effectively nothing more than schools of hypocrites to further pauperize the poor and the exploitation of government rules to feather the bed of the insiders and allow our betters to continue their consuming ways unabated, is dealt with in greater detail in my book on *Climate Change and Environmental Equity: How We Should Do Whatever We Can for the Environment, Provided it Does Not Increase the Cost of Living for the Poor or Underline liberal democracy.*

The Green New Deal also talks about building wealth and community ownership. It is not clear what *community ownership* is supposed to mean. Does that mean the bureaucrats run something and own something related to the economy? We have public utilities that are regulated by the state but are, at core, a private enterprise. Community ownership of a means of production is not a promising area when the record on the Welfare-Industrial Complex is reviewed, noting how it has decimated family formation in poor urban and rural communities. Publicly owned enterprises would be ripe for political patronage and the favor mill, which is the opposite of economic efficiency. The politicians don't pay; the citizens do. *Community ownership* could also be a code word for the Marxist concept of the state owning the means of production. Marxism prescribes the dictatorship of the proletariat and "to centralize all instruments of production in the hands of the state."[76] Then the Deal goes to "high-quality union jobs that pay prevailing wages, hires local workers…and guarantees wage and benefit parity for workers affected by the transition." It does not explain why a distinction would be made between union and nonunion jobs, but it is clear about overpaying for work. *Prevailing wage* is where the government makes contractors on government jobs pay higher wages than they otherwise would.

---

[76] Karl Marx and Friedrich Engels, *The Communist Manifesto*, trans. Samuel Moore (London: The Merlin Press, 1848, 1998), 19.

The result is that instead of retrofitting three public schools with better insulation, you only retrofit two. That is two-for-the-price-of-three legislation, which squanders public resources. If you are wondering why the lead paint at your school has not been remediated, it is because prevailing wage requires that the work be done at a higher rate to reward those lucky enough to receive that prevailing wage. But it is a violation of the principles of good government to spend more on a project than absolutely necessary.

The Green New Deal also talks about guaranteeing paid vacations to all people of the United States. You have to be a Pollyanna to believe all the wonderful things that are promised. One thing that is certain is, when energy, manufacturing, and farming are to be done to the highest technological level available, that is going to cost money and can put businesses out of service if they compete with the likes of companies out of China or India with limited environmental enforcement, prodigious pollution, and subsidized industries, in the case of China. That is a perfect storm of higher-cost goods and unemployment in industries forced out of business by having to meet the highest technological standards, which costs money. In the meantime, competitors will undersell our industries. And when the economy is weak, the first people to take it in the neck are the poor, who have the least economic resources available to weather a storm, and that disproportionately affects African Americans. How do higher costs for heating, cooling, electricity, transportation, clothes, food, and housing help blacks in America? They don't. It is one thing to champion a cleaner environment, which we all want for our children, nation, the world, and ourselves, and it is another to put that burden on the poor. Proceed with Godspeed, keeping the environmental equity requirement in mind, that we will do whatever we can for the environment, provided it does not raise the cost of living for poor people. And the cost of living includes being employed and earning a living.

The Green New Deal is an example of taking a gun and aiming it at your own foot and pulling the trigger. If the entire United States economy were shut down in 2020 and there would be no more carbon dioxide emissions from the country, then barely staggering to survive by the vagaries of the wind and sun and the few atomic plants that would be allowed to remain open, there would be less than a 0.2-degree-Celsius change for the better in the temperature of the world by 2100 and the sea level rise would only be improved by two centimeters![77]

Guess who would suffer most for the shutdown of the United States economy? The poor! The poor have the least amount of resources to deal with a stagnant economy and increasingly expensive utility bills for electricity and heat and how to move about. Not everyone can afford a Tesla. Before you sacrifice the United States economy and before you sacrifice the poor in America, appreciate that if the United States economy were turned off tomorrow, the impact on climate change would be negligible. Without a robust American economy, military, and political system, the totalitarian regimes of the world, such as China, North Korea, and Cuba, as well as the authoritarian regimes of Russia, Iran, Saudi Arabia, and Venezuela, would have freer rein to impose their illiberal hegemony on their neighbors and around the world, such as the Russian invasion of the Ukraine in February, 2022. That is neither a safe nor secure future for the citizens of the United States or the citizens of the world.

And while we are on the subject of the environment, there was a discussion/debate on whether it would be more efficacious or less efficacious for the United States to stay in the Paris Climate Accord, which was signed outside of Paris, France, in 2016, with the stated goal to reduce carbon emissions through voluntary targets by its signatories, as no enforcement mechanism was included in the accord. The accord also called on President Trump to notify the other signatories that the United States would exit the accord in 2017, which

---

[77] Kevin D. Dayaratna and Nicolas D. Loris, "Assessing the Costs and Benefits of the Green New Deal's Energy Policies," The Heritage Foundation, July 24, 2019, citing "Technical Update of the Social Cost of Carbon for Regulatory Impact Analysis," Interagency Working Group on Social Cost of Carbon, Technical Support Document Under Executive Order 12866 of President Barack Obama, May, 2013, "Emulation Coupled Atmosphere-Ocean and Carbon Cycle Models with a Simpler Model, MAGICC6, Part I: Model Description and Calibration" *Atmospheric Chemistry and Physics*, vol. 11 (2011), pgs. 1417–1456, and "MAGICC/SCENGEN," University Corporation for Atmospheric Research.

would not take effect until 2020. The Biden administration canceled America's withdrawal from the Paris Climate Accord upon his assuming office in 2021. Without regard to what the United States was doing, in 2017, *Nature* magazine reported two studies that found out the major industrialized countries were not doing enough under the Paris Climate Accord and the members would miss the goal of keeping the global temperature rise by 2100 to no more than 1.5 degrees Celsius.[78] So the agreement was already failing by 2017. By 2020, Earth.org warned that the commitments agreed to in the Paris Agreement were woefully short of what was needed and that the signatory countries had to step up "with cuts needing to increase at least *fivefold* [italics mine] to reach the 1.5 degree Celsius goal."[79]

Nonetheless, the United States experienced the largest decline in carbon dioxide emissions in 2017 for the ninth time in the twenty-first century.[80] This happened at the same time as China and India continued to increase their carbon dioxide outputs. China and India in 2017 accounted for almost half the increase in global carbon output, which is right on track with the Paris Agreement, which allows China to keep emitting more carbon dioxide through 2030, and India has no hard goal of reducing their emissions. And somehow this would turn out to be a fair deal for America's poor? Who allowed voluntary targets on China and India and promised transfers of monies from the United States to developing countries in the pact, under the extortion terms of "If you don't pay them money, they will pollute more"? The main reason that United States carbon emissions were declining year over year, even with an increasing economy, was the steady displacement of coal for electrical generation with cleaner natural gas. The cheaper and cleaner natural gas came about as a result of developments in hydraulic fracturing and horizontal/directional drilling.[81]

---

[78]   Wikipedia, s.v. "Criticism, Paris Agreement," accessed November 12, 2020.

[79]   Yi Yeung, "Current Emissions Commitments Not Enough to Meet Paris Targets—UN," Earth.org, March 27, 2020, accessed November 12, 2020.

[80]   Mark J. Perry, "Chart of the Day: In 2017, US Had Largest Decline in CO2 Emissions in the World for 9th Time This Century," American Enterprise Institute, July 12, 2018.

[81]   Ibid.

With fracking and horizontal drilling, the United States went from importing 60 percent of its oil in 2006 to becoming a net exporter of oil in 2019.[82] Although *The Washington Post*, makes the obvious point that other oil suppliers still matter to the US, the United States still became a net exporter of oil, and that can help the economic security of the poor versus importing 60 percent of the country's oil, not to mention the strategic benefit to the United States when facing the energy dislocations from Russia's invasion of the Ukraine in 2022.

47. In the rush to address climate change, why do you ignore environmental equity, which states we should do whatever we can for the environment, provided it does not increase the cost of living for poor people, and require renters who are disproportionately black and Hispanic to subsidize the electricity of well-to-do homeowners, who can afford to put solar panels on their roofs? While the Hispanic American community has begun to increasingly underpin the United States residential property market by buying homes and apartments, blacks and Hispanics still make up a higher proportion of renters. And usually, renters have to pay for their own utilities, such as electricity, water, home heating oil, natural gas, internet, and cable television. This is as it should be, to give an incentive for people not to waste heat, air-conditioning, or water. Otherwise, people might just leave their windows open in the winter for fresh air or turn the AC down in the summer to lower temperatures if they don't have to pay for that choice. Utility bills are part of what poor people must pay monthly. You should not try to increase those utility costs but rather reduce them.

So why have you supported policies that allow well-to-do homeowners to sell electricity to the public utility at retail prices, whether the utility needs the electricity or not, and allow the homeowner's meter to spin backward so that, if all works out, the homeowner owes nothing to the utility at the end of the year for electricity consumed?

---

[82]   Jason Bordoff, "No, President Trump, the US Isn't Energy Independent. Middle East Oil Still Matters," *The Washington Post*, January 10, 2020, accessed November 12, 2020.

Yet when storms come and power grids need to be re-established, or the sun doesn't shine on solar panels, the well-to-do homeowner can draw electricity from the public grid, which electricity they so desperately need for their wine cooler, hot tub, landscape accent lighting, elevators, radiant floor heat, or inefficient electric heat. During a storm, homeowners and renters alike expect a utility to send workers into the field to re-establish power using workers who get paid salaries and earn sick pay, health benefits, pensions, disability benefits, etc. to go out during and after the storm to re-establish services, yet the renter is the one who pays for all of it and the well-to-do homeowner with solar panels pays for little of it.

Before and after major storms, there are teams of bucket trucks on the highway caravanning from one state to another. Then when the repairs are complete, the bucket trucks head back to their home state. There is no need to have an oversupply of these bucket trucks and trained technicians in every state when storms usually roam around between hurricanes, tornados, and floods. Just send the trucks and workers to where they are needed. Sometimes you will see them heading to a disaster area such as New England after an ice storm, or heading home after fixing flood or wind damage to power lines in other states. Thank heavens these technicians and trucks exist! We sit inside our homes on bone-chilling February evenings, waiting impatiently for the power to get turned back on so that our heating systems might work. What a relief when it happens! We should be so glad there are people who get up in bucket trucks in the middle of the winter and at night. And who pays for these trucks and personnel? The electric utilities pay. Who pays the electric utilities? Companies and individuals who have electric meters pay based on their consumption, measured by meters. If a citizen has solar panels on the roof, it is possible that the electricity generated by those solar panels might spin the meter backward, as it sends electricity back into the electrical grid, and lets that homeowner pay less for these bucket trucks, personnel, wages, benefits, pensions, disability, sick days, and health benefits of the people working for the utility or who subcontract to the utility.

If you are well-to-do and own your own home, you can get a loan to put solar panels on your roof. With government credits for installing solar panels on their roofs, owners can make an agreement with the installation company whereby the homeowner assigns their government tax credits to the company selling the solar panels. At the same time, the system has been gamed so that the electricity that comes off these roof panels can spin the meter backward. And to make it even better for the lobbyists and owners, the utility has to buy the electricity at the same retail rate that they sell the power to the consumer. Customarily, an electric utility either generates its own power or it pays a wholesale rate for the electricity from another supplier. They buy power produced by natural gas turbines, coal-fired boilers, atomic reactors, dams, or windmills, for example. The utility hopes to pay their people, maintain their equipment, fund pensions for their workers, heat their own offices, etc. by selling electricity. The utility has to earn money.

If the homeowner with solar panels on his or her roof can sell the solar power back to the utility at retail rates, then all they have to do is have their meter end up where it started at the beginning of the year and they owe no money for electricity used. They are still likely to have a monthly service charge for being hooked up to the electrical grid. But it is the people without solar panels who end up subsidizing the fantasy of net-zero homeowners who pretend to use no more electricity than they produce, yet they have the luxury of having access to the electrical grid 24-7. This is not fair to the renter. Nobody is putting solar panels on the roofs of single-family residences so that renters have lower utility costs. Why do you support this inequitable and regressive policy for African Americans, Hispanics, whites, and Asians who rent? Why do renters have to pay for more of the upkeep of the entire electrical grid while the well-to-do have their consumption subsidized?

It is not as though the excess electricity that the homeowner spins back into the grid is necessarily put to use. Know that there are few efficient places to store surplus electricity. Electric utilities have to supply their network at whatever their customers are demanding, and any excess electricity gets driven into the ground, dissipates, and is lost forever. The rigged system to sell more solar panels to US home-owners through subsidization of homeowners by buying the power produced at retail rates is unfair to renters. In order to always meet peak demand, utilities have providers of emergency power standing by. Natural gas power plants and atomic power plants only get paid for the power that they produce. What would be slightly more equi-table to the poor is if the rates paid for electricity being spun back into the electrical grid would be credited at wholesale rates. That at least helps the numbers work for the solar panel investments already made versus curtailing the program entirely. But the burden of find-ing carbon-neutral energy sources should not be placed on the backs of the poor through higher utility rates. This raises the question on whether the poor were even consulted when this electricity buy-back program was enacted. The poor should at least be allowed into the room to comment on how it might affect them. You cannot make this type of legislation without thinking how it might affect renters unless you reward the power of insiders to game the system for their connected supporters. Remember environmental equity, that we will do whatever we can for the environment, provided it does not raise the cost of living for poor people. Had the principle of environmen-tal equity been consulted before this legislation or utility rule was passed, it would have failed and the utility rates for renters would not have been increased to benefit the well-to-do.

48. While we all should want to help the environment, and many have said that they would like to address undefined *structural racism*, do you make any connection between the environmental pol-icies you vote for and how they make life more expensive for poor people or how they eliminate existing jobs? Would you second-guess your environmental choices if they increased black unemployment or if they increased the cost of living for the poor in general and blacks in particular?

The cognoscenti speak in hushed, knowing tones how they will do away with carbon-based energy, while they rely on it to carry on their fast-paced life of flying between cities and countries, driving their own cars, living in their own house(s), eating out, going on vacation, consuming ample clothing, and running their air-conditioning. Like these cognoscenti, is your public stance opposing carbon energy taken to make you feel good and improve your social media posts and make your social media profile appear particularly enlightened, although it contradicts your carbon-intensive lifestyle? Remember that it is categorically false for a Tesla store to represent that their cars are "zero-emission." During the manufacturing process, Tesla vehicles consume not only electricity generated by natural gas, coal, or petroleum but also natural gas, coal, and petroleum to build the large batteries that go into them. And making these large batteries is a particularly dirty process, not to mention the chemical challenges of recycling an electric car at the end of its life. Electric car aficionados don't even want to contemplate the global supply chain of cobalt needed for the lithium-ion batteries that power their smooth rides. The global supply chain goes right through the child labor employed in cobalt mines of the Democratic Republic of the Congo.[83] Ten-year-olds earn $3.50 to $10.00 per day in open holes in the ground.[84] You should not be so confident in the greenness of your choices for child labor or for the environment or your record of raising the cost of living for impoverished communities through higher utility bills and fewer jobs.

[83] Sean Fleming, "The Hidden Cost of the Electric Car Boom—Child Labour," World Economic Forum, September 24, 2018, accessed November 12, 2020.
[84] Ibid.

Chapter 14

Environmental Hypocrites

49.   S CHOOLS OF ENVIRONMENTAL studies at colleges and universities promote themselves as champions of the environment, yet a more accurate description might be the school of hypocrites to further pauperize the poor. The University of Michigan's School for Environment and Sustainability claims a focus on "solving the climate crisis and crafting a world that is economically robust, environmental sound, sustainable and just."[85] What is "just" could certainly be open for discussion. But does their school encourage increasing the cost of living and diminishing the job prospects for the poor as well as eliminating whole industries that employ the poor? Does it include subsidizing the lifestyles of the well-to-do so that they can buy $135,000 Tesla automobiles and still demand a $7,500 credit from the government? Does the University of Michigan's School for Environment double down by using air-conditioning for their lecture halls or professors' offices? Do the students go for UberEats so that they can get their single meal delivered to them by somebody driving a car around? Or perhaps they cannot be bothered to hang their laundry out to dry because that is not part of

---

[85]   University of Michigan School for Environment and Sustainability, "Mission," School for Environment and Sustainability, accessed November 16, 2020.

their "sustainable" lifestyle while they make a stop to pick up a single serving of coffee on their way to wherever? A coffee they could have brewed at home. But now they can throw their "sustainable" coffee cups, which were served as two cups with a nice holder sleeve on top of that so that it would not discomfort their tort-ready fingers, into the trash. Yes, but they insisted that no plastic straws should be used while they increase the trash stream. Their delicious coffee was harvested even deeper into the forest or rain forest to achieve an even greater robust flavor—"sustainably," of course. Did you know that 10 percent of the "profits" on the sale of this "sustainable" coffee would be given to somehow help this community that is even further off the grid that brought you this divine joe? Ahh. It must feel good to consume products that shout "sustainability" all the time, so that your conscience is clear of your daily environmentally wasteful ways. Shall we buy some "distressed" clothing to accentuate our vagabond look? *Distressed clothing*, by definition, requires more energy and chemicals to produce, but no matter if the consumer can feel better about their fashion choices. Would this all fit within the "sustainable," environmentally sound, and just world envisioned by the University of Michigan's School of Environment and Sustainability? Yet ye are mostly hypocrites! Do not watch what they do but listen to what they say and lecture.

Consider that air-conditioning did not exist years ago. It takes energy to air-condition your office, your car, and your home. It would be fair to say that most schools of environmental studies meet in air-conditioned buildings. Why? It hurts the environment. Many teachers and students get to their environmental schools with air-conditioning in their cars and public transportation. That wastes energy. In addition, the teachers, professors, and students use air-conditioning in their homes and apartments versus the old-school option of fans, showers, and open windows. Air-conditioning is a comfort that people in developed countries have come to appreciate, rich and poor. Would a poor person be begrudged for his or her desire to also live or spend part of their time in air-conditioned comfort? Is that only something that people in environmental study programs should enjoy? Should it be made more or less expensive? If it is made more expensive, then poor people will have less of it. Is that just? Is that what *sustainable* means? If environmental laws make it more expensive to run a business or bring a product to market in the interest of lowering carbon emissions, how much value should be placed on raising the cost of living for poor people and/or diminishing their pay or ability to get a job in such a business? Politicians make a lot of noise about all the new jobs that would be created in new environmental businesses to offset putting people out of work in other industries. That is talk and good politics. It seems, however, that relying on politicians to deliver the goods is concentrating too much power in the government at the expense of businesses that actually hire people, pay people and are the best vehicle toward building economic independence for the poor. The end effect of regulating and delaying projects and business may help the environment, but it always raises costs and thereby disproportionately affects African Americans. And did you say you wanted to try a different path, or just the same path you have walked for years, expecting a different result?

Chapter 15

Houses and Apartments Made More Expensive to Satisfy Special Interests and the American Dream Put Further Out of Reach for African-Americans and Others

50. WHY DO YOU kill construction and supply jobs for the working poor and middle class by making more rules to renovate an existing house or build a new house, which makes them more expensive to build? In the town of Greenwich, Connecticut, for example, the combination of environmental, building, and zoning rules has increased the time to get a permit from two months to six to seven months in order to build a new house over the past twenty years. Every delay, every new certification by an engineer, every new round of building plans cost money and make it less attractive to build a home to rent or sell. It may be a development that includes some affordable housing units. It may be the simple law of supply and demand that the more housing you have, the less expensive it becomes overall, which helps make housing more affordable to the poor. There are no circumstances under which having fewer housing units available lowers the cost of houses for the same number of people. The fewer housing units you build, the more expensive housing becomes for the poor. Look at the lofty real estate prices in California, which is captive of the administrative state and extensive rules. In 2020, the poor and the not-so-poor were living

in cars and vans on the streets of Los Angeles and San Francisco, progressive meccas. How is that fair to the poor and the not-so-poor when the administrative state chokes off the supply of housing and blames it on companies that actually provide jobs? That is the mark of a good politician: make a mess of things and blame it on someone else. San Francisco and Los Angeles have some of the most expensive real estate in the nation, but 2019 and thereafter saw an increasing number of citizens living in the streets, in their cars, and on the couches of friends and families as the restrictive government regulations have choked off building enough housing for all their citizens over a course of decades.

The advocates for all these restrictions have sincere objectives but add yet another layer to the ever-tightening regulation of building shelter for our citizens, rich and poor. The houses for the well-to-do become more expensive through time delays, further engineering submissions, greater building code requirements, and higher costs of compliance. The middle class have to compete for fewer new houses built and higher costs to add to what they already have, if they are fortunate enough to be homeowners. And the poor are left holding the bag as the short supply of housing increases rents and purchases for everyone, and as the poor have fewer resources by definition, there is little they can do. The politicians then come trotting out to promote rent freezes, no evictions, and rent control for a problem that the politicians created themselves. What gall! But if they can say it with a straight face and sound as if they are being compassionate, then more votes for them and fewer houses and apartments built into the future as the incentives to rent are diminished by rent control. What a perfect combination for these cynical statists—create housing shortages through increased bureaucracy and rules; promote rent control or rent freezes, thereby creating even fewer available houses and apartments for rent; make it more expensive to build new housing stock; and then ask for re-election based on railing against the housing shortage and high free market rents that the statists created themselves.

51. Why do you ladle so many new rules into the permitting process for commercial and residential projects so that what was once a two-month permitting process is now more like a six- to seven-month process, thereby increasing costs and killing countless projects and therefore jobs for African Americans, Hispanics, Asians, whites, and others in the construction and supply businesses, not to mention the tax revenue lost by the municipal governments and increasing the cost of the most expensive thing we ever buy, a house, disproportionately affecting impoverished communities. Does it make you feel warm inside? Do you sleep better knowing you have made their lives more difficult? In 2000, one could make it through the permitting process in a coastal flood zone in Greenwich, but not directly on the water, in two months. That included the coastal review authority, sign-off by Inland Wetlands if no wetlands were on the property, sewer department permit, highway department permit, zoning enforcement review, floor area review, and building department review. By 2020, it took six months or more for the same effort. There are no appreciable benefits to the community, and certainly none to the property owner. Time is money, not just in the number of extra months that someone has to pay mortgage, taxes, and insurance on an unusable property but also in that professionals must be paid to process mind-numbing paperwork for six to seven months versus for two months. It inherently costs more. And it is still the same house. The same number of people can find shelter in this house in 2020 as they could in 2000. There has been zero appreciable benefit to society.

This is merely obeisance to the administrative state. Just imagine if a Realtor were to show you properties and you asked the Realtor for the difference between the cost of buying a used house and renovating it to what you want or buying land or a house and knocking the house down and building what you want. What are the cost differences? New houses are invariably more expensive than used houses, but by how much more? When you add four months into the equation for either project, though the new house usually takes longer to get through the permitting process, as there are more minimal environmental calculations, that does not only add four months to the project, which most of us do not have the luxury of absorbing, but also affects your life by an additional four to five months. Children have to go to school. Temporary housing may have to be found for a longer time, as well as carrying two properties for a longer period, which costs more money.

In the not-too-recent past, the Realtor might have told his or her client that they could contract to buy a property and, while they waited two to three months to close, could design their house and start the permitting process, then after they closed on the property, they could get their permit within a few months and build their house or renovate and add to their new house and be in their new house or the renovation/addition one year after closing. Now the Realtor will tell their customer that it would not be twelve months but closer to eighteen months since the permitting and inspections will be so long. This dislocation for more time will dissuade even more citizens from building their own home. What a tragedy! Where the politicians have teamed with the professionals to make an ever more intricate web of regulations and certifications, the professional engineers and architects have placed the American dream further away for the poor of all colors! The engineers might think themselves clever by layering up all these requirements that call for the services of an engineer, whether environmental, civil, and structural, but they have actually given themselves less work because there are fewer projects. So while they feast on the fees that they can impose on the few sorry rubes who come through their door, so many other citizens are locked out of even dreaming of one day building or owning a new or completely renovated home.

The proponents of the administrative state seek to control ever more of our lives and economy, counter to the principle that they are supposed to be working for the common good. Their critics say that the statists are working, mostly to amass more power and votes so that they can stay in power. The advancement of the poor is a secondary consideration, if at all. What gets lost in this regulatory morass is that there are factions that are working to improve their chances and not just the statists. Society wants a consumer to know before they buy a house whether it is in a one-hundred-year flood zone and whether that will involve flood insurance. A consumer should also know whether the house or apartment they buy is located in a polluted area. That is as it should be, and it does not slow a real estate transaction. But what other rules prevent an electrician who works for somebody else to go out on their own to start their own business and realize the American dream? Is there a noncompete clause that forces them out of where they live so that they would have to move? What is behind the phase "I am trying to help you"? Is the statist or faction trying to service themselves more than the citizen? We should not be impressed by the flyer received in the mail that touts all the laws that the politician passed. What have they done to lessen the burdens on creating jobs for African Americans and other Americans? What has the politician done to make it more likely that an African American or other American can engage in a trade or business?

What happens when a house or apartment is not built? Jobs are lost for excavators, foundation contractors, framers, landscapers, concrete producers, lumberyard workers, truck drivers, carpenters, plumbers, electricians, air-conditioning and heating contractors, insulators, wallboard installers, wallboard suppliers, finish carpenters, door and window manufacturers and suppliers, siders, roofers, copper workers, masons, well drillers, septic installers, interior designers, bathroom supply house workers, kitchen appliance suppliers, garage door sales and installation workers, salespeople, refuse collectors, and back-office people to make all these companies work. Do you see yourself as one of these people? Do you work for one of these people? Do you need an advanced degree to do any of these jobs and do them well? Of course not, but the statists and their allies on the inside systematically try to reduce your job opportunities and your opportunities to start and own your own business and machinery.

Yet the statists will tell you that they are appalled at something referred to as systemic racism. Just don't tell the statists that this is just one example of systemic racism, as all these rules, delays, and denial of opportunities disproportionately affect the poor in general and the African American community in particular. Job opportunities are reduced. Ownership of businesses is reduced. But the statists press on every month and every year, putting in more restrictions to show how well they can cut and paste requirements from other states and jurisdictions into their own states! "Look at me. Look how many more requirements I can saddle our community and poor with to further diminish their economic chances." And you claim to oppose systemic racism? You are systemic racism! Look in the mirror and know thyself. You are the problem, not the poor.

52. And to add insult to injury, the administrators in the zoning department of the town of Greenwich will answer an inquiry on whether a certificate of occupancy can be issued after a house is finished so that a family can move into their new home or renovated home with the following: "We do not object to the issuance of a certificate of occupancy." This is outrageous! After having made the homeowner slog through unnecessary and burdensome regulations and shepherd documents around the local municipality and to hire engineers, surveyors, and a whole slew of workers to build a house in order for the homeowner to get closer to pursuing their happiness, under the Declaration of Independence, of owning a new home or a newly renovated home, the administrator "does not object" to the family getting permission to move into their own home? This is upside down! Our God-given rights set forth in the Declaration of Independence allow us to pursue our happiness, and the human rights set forth in our Bill of Rights are not beholden to a government administrator who decides whether you will enjoy your God-given rights. It is not the zoning department's place to object to your God-given rights! It is the role of the zoning department and, by extension, all government agencies, to help, assist, and accelerate a citizen's realization of the happiness they pursue. You work for us; we do not work for you! Although some government agencies do seek for the citizen to prostrate themselves before the administrative state with the hope that the state will grant the citizen what is already rightfully the citizen's, the right to pursue their happiness. Flipping the script that the citizen must come on bended knee to the state for the citizen to pursue their happiness is a structural problem that permeates not just the zoning department of the town of Greenwich, which "does not object" to the citizen pursuing their rights under the Declaration

of Independence and our Constitution, but also many departments throughout the government. Will you change that mindset or double down on the subjugation of the citizen to the state or allow self-interested groups to get rules through to benefit themselves?

53. Why do you make homeownership more difficult and unaffordable for American citizens? Prior to 1971, Connecticut did not have a state building code, although various communities had their own local building codes that might address how a home is to be built. How far have we come since then? In 2020, Vermont still did not have a state building code for owner-occupied single-family homes, although various towns might have their own municipal building codes. Vermont still had requirements for installing septic systems and wells, as both are critical for the health of its residents, but Vermont trusts its people to build houses well enough that somebody else would be willing to live in them. Maybe you hit your head on something because it is not tall enough or you are too tall, but that was deemed okay by the people who built the house or who bought it. The important thing is to keep the cost down in an area where work is not easy to get, as it is on the economic periphery of American commerce on the Canadian border, and tourism and second homes can only take an economy so far. It is unlikely that any reader would change their Airbnb reservation for a weekend rental to view the beautiful fall foliage once the reader learned that there may have been no building code for the quaint house they have rented at the edge of a field with a view over a pond, to the myriad of fall colors still hanging onto the trees and carpeting the floor of the forest. Maintained homes do not fall down in Vermont. People live their entire lives in houses built without a building code in Vermont. How sacrilegious for a statists to live in a house that has not been permitted or approved by the state! Do not fear. Those houses are safe, and Vermont is a wonderful place to visit at all times of the year. And the quality of houses is tested in Vermont much more due to subzero weather than houses in warm climates, which rarely face such conditions.

Despite this evidence, the engineers and special-interest groups who manufacture new and improved products for houses get together every year and dream up ways to make the American dream less obtainable for our citizens. These engineers and manufacturers have indeed come up with new products for homes to make some elements of building safer and better. There are certainly improvements in fire and electrical safety that are a step forward. Many of us are familiar with GFI outlets in our kitchens and bathrooms that trip when short-circuited. They are a neat advance in safety. There are some framing techniques that make it harder for fire to spread quickly in a home. Fire and smoke detectors are a recent and inexpensive development. One of the biggest advances in energy efficiency has been open- and closed-cell spray foam insulation. The sealing and insulation quality of spray foam transforms an ordinary house into a twenty-first-century house. But there are also fasteners that are better than old fasteners. Engineers compete with their slide rulers to show how a house can be made even stronger to withstand a direct hit by a hurricane or tornado. The efficiency of water heaters and furnaces has improved. Heat pumps have become more efficient. Windows have become better at not letting as much cold into the house and to shield sunrays in warm climates, which would heat up the indoors. Siding material has become more diverse in finishes and materials that an exterior really can become maintenance-free and still look good. Home entertainment systems and smart wiring for connected homes are here to stay. How about controlling the heating, cooling, music, and security system from the convenience of your own smartphone? It is all available and was not imagined thirty years ago. Building science keeps advancing, and new products are developed. How better to keep up with and surpass the Joneses than with the latest advancements that were not even available when the Joneses bought their house? This is as it should be, particularly in a free market system, where the citizen consumer and privately owned companies decide what people like and what will be built. Imagine if a bureaucrat told a company what they would build or would tell a consumer what they would buy.

In a perfect world, marketing and the merit of the newly developed products would be enough to find a market for the new good. But that is not enough for some. In order for the manufacturers to get the public to buy their products, they get our professional engineers to put these new products into model building codes. Every few years this conspiracy of interests puts out an even more expansive and expensive model building code and energy code for consideration by the fifty states. There is no federal building code. Each year one or more states bend the arm of its people and adopt an even more stringent and expensive building code. This is reported as progress by the press since it is a newer code and will make buildings less susceptible to direct hits from tornadoes or right in the path of a hurricane, and "sustainable" and "energy" features are mandated into ever-newer codes. The statists even have inspectors now inspecting how well plywood is nailed before they can cover the exterior plywood with a building wrap, like roofing felt or house wrap. This is all madness in the name of building science!

You need to step back and look at how a Realtor views the housing market. A Realtor will sell you any house or apartment that you want. They will sell you a house made in 1880, 1890, 1900, 1910, 1920, 1930, 1940, 1950, 1960, and 1970. And you will buy them. Perhaps you have heard of midcentury modern houses, which have picked up in popularity for their open and breezy floor plans. Have you not heard of the advice to buy a 1930s house because it has good bones? Well, all these houses were built before the Connecticut State building code was enacted in 1971. Imagine that. And they still haven't fallen down. Even the shoddy houses haven't fallen down! Who wouldn't jump at the opportunity to move into a midcentury modern house from 1955 that has been updated with a new kitchen and bathrooms and had the floors refinished and a new paint job added? Wait. The house was not built with the most recent building code. Is it safe? Ask the people who live there. It is safe and offers a great life, and yet the statists keep making the American dream harder to realize. We can make automobiles safer for the occupant, but we chose not to because of the extra costs associated with bigger air bags, more generous impact zones in the front, side, and rear of the vehicles. There could be more extensive passive monitoring in cars, such as was found in the high-end Tesla automobiles that had encouraged some to take their hands off the wheel and take a nap while underway, if viral videos are to be believed. But a cost-benefit analysis is made as to the extra cost and the amount of lives saved. By the same token, a house can be made safer and more durable from a direct hit by a tornado or very high winds. What may be advisable for a house in Florida, situated on the Atlantic Ocean, is different from what might be required for a house in the middle of Massachusetts. Double-wide homes, which are a combination of two factory-built sections of a house that are bolted together on a foundation and their cousin, the trailer home are highly affordable and practical forms of housing, but they can also be more susceptible to high winds and tornados in all parts of America, but they should definitely remain in the mix as affordable means of housing.

In Connecticut, some towns make you fortify shear walls. A shear wall is where an engineer has calculated a wall in a house with significant forces tugging, pushing, and pulling on it. Instead of just having plywood nailed on the exterior of this wall, the builder then has to nail plywood, which may be of a thicker variety, on the inside of that same wall. This means that the plumbing pipes, electrical wires, low-voltage wires, and insulation all have to be installed and inspected before plywood is fastened on the inside wall, which is then customarily covered with wallboard, which is what we paint, but is also a barrier to fire. This takes time. This creates delay, and it wasn't required decades before. Then there is the practice of making one have metal straps preinstalled into a poured concrete foundation sticking out of the foundation, which straps are then supposed to be nailed into the two-by-four or two-by-six framing members that make up the exterior walls to make it less likely that the house can be lifted from its foundation. Or there are threaded steel rods drilled and epoxied into the foundation that are then bolted into framing members on the first floor. But wait, the town wants to inspect how well the framers nailed the exterior plywood into the sill plate and vertical framing members before you can apply house wrap, such as roofing felt or a plastic type of house wrap. Then there are straps that they want you to nail on the outside of the building between the first floor and the second floor, so you need to make sure that the framing members of the first floor line up with the faming members of the second floor to receive the straps. The mid-century modern house from 1958 did not have any of this nonsense, and yet it is still standing and beckoning its next family to make a home and memories there.

The Special Study for Housing Economics of the National Association of Home Builders put the changes to building codes from 2011 to 2021 at 10.8 percent of the cost of actually building the home.[86] This 10.8 percent does not even encompass the added costs in Connecticut since the first state building code of 1971. Yet the statists and insiders with their able lobbyists continue to push to make housing less affordable and less available. The 2021 National Home Builder survey did not stop with just the changes to building codes; it found another 7.7 percent increase for architectural design standards beyond the ordinary. The shear wall example above is but a sampling of this madness as architects in Connecticut have to submit shear wall calculations and how to remedy them. The fees paid by builders after they buy the buildable lot to construct a house then have to make their way through further permitting processes for wetlands' permits, if applicable, coastal zone permits, building permits, highway permits, and sewer permits. The price and number of permits needed tend to go up as opposed to go down or disappear. Standards of the Occupational Safety and Hazard Administration have also tightened to apply occupational standards from indoor work to outdoor work or airborne particles that may be unnecessary can also add marginal costs.

This National Association of Home Builder survey of the impact of regulation on new home prices had been done in 2011, 2016, and 2021. Their survey of the average cost of regulation in the price of a new home from development of the lots through the actual construction of the new homes went from $65,224 in 2011 to $84,671 in 2016 to $93,870 in 2021. None of these costs reflect the actual ele-

---

[86] Paul Emrath, "Government Regulation in the Price of a New Home: 2021," May 5, 2021.

ments of a new home, such as the concrete for the foundation, lumber for the faming, nails, glue, and bolts to hold it together, shingles for the roof, windows to look through, appliances and countertops to prepare and cook a meal on, asphalt for a driveway or grass seed, and plants for a yard. The former is all money that is consumed in dealing with the regulatory state. The regulatory state is an important watchdog for the resources of the community and to ensure a minimum of construction standards for the health and safety of the community. But that was being done already in 1971, fifty or more years before. What has been ladled on top has been excessive and has made housing less affordable and available for the poor and middle class! How does one right the ship so that this debacle of feathering the bed of the insiders and strengthening the hand of the statists who promote the state over the citizen is pushed back so that the interest of the poor and middle class to housing and decent jobs in the housing industry is returned to the fore?

The Connecticut building code should be set back to 1971, with some of the fire, electrical and energy improvements developed in the meantime retained. If a builder wants to build a house to the latest-model building code and believe that will sell to the discerning consumer, then let them. They should be free to throw their money out of the window and build to a 2020-model residential building code. Let them do that and find the customers who are willing to pay for such nonsense. But don't systematically make it more difficult for those less fortunate than these well-to-do consumers who dream of owning a new home or apartment or raising their family in a new or renovated home or apartment. This disproportionately affects African Americans, and it definitely causes fewer houses to be built.

Fewer homes built reduces job and business opportunities for all Americans generally and African Americans specifically. Statists should also think of the tax revenue lost from fewer houses being built. There are less permit fees paid. The tax base relies more on the older homes, where older people might live, versus the new and more expensive new homes. Then there is the tax revenue that flows from more goods and services being sold and more income being earned. It has been said that in the state of Connecticut, if all the people that have been chased out of the state by the increased taxes in Connecticut, just their income taxes would have been enough to make up for Connecticut's chronic budget shortfalls. But there are some in government, for whom there is never enough money pulled in from businesses and citizens of the state. Let the free market determine what builders and homeowners put into their homes. Under the scenario of a simplified building code, there will be more houses built, and they will be less-expensive homes. Don't require a homeowner to bury $55,000 of useless building and drainage requirements in their yards, never to be seen again. First you have to have the $55,000 to bury, never to be seen again. Since the average net worth of an African American is less than that of a white American, these myriad requirements systematically put homeownership and jobs and businesses in the trades further out of reach for African Americans, and by extension the American dream. This is but another form of systemic racism. We don't have your resources. Don't make us live in your gold-plated world, as some of us cannot afford it.

To improve upon this dismal state of affairs, the building code in most states should be put back to the first building code that that state adopted. In the case of the state of Connecticut, that would be 1971. To ask the other states to actually abolish their building codes is to short-circuit too many statists, as they cannot imagine a world not in the cold, steely embrace of the state. Remember, the state cannot hug or love you; only a human being can hug and love you. The state can never be our parent, guardian, brother, or sister. If a state's residential building code were brought back to the state's first code, that does not prohibit including advances in energy efficiency, fire, and electrical safety. But requirements to have two garden hose outlets on a house, or two outside electrical outlets, could be reduced to one each. If a builder or a consumer wants to pay for it, then that becomes a free market decision, which is a decision free of coercion, otherwise known as someone exercising their free will. That is a better future than the coercive nature of the administrative state: "Do as we say, or else." Electrical outlets within twenty-five feet of a heating or cooling appliance or a light in a utility closet could be eliminated. Horror that a tradesperson would actually have to bring a shop light or extension cord when they go to work on a property. All these things add cost. No, the town should not have to look at how many nails were shot into plywood before it can be covered. Shear wall calculations will not have to be made or inspected where none were required before. The houses are still standing.

Action could go further to make new homes less expensive. A whole new "affordable housing code" could be enacted within the original building code. This would be an option for citizens to build affordable houses for themselves. Any house 3,800 square feet and less, excluding garage space of less than 900 square feet could qualify for affordable home building. Preliminarily, the house could be built with two-by-four studs provided open-cell spray foam insulation is used to a depth of three inches in the walls. The roof would have to be insulated by open-cell spray foam insulation from a minimum of nine inches from the roof ridge to the plate so there is no freezing attic in winter and boiling attic in summer. Spray foam insulation would obviate the need for any blower door tests to see how tightly the house is built for outside air intrusion. All heating and cooling machinery and ductwork would be installed in the conditioned space. At most, 10 percent of ductwork could be installed in unconditioned space that is exposed to the cold in the winter and the heat of the summer. Basements would not have to have open vents to allow warm, moist air in in the summer and cold, frigid air in in the winter. Appliances that require air to run a heater would use outside air. In areas that have not seen frost below two feet in the winter at any point in the last fifty years, they could start their foundations at 2 feet below grade as opposed to 3.5 feet, with water, sewer, and septic still delivered at the depths required today. "Smart framing" of placing headers in the floor system above and eliminating headers over doors and window, as well as cripples, would be encouraged to lessen the wood consumed to build a home. Twenty-four-inch on-center roof rafters would be encouraged to also limit the amount of wood consumed and increase energy performance. This also reduces thermal bridging of interior warmth to the outside through the wood, as spray foam insulation is a better insulator. Only one outside garden hose outlet and electrical outlet would be required. No additional outlets would be required for lazy tradesmen who don't like to bring their own extension cords or droplights. Arc-fault breakers in bedrooms would be eliminated to what was allowed previously. Permitting would be by certification by licensed engineers as to adherence to building codes, with a municipality given fourteen days to point out deficiencies, if any, before a building permit is issued at the end of these 14 days. A municipality is able to point out any code deficiencies they missed in the first fourteen days at any time after issuance of the building permit.

This "affordable housing code" within the building code would reduce the cost of building a home but still bring the revolutionary technology of spray foam insulation and efficient water and home heating units to homes made for lower-income people. This would lower the lifetime operating expense of the home to the home-owner as well as the renter. These new technologies also improve the comfort in winter and summer in the home for the occupants. By decreasing the time that one has to wait to get a permit and the time to build a home, as well as the actual cost to build the home, the quantity of new homes built with newer technologies and greater energy efficiency than our existing housing stock can be increased. More homes means a lowering of prices under the laws of supply and demand. That could be a way to address the amorphous *structural racism* that was talked about after the killing of George Floyd but, in this circumstance, boils down to *structural statism* that makes life harder for the poor in terms of affordability and in terms of job and business opportunities.

Chapter 16

Job Training or Jobs: Which Is More Important?

ECORD LOW UNEMPLOYMENT for the black community is a
social good and something that should be worked for, as
would record low unemployment for all strata of society.
Which of two routes will you continue to pursue after the killing of
George Floyd: job training or a strong economy? You can only follow
or promote one; you cannot say both, as then you are speaking like
a politician who promises you everything under the sun. What are
the principles of the politician? For those of us who are older, it is a
standard plank of politicians that they will lower your taxes and they
will eliminate waste and fraud in the government. When the citizen
hears that, his or her eyes should gloss over. "We will put the government's information online, and thereby the government will be made
more transparent. We will have Freedom of Information Act requests
so that the government will provide documents and information to
the citizen, who is theoretically the sovereign." Yet after the killing of
George Floyd, we learned the inconvenient truth that curtains have
been drawn in front of certain operations that will not be shared with
the public as they are personal or they involve disciplinary matters
that are still ongoing or it is part of an ongoing investigation and
cannot be compromised, etc., etc. The statists are adept at putting
up shields to protect the state. But let the politicians continue to tell

you that they will give job training and relocation resources so that people can move to where the jobs are. That is all well and good and has its place, but what are the guiding principles?

Shall there be a vigorous economy sucking employees up out of the populace because their businesses need them? Or will it be a slower economy with higher unemployment due to higher rates of taxation and regulation for all things business? So that the "compassionate" government can go about making things better as they see it, spending the citizen's money as the politicians see appropriate, as opposed to leaving it in the citizen's purse or wallet for the citizen to spend as they see fit. As the politicians increase the cost of food, housing, transportation, clothing, and recreation through heightened sales taxes, user fees, environmental surcharges, licensing requirements, certifications and recertifications, eligibility requirements, remedial measures, "revenue" measures, and outright favoritism of businesses and individuals who have contributed time or money to their campaigns or allies? The latter is not government of, by, and for the people; it is run by statists for statists, and unless a citizen happens to be on the inside, the citizen will be on the outside looking in. Will you continue to give more power to these "compassionate" yet, at the same time, cruel statists?

A truism is that the power to tax is the power to destroy. Try as you might, if the statist wants to destroy your business, your community, your state, they can do it with a thousand small fees, taxes, and revenues until the citizen has been driven to his or her knees. Some will not be able to leave as they have neither the resources nor the contacts to start afresh somewhere else. There sits the cynical "compassionate" politician, lording over the poor souls who are left in their political fiefdom. Look at failed cities and who has been running them and for how long. Yet these "compassionate" politicians can rail against the system as it is always the system that has upended their plans at improvement. More of the same.

One is not supposed to use *never*, as there are always exceptions, but these political machines that have been in power for decades *never* say that they will back away from the statist playbook of more state, more rules, more regulations, more government guidance, more state employees, more taxes from their citizens and from state or national governments coffers, and more gatekeeping by the local government. The reason that these political machines have failed their constituencies is never admitted, as it is always something else. Witness Bridgeport, Connecticut, the largest city in the state of Connecticut, which sits on Long Island Sound and has two major highways passing through it, with many high-quality secondary roads leading into it. Then there is a four-track railroad that goes through it with Amtrak, commercial and commuter trains, constantly stopping and going through Bridgeport and an able workforce. Yet despite decades of aid from the state capital of Hartford and from Washington, DC, it consistently underperforms its potential in people, location, and capital. Its mayor, Joseph P. Ganim, a gregarious and positive man, was convicted in 2003 of racketeering, extortion, bribery, and mail fraud, among other felonies, in connection with a six-year scheme to shake down city contractors for more than $500,000 in cash, meals, clothing, wine, and home renovations.[87] He did his time and redeemed himself. He was even re-elected as mayor. In 2017–2018, he ran for governor of the state of Connecticut as a Democrat. In 2020, he was still mayor, and his chief of police, Armando Perez, resigned in September 2020 after federal authorities charged him with rigging the city's 2018 police chief examination to guarantee that Mr. Perez would get the position, according to the *Hartford Courant*.[88] The point is not specifically about Mrs. Ganim or Perez but rather on how these machines can take hold of a political jurisdiction and not let go. The clutches of the "compassionate" statists are so strong that the jurisdiction cannot be wrested from their death grip for the benefit of the citizens. This is the cautionary warning for choosing between a strong economy to lift all boats and the "compassionate" politician, who is touting job training or other government policy that is going to make everything better.

---

[87] Paul Von Ziebauer, "Bridgeport Mayor Convicted on 16 Charges of Corruption," *The New York Times*, March 20, 2003.

[88] Edmund H. Mahony, "Bridgeport Police Chief Resigns after He's Charged with Fraud and Accused of Rigging a Promotional Exam to Guarantee Himself the Position," *Hartford Courant*, September 10, 2020.

A glaring example of how broken Bridgeport's political system is lies right beneath the busy elevated I-95 interstate highway that rumbles through Bridgeport on recently expanded and smooth four-lane highways with generous exit and entry ramps. Right there below I-95, on what is partly Steel Point, is a very desirable piece of real estate. Before the COVID-19 pandemic, it had the makings of what urbanization was looking for. It had an easy exit and entrance onto I-95. The Bridgeport train station for Metro-North and Amtrak trains was a short ride away. It had water on two sides and faced the sun from the south. There had been homes and neighborhoods on this point decades before that had fallen into disrepair, and these houses had been mostly cleared and the area left desolate until deals could be made. Lest you think that these "deals" would benefit the citizen, you would be wrong. A concept in real estate is finding the highest and best use for a property. It does not make sense to build a single-family home in downtown Manhattan, as that would be an underutilization of the property for just one family, considering how expensive the land would be. Rather, an office tower or a residential apartment building is more likely to be the highest and best use of the land. Perhaps there might be offices in the lower levels and apartments in the upper levels? Maybe there would be a hotel stuck in there somewhere? Depending on the zoning for the area, the real estate people would try to calculate the best use, which in the end usually produces the most dollars since the economy rewards the efficient use of our resources. And more money coming out of that development will give rise to more property taxes to the municipality. If more workers come in to work there, then that will help restaurant and shops in the area that might sell to these workers. If it is an apartment tower, the residents are likely to be residents of the city, and they would then pay income taxes, not just to the federal government and Albany, New York, but also an income tax to the city of New York. Similarly, the fertile farmland of Iowa away from a major city is not the place to build a condominium complex on if there are no amenities nearby. Probably not the highest and best use of the land. In Greenwich, Connecticut, there has been a slow gentrification of downtown areas of Greenwich that are in multifamily zones. What had once housed single-family homes or smaller multi-family homes are now being knocked down to make room for town-homes containing four homes built to every available square inch. Properties on or close to the train tracks, with the smell of asbestos dust from the train's brakes in the air, are being replaced with luxury condominium buildings within earshot, smell, and view of six lanes of onrushing traffic on I-95. In other circumstances, the hypocrites of environmental studies postulate that poor people have been rel-egated intentionally to polluted housing sites near train tracks and highways; but if it is done in gentrifying areas in Greenwich and Stamford, it is called gentrification. Who knew that the exact same piece of real estate could be two things at the same time, depending on the political views of our betters?

Pre-COVID-19 pandemic, what would be the highest and best use of urban land with an elevated highway on one side and water on the other two sides? Wouldn't that be a clear slate for private enterprise to put in high-rise apartment buildings right on the water? Isn't that one of the biggest sellers of real estate? Water? Then you have south-ern views toward the sun and out to Long Island Sound. Wouldn't there be some office buildings so people could live and work in the community? There would certainly be some waterfront restaurants for people to come from outside to enjoy the water. Maybe some docks so that people can have boats to drive or sail out to Long Island Sound? Cars would be parked in parking garages. There would be regular shuttles to the nearby Bridgeport train station. Or perhaps part of the parcel would be returned to affordable, tightly sited sin-gle-family homes with modest gardens in back and a one-car garage. A whole variety of possibilities is offered by free enterprise in coop-eration with the city and state to lay roads and public utilities. There could even be waterside parks and walking trails. That, however, is not what became of Steel Point. Far from it. If statists are in it for themselves, they need to assure their re-election. They need to make sure their friends, supporters, and sycophants are provided with jobs and benefits. "Did such-and-such contractor donate to my cam-paign?" "Did such-and-such contractor donate to the local political party?" "Who works for that contractor?" "If the contractor were to 'win' this contract, what is the likelihood that the contractor will hire my niece or nephew?" "Whom will they buy supplies or services from? They need to keep the system going." Did this happen at Steel Point? I don't know. You be the judge.

In 2020, if you cruised by on I-95 or if you stopped in to admire the Bass Pro Shop that is now located there, you will be impressed with the amount of parking lots and roads! That is correct, parking lots for the Carefree Boat Club at Bridgeport, the Bass Pro Shops, and Chipotle Mexican Grill. You cannot make this up. One of the last uses for prime urban property on the water and convenient to highways and mass transit is for parking lots! That would make about as much sense as planting corn or wheat there on a farm! You can't make this up. Most anyone will tell you that it is possible to have parking lots with upper and lower levels or under the Bass Pro Shop itself. This is what happens when "compassionate" politicians who claim to be champions for the poor and the least among us have and hold power and ask you time and again to support their compassionate view of more government. Would free enterprise have done a better job developing Steel Point in cooperation with the city and state? Unequivocally, yes.

Politicians say they represent everything and everyone and can do a better job than their opponent. At the end of the day, you can either support historically low unemployment for African American men and women and historically low unemployment for Hispanic men and women and historically low unemployment for white and Asian Americans, or you can support job training for African Americans, Hispanics, whites, Asian Americans, and others in the effort to help the less-fortunate among us. The catch with the job training, however, is that there may be no job at the end of the job training program. There may be no position that needs filling. And for ex-cons, many of whom are African American, there is even less likely to be a job at the end of the training program. But the politician got the votes and was able to market his or her compassion as he or she was able to promote "job training." None of us want a situation where a person goes through job training and there is no job at the end of the process. Not a make-believe job where somebody gets a check for not doing anything, but rather a job where the trainee shows up and does actual work and contributes to society and feels like they are contributing. But the jobs-training politician can only deliver one thing, and that may be job training. The jobs-training politician cannot deliver an actual job or an economy that lifts all boats, because the jobs-training politician puts the state before the citizen.

Is record low unemployment more important or less important than job training programs? This is not an idle question. *Job training* is a throwaway line for politicians immemorial. It is true that when the requirements of the economy change, whole swaths of the economy can find itself out of favor. A factory might close. A technology might end. The worker needs new skills and might need to relocate to another area of the country where there is more opportunity. Those are legitimate concerns, but *job training* is mentioned repeatedly by politicians. We can all be for job training. But what are we training for? A job. A job is more important and emotionally satisfying than job training. When you do a job, no matter what it is, you are giving back to society. You can feel satisfaction for doing your job reliably and consistently. Prior to the COVID-19 coronavirus outbreak, the United States had low unemployment. Many employers were looking for workers. Job postings were not being filled. That can slow a company down, but it can also make companies grab for more workers. At the same time, black and Hispanic unemployment hit a fifty-year low! And that is a good thing. The wages of the lowest quintile of workers were finally increasing at a faster rate than those of the quintiles above it. That had been a long time coming, as low unemployment rates would heat up the wages at the low end. Then there is the historic problem for ex-convicts to find gainful employment in the economy when they get out of jail. Some of these ex-convicts might bring substance use issues with them as well as other isms, but jobs are key to re-enter into society, earn your keep, and give back. In a strong economy, ex-convicts were getting and holding actual jobs. This is a social good. So if you want to look at structural racism, you need to decide whether low unemployment or job training is more important. You cannot waver and say both, as that avoids the hard question. That is a cop-out. If job training is more important, then the strength of the economy takes a back seat. If a strong economy with record low unemployment is more important, then job training takes a back seat. As a realistic matter, with a tight labor market, companies will run their own job training to get the people they need.

Before the COVID-19 pandemic from China struck in March 2020, it was pretty clear that President Trump would win re-election the following fall with record-breaking numbers for black unemployment, Hispanic unemployment, wealth created in the black and Hispanic communities, more drops in child poverty, and a long-awaited increase in the income of the lowest quintile of workers compared to the other four quintiles after lagging the income growth for the upper four quintiles for years. The record numbers kept racking up, which gave credence to a rising economy lifting all boats and not just an economy that benefits the elites, who are tied into the corridors of power in Washington, DC. Only the COVID-19 pandemic and the president's feasance or nonfeasance, in the eyes of the beholder, delivered a close election to former vice president Joe Biden by 51 percent to 47.31 percent, leading some to question whether Libertarian candidate Jo Jorgensen siphoned off enough votes in contested states so as to deliver those states to Vice President Joe Biden. Quixotically, the party of the losing candidate, the Republican Party, picked up at least ten seats in the United States House of Representatives. When does it happen that the winning presidential candidate has no coattails to bring more of his party with him or her? If you have to choose between a strong economy that lifts all boats or job training with no guarantee of a job at the end of the training, which one do you choose?

Yes. So how could one support President Trump in 2020 and before in view of the many inartful tweets and comments he made that stepped on many toes? Because the best way to help the least among us is through a strong economy with rising wages for all. The best way to help the poor is to increase their participation in the job market, to get more citizens on the ladder of success. By remaining within government aid programs created by the Welfare-Industrial

Complex, a citizen cannot rise up and out to be on their own. The only way that a citizen can rise up and out is by stepping their feet outside of the Welfare-Industrial Complex in that first job, in that second job, often at the same time. Nothing is more certain than the likelihood that the citizen will still be a client of the state ten years hence if he or she never steps his or her foot outside of the Welfare-Industrial Complex. The state can lift you off the ground and put you on your feet, but if you sit down again after the state turns around, then there is little that can be done for you.

To choose a strong economy and a bias for jobs for American citizens was a rational reason to have supported President Trump. Consider that one definition of *African American* is a black in America who is descended from the slaves brought to the British colonies on these shores and to the United States of America. All these black citizens have been born in the fifty "united states" and the District of Columbia.[89] When the Trump administration worked against illegal immigration and harboring illegal immigrants in the United States, it was done in part to help the job and wage prospects of American citizens. If the proponents of illegal immigration and sheltering illegal immigrants believe that America has acquitted itself of the racial injustices heaped onto the African American community in our history, that the interests of African Americans should be pushed to the back in favor of illegal immigration, then they should say so. Because an illegal immigrant will work for lower wages and longer hours than a citizen born in America in general, as whatever condition the illegal immigrant finds herself or himself in in the United States is still better than what that person was experiencing in the country that they left. As a result, illegal labor competes with poorer African Americans in the workforce and lowers the wages and job opportunities available to these same African Americans. That is a quandary for anyone compassionate for the travails of an illegal immigrant, two-thirds of whom are Hispanic and one-third of whom are Asian,

---

[89]   This is an overgeneralization for simplicity, as Hawaii and Alaska became states in 1959. Arizona and New Mexico became states in 1912. Oklahoma was the forty-sixth state in 1907. There are many African Americans alive in 2020 that were born before 1959 in what had been territories.

but also the economic challenges that remain for many in the African American community. Is it wrong to ask whether we should first try to correct the economic imbalance of black America to the rest of America? Remember that blacks have one-eighth the economic net worth of whites in America. That needs to change. That cries out for attention above the concerns for illegal immigrants, who are not even citizens. We must do better for those born here. Legal immigrants to the United States from any country, whether it be Belize, Mexico, China, India, Nigeria, Kenya, Australia, Poland, Russia, South Africa, Pakistan, etc., will not begrudge a nation's effort to help those actually born in the United States. And that relates not just to our urban poor but to our rural poor as well. There are many communities that have seen their industry, such as coal, shoemaking, manufacturing, and farming, take a hit through relocations to other parts of the US or overseas or changing market conditions, preferring one technology or resource over another. It is not wrong of a supporter of President Trump to look past rhetoric that offends some to focus on what policy changes might help the economic chances of their fellow Americans. To support these policies does not mean that one is against immigration, as we are mostly a land of immigrants, descendants of slaves, and indigenous peoples. Legal immigration is a core tenet of our strength, but illegal immigration saps at our *rule-of-law* system. Without the *rule of law*, our country is like any other *rule-of-man* country just going with what the current people in power say.

And how did the Trump administration do with a focus on the economy? The numbers were encouraging until the worst pandemic since the 1919 Spanish flu influenza struck the United States and the rest of the world in March 2020. The United States Census Bureau at the United States Department of Commerce puts out an extensive report on income and poverty in the United States annually. The 2019 report merely added to numbers that had been collected annually since 1959 in interviews and data collection from families and individuals across America. Most of the categories of data go back to 1959, but other categories started to be collected some years later. Those living at the end of 2019 sensed that with national unemployment running at about 3.5 percent and record low unemployment for blacks at 5.5 percent in September 2019, dropping from 6 percent.[90] The previous record black unemployment had been 5.9 percent in May 2018, during the Trump administration. The unemployment rate for black women had dropped to a record 4.4 percent from 5.2 percent, another record low, while the unemployment rate for black men had increased to 5.9 percent from 5.8 percent, which had been a record low from black male unemployment.[91] The unemployment rate for Hispanic or Latinos had dropped to 4.2 percent in August, which was equal to a record low hit earlier in 2019. White unemployment had gone up to 3.4 percent from the previous month's 3.3 percent. "This [was] the smallest gap on record between the respective unemployment rates for blacks and whites."[92] According to CNN, Valerie Wilson, director of the program on race, ethnicity, and the economy for the Economic Policy Institute, said "the record low unemployment rate for African Americans is undeniably good news." Maggie Fitzgerald at CNBC reported a like story in October 2019 that black and Hispanic unemployment were at a record low.[93] She cited the United States Labor Department report to state that "there have never been more Black and Hispanic Americans in the workforce." "The best numbers that we've ever had: African American, Hispanic American, Asian American, Women, everything. We have the best numbers that we've had in many, many, many decades," quoting President Trump.[94] The unemployment rate for Asian Americans was down to 2.5 percent and was 3.1 percent for adult women. Truly good numbers.

That is not the end of the inquiry, nor was anyone declaring victory or saying the battle to improve the economic condition of the black community was over. This was a start and a step in the right direction. That is how one could support the economic pol-

---

[90] Chris Isidore, "Black Unemployment Rate Falls to a Record Low," CNN Business, September 6, 2019, accessed November 17, 2020.

[91] Ibid.

[92] Ibid.

[93] Maggie Fitzgerald, "Black and Hispanic Unemployment Is at a Record Low," CNBC, October 4, 2019, accessed November 17, 2020.

[94] Ibid.

icies of the Trump administration, if one believed that a stronger economy could do more to improve the condition of the black community than supporting the politicians who tout job training. What will job training get the citizen if there are no jobs on the other end? What will job training get the hardest to employ, the ex-cons, if there are no jobs on the other side? Consider the Bloomberg News story titled "Ex-Cons Find Second Chances Easier to Get in Tight Labor Market," in July 2019. That makes sense. You are running a business and you have trouble finding enough people who can work for your business. Many ex-cons have the skills and ability and are worth taking a chance on.[95] Granted, an ex-con will probably have gone through some sort of training program or a community organization for placement, but the point of job training is a job. On the other hand, if there is a strong economy, the economy will encourage and demand job training to get the people the economy needs. A robust economy with "Help Wanted" signs posted everywhere can be the strongest social welfare program for our entire nation in general, and for minority communities in particular.

Unemployment at a fifty-year low was nothing to sneeze at. Record low unemployment for blacks was nothing to sneeze at. To promote policies to improve these numbers is meritorious. It should be noted that the labor participation rate for blacks in August 2019 at 58.8 percent was not as high as it had been in March 2000 at 61.4 percent.[96] The objective measures for the economy and for blacks and Hispanics were at record highs by the end of 2019. Even a liberal stalwart like the people behind *Saturday Night Live* ran an opening skit for their iconic comedy series that questioned the chances of any of the Democrat candidates for president during the early part of the 2020 Democratic Party primary season. They satirized a debate by the Democrat candidates for president in New Hampshire in February 2020 by introducing them as thus: "Let's meet our future

[95]   Leslie Patton, "Ex-Cons Find Second Chances Easier to Get in Tight Labor Market," Bloomberg, July 16, 2019, accessed November 17, 2020.
[96]   Ibid.

MSNBC contributors!"[97] That is telling of the mood at that time. With such low unemployment for whites, blacks, Hispanics, Asians, and all Americans, the chances of a Democrat winning the White House were slim before the COVID-19 pandemic hit the next month of March. If one were to remove the pandemic, Vice President Joe Biden would not have won the presidency the following November.

Some have countered that the Trump economy was merely an extension of the economy that President Barack Obama handed over after eight years at the helm. His presidency was born in the worst economic downturn in the United States since the Great Depression of 1929. It became known as the Great Recession of 2007–2009. President Obama served from January 2009 until January 2017. The unemployment rate in January 2009 was 7.8 percent and increased to 9.8 percent by January 2010. Then it declined annually during President Obama's two terms to 4.7 percent as he left office in January 2017. In the Trump years, the rate declined to 4.1 percent in January 2018, 4 percent in January 2019, and then 3.6 percent in January 2020.[98] National unemployment rates for the January reading had gone to 4 percent or below since 1948 after World War II and the Great Depression: in 2000 at 4 percent, 1970 at 3.9 percent, 1969 at 3.4 percent, 1968 at 3.7 percent, 1967 at 3.9 percent, 1966 at 4 percent, 1956 at 4 percent, 1953 at 2.9 percent, 1952 at 3.2 percent, 1951 at 3.7 percent, and 1948 at 3.4 percent.[99] It is not easy to get below 4 percent and hold it there. But for the COVID-19 pandemic, it was likely that a sub-4 percent unemployment rate would have continued, and the benefits to the lowest quintile of workers would have continued as well.

For Americans in general, the median US household income in 2019 rose by $4,379 to $68,709. That $4,379 increase was 50 percent more than during the entire eight-year presidency of Barack

[97] Tim Hains, "Saturday Night Live Mocks 2020 Democrats in NH Debate Skit: "Let's Meet Our Future MSNBC Contributors," RealClearPolitics, February 9, 2020, accessed November 17, 2020.
[98] "US Unemployment Rate by Year," Multpl.com, accessed November 17, 2020.
[99] Ibid.

Obama.[100] Citing the US Census report "Income and Poverty in the United States: 2019," the median household income increased for blacks at 7.9 percent, Hispanics at 7.1 percent, Asians at 10.6 percent, and foreign-born workers at 8.5 percent, versus whites at 5.7 percent and native-born Americans at 6.2 percent. Median earnings for women increased by 7.8 percent compared to 2.5 percent for men. Overall, 2.2 million more Americans were working.

Poverty fell 1.3 points to 10.5 percent, "the lowest level since 1959, and declined more for blacks (2 percentage points), Hispanics (1.8), Asians (2.8), single mothers (2.6), people with a disability (3.2), and no high-school diploma (2.2)."[101] Table B-5 of the US Census report showed that the poverty rate of 18.8 percent in 2019 was the lowest rate ever recorded for the black community since these records had been compiled in 1959, when it was 55.1 percent (see Appendix B, "Income and Poverty in the United States: 2019, US Census Bureau," September 2020, Table B-5, "Poverty Status of People by Family Relationship, Race and Hispanic Origin: 1959–2019")! The poverty rate for black families with a female householder and no spouse present was at 29.5 percent, which was also a record low since records had been kept in 1959, when it was 70.6 percent. The poverty rate for black families with a female householder skews the numbers from 17 percent of all black families in 2019 below the poverty line, which had been 54.9 percent in 1959. Lowest in history was movement in the right direction.

The statistics for Hispanics only go back to 1972 but showed a historic low poverty level of 15.7 percent in 2019 for all Hispanics as opposed to 22.8 percent in 1972. The poverty rate for Hispanic families with a female householder with no spouse present was 28.7 percent in 2019, compared to 53.5 percent in 1972, also a historic low. Commensurate with these improved rates, table B-6 showed the decline in child poverty rate from 18 percent in 2016 to 16.2 percent in 2018, and finally to 14.4 percent in 2019. In eight years of the

---

[100] Editorial Board, "The Higher Wages of Growth," *The Wall Street Journal*, September 17, 2020, A16.
[101] Ibid.

Obama presidency, child poverty went from 20.7 to 17.5 percent, and in the three years of the Trump presidency through 2019, it went from 17.5 to 14.4 percent (see Appendix B, Table B-6 of US Census Report). This is all good work. The faster, the better. The point to be made is that it was not irrational to support a presidency focused on economic growth in the belief that a stronger economy would lift all boats better than policies that accentuated more power to the state with regulations and aggressive income redistribution plans. Income redistribution plans tend to discourage work, as there can be less incentive to work, for fear that a citizen might lose qualifications for such-and-such a government payment or subsidy from the Welfare-Industrial Complex. Don't forget, the Welfare-Industrial Complex is run by and for people who have a vested interest in the Welfare-Industrial Complex to keep going so that the wages, benefits, health-care benefits, sick days, personal days, disability eligibilities, paid personal days, holidays, and pension benefits go on unabated. The Welfare-Industrial Complex is no cottage industry; it is a behemoth that does not appreciate it when citizens question its efficacy. It is exasperating to look at the poverty rate chart of the US Census Bureau since 1959 and see how the rate declined from 22.4 percent in 1959 to 12.1 percent in 1969, and then once the Great Society Programs of Lyndon Johnson began to alter people's behaviors, the decline in poverty rates stopped.[102] It had dropped ten points in ten years. Since then, the national poverty rate bounced in a range between 11.1 percent in 1973 and 15.2 percent in 1983, 15.1 percent in 1993, and 15 percent in 2012. The rate usually went up after a recession. The rate of 10.5 percent under President Trump was then a historic low in 2019. For black Americans, who make up disproportionately more of America's poor, the poverty rate had been 55.1 percent in 1959 and went down to 32.2 percent in 1969, a 22.9-point drop in ten years! Thereafter, the black poverty rate did not get out of the thirties until 1995 at 29.3 percent poverty rate. That was twenty-six years to reduce black poverty another 2.9 points, all the

---

[102] Jessica Semega, Melissa Kollar, Emily A. Shrider, and John Creamer, "Income and Poverty in the United States: 2019," US Census Bureau, September 15, 2020, figure 7.

while that structural statism was growing with annual increases in the size and scope of government, and the Welfare-Industrial Complex churned on. During the presidency of Bill Clinton, welfare reforms were enacted "to end welfare as we know it," which was a pledge from President Clinton's campaign. The Personal Responsibility and Work Opportunity Reconciliation Act of 1996 was signed into law. Aid to Families with Dependent Children was replaced with Temporary Aid to Needy Families. There were changes to limit government benefits to five years or allow states to have tighter limits. Workfare was required, where certain people had to either be working or participating in community service programs or receiving vocational training so that they could work. If you didn't work or volunteer, then you could be kicked off the welfare rolls.[103]

The black poverty rate declined from 33.1 percent in 1993, the first year of President Bill Clinton, to 22.7 percent in 2001, the last year of Bill Clinton's presidency, "ending welfare as we know it." That was a reduction of 10.4 points, a significant reduction in poverty in the black community.

The statists cannot bear the suggestion that anything but the state can ameliorate poverty, and have been busy trying to rewrite the progress made during that period in reducing poverty with a bipartisan coalition of politicians who were willing to seek common ground. For the next fifteen years, black poverty as measured by the US Census Bureau bounced between 22.7 percent and 27.6 percent and was still stuck at 26.2 percent in 2014. In the last year of President Obama's administration in 2017, it had gone down to 20.2 percent, 2.5 points lower than the 22.7 percent scored in the last year of President Bill Clinton in 2001, sixteen years before. Under President Trump, the black poverty rate declined to 18.8 percent in 2019, the lowest number on record, which was 1.4 percent below the beginning of his administration, with a decline each year. This is progress. While political partisans will argue, progress has been made. But much more needs to be done. It is not irrational to choose

---

[103] Alana Semuels, "The End of Welfare as We Know It," *The Atlantic*, April 1, 2016, accessed November 17, 2020.

the politician who promises a stronger economy versus the politician who stresses job training to increase the economic conditions of communities with very real and substantial socio-economic disparities.

Real incomes grew for Americans between 2016 and 2019 according to the United States Federal Reserve.[104] While the lower quintiles had lagged behind the upper quintiles in income growth, the years 2016–2019, with a robust economy, saw the bottom quintile experience higher wage gains than the upper quintiles. Wealth continued to grow for families with either a high school diploma or some college. "Those with a high school diploma and those with some college saw increases of 5 percent and 10 percent, respectively."[105] The college-educated had a higher drop. "Families without a high school diploma saw a 9 percent increase in their median income, while families with a college degree saw a 2 percent decrease."[106]

According to the Federal Reserve, the net worth of all families rose 18 percent in the 2016–2019 time frame.[107] Wealth among lower-income Americans also increased. The net worth of assets minus debt for the lowest-income quintile increased 32.5 percent, and for the second lowest quintile, 30.7 percent. Net worth increased among blacks at 32.1 percent, and for Hispanics 63.6 percent, in that three-year time frame, while it increased 4 percent for whites.[108] Even with these gains, the typical white family and typical black family have not yet recovered to pre-Great Recession levels of net worth. "Only the typical Hispanic family [saw] an increase in wealth relative to before the Great Recession, rising by about 39 percent."[109] The increase in net worth may have taken the form of saving more money, such as in stocks or in their own business.[110] Nonetheless, the net worth gap

---

[104] Neil Bhutta et al., "Changes in US Family Finances from 2016 to 2019: Evidence from the Survey of Consumer Finances," *Federal Reserve Bulletin*, vol. 106, no. 5, September 2020.

[105] Ibid., 9.

[106] Ibid.

[107] Ibid., 10.

[108] Ibid., figure 2, "Black and Hispanic families experienced faster growth in wealth over the last two surveys after experiencing larger declines in wealth caused by the Great Recession." FEDS Notes: "Changes in US Family Finances from 2016 to 2019," September 28, 2020.

[109] Ibid. FEDS Notes: "Disparities in Wealth and Ethnicity in the 2019 Survey of Consumer Finances," September 28, 2020.

[110] Editorial Board, "The Wealth Gap Shrinks," *Wall Street Journal*, September 30, 2020, A18.

between white and black Americans still persists at about eight times that of whites compared to blacks, which is why the reduction of structural barriers imposed by the state, also known as structural racism, needs to be pursued to increase the ability of black Americans to own businesses, trades, licenses, real estate, machinery, and equipment. Home ownership for all socioeconomic groups declined during the Obama administration after the impact of the Great Recession. There was slight improvement of 1.4 percent in home ownership overall between 2016 and 2019, with a 2.3 percentage improvement for blacks and a 1.8 percentage improvement for Hispanics. Growth in business equity for blacks increased by 138 percent, and for Hispanics by 63 percent, in those three years, which is hopefully a harbinger of better news into the future. True, that if you start with little, a modest increase can appear to be a large increase, but it is in the right direction. The introduction of the gig economy and the internet make starting your own business easier, and perhaps that has added to the increase in business equity for blacks and Hispanics.[111]

A brief observation is in order for the efficacy of family and how it can help against poverty. Looking at the same table from the US Census Bureau's "Poverty Status of People by Family Relationship, Race and Hispanic Origin: 1959–2019," it is encouraging for the downward trajectory of poverty for black families. It is almost like a stepping-stone lower for each year. From 2014 through 2019, the poverty rate for all black families went from 24.6 to 22.2 to 20.2 to 19.8 to 18.8 to 17 percent. Far above what it should be, as for all races in the United States the rate of poverty had declined to 8.5 percent by 2019.

It is not inherently wrong to support and believe in the ability of a strong economy to improve the economics of the African American community. If one favors just enough government rules and regulations to balance the interests of the citizens with the interests of a vigorous free market, then more equitable growth will follow. Structural racism, on the other hand, is better able to flourish in the thicket of more government rules, regulations, and programs. Self-

---

[111]   Ibid.

interested factions and statists will continue with programs that don't work so long as it keeps them elected or in power. Improvements in the economic condition for black Americans after World War II happened, and once poverty records were kept starting in 1959, a full drop of almost twenty-three points in those below the poverty line occurred between 1959 and 1969 from 55.1 percent to 32.2 percent! Then it came to a screeching halt when it vacillated between 35.7 percent and 30.3 percent for twenty-four years, until another drop of 10.4 points came with welfare reform and a strong economy under President Bill Clinton from 1993 to 2001, when it dropped from 33.1 percent to 22.7 percent! And then it stopped again during the administrations of Presidents George W. Bush and Barack Obama and stayed in a range from 27.6 to 22 percent. Only at the end of President Obama's eight years in office did the poverty rate start to move below 22 percent, where it had left off in 2001.[112] The black poverty rate then went to 21.2 percent in 2017, 20.8 percent in 2018, and 18.8 percent in 2019. That is the trend that should be kept up. It has taken too long to even get to 18.8 percent. The COVID-19 pandemic will set that progress back. But is progress more likely to be reduced further by a heavier hand for the state in the economy and for even greater Welfare-Industrial Complex programs, or should the emphasis be on a strong economy to continue lifting all boats?

54. Why do you support special interests that already have a stake in the economy in the ownership of a business or bank? And yet you make it more difficult for African Americans to start their own businesses or banks by padding ever more requirements onto what it takes to open and run a business than the existing businesses had to face when they began. If we look at the historical fact that white Americans have a greater net worth than black Americans by a multiple of eight, which makes it easier to help their own children with a college tuition or a down payment on a home or seed money to

---

[112] These poverty rates are based on the annual rates published by US Census Bureau and are not based on monthly amounts. See table B-5, "Poverty Status of People by Family Relationship, Race, and Hispanic Origin: 1959–2019," page 63 of Income and Poverty Report, US Census Bureau.

start a business, why do you make things consistently more expensive to run a business to accumulate wealth? It is accurate to say that an existing business with existing clients, existing banking relationships, existing relationships with suppliers, and existing relationships with government regulators is better poised to absorb additional mandates of what a business must do in terms of paying their employees, the kind of benefits and their extent for employees, licensing requirements and certifications by the state, and licensing or certification fees than a business that has not even been started yet. In economics class, this was referred to as barriers to entry. How many more things does a businessperson have to get together in order to enter into a business? Existing businesses may support greater government mandates or minimums since the existing business is more likely able to absorb the additional cost, provided it also helps reduce the number of businesses competing for that share of the market. If it becomes too onerous, then nobody else will enter that field and the existing firms will have the business to themselves. One cannot even imagine how many banking regulations there are today to consider starting a bank, unless you have deep-pocketed resources. Those exist but usually rely on people who are already in the business. Since blacks historically have fewer resources and were not traditionally owners of banks or large concerns, it makes it harder to make new ones that are owned by blacks. Thus, the more requirements, fees, and minimums are placed on any endeavor accentuates the disadvantage faced by African Americans from past history. This does not mean that blacks have not started their own businesses and have done so successfully; they have and continue to do so. But by reducing the barriers, more can do so.

The talk of owning and running a business may not be for the majority of people, but owning and running a business is key to establishing wealth. In addition, there is a chance that a black-owned business may also hire other blacks or provide more services within the black community. If you want to make a change after the events of 2020, then change would be making it easier for all Americans to start a business, learn a trade, own machinery and equipment, own commercial and residential real estate, build a legacy for their offspring, found a bank, and acquire more professional licenses, such as those of a doctor, lawyer, and tradesmen. By taking a harder look at what rules, minimums, fees, and taxes are on the books, America can make it easier for all Americans to improve their lot. One should want to increase the number of teachers, professors, and entrepreneurs in the African American community.

All these requirements for licensing, building, and permitting make life more difficult for the American citizen in general, and African Americans in particular. This would make any level of licensing and permitting beyond the bare minimum disproportionately affecting poor people. This could be called systemic racism but is definitely systemic statism, the state making the life of a citizen more difficult. What would it take to get you away from your embrace of statism, lording over the citizen? It is not too late to alter your past political choices and dismantle this carefully crafted systemic statism/racism. But only if you are serious.

Chapter 17

The Vilification of Black Men Must Stop

55. **D**O YOU BELIEVE black lives matter? It is certainly hoped that you do. This is not a competition of one life over another. Social justice is not a competition. "Black Lives Matter" can be a simple expression that the life of a black citizen does matter, and not get caught up with the political orthodoxy of some extreme groups. After the killing of George Floyd and Breonna Taylor, how will anything change? The risk is that nothing happens for all the people mounting their personal soapboxes to let the world know how enlightened they are. Don't tell me how woke you are; tell me that you will eliminate and reduce all the structural statism barriers mentioned above that stand in the way of blacks in particular, and everyone else in general. What barriers will you remove to allow the poor to get their foot on the first rung of the ladder of success? Don't keep raising up that first rung or removing it entirely so that the citizen can't even get their foot on the ladder of success but instead is relegated to a lifetime of dependence on the state. If you fail to take these barriers down, then you would appear to be so attached to your past political preferences that have created much of what is structural statism and you are too proud to admit error and remove your past contribution to structural racism.

56. Do you believe that it benefits our black grandfathers, fathers, brothers, sons, nephews, uncles, and friends to gratuitously vilify men? Then why do you do it? Why is it okay to habitually denigrate men as predators or aggressors? This does not help men in general and black men in particular. In fact, with reference to the black community, it plays to old stereotypes. So why do you insist on continuing to make these men's lives more difficult with your prejudices and assumptions? It is not okay to reflexively say that men are bad. That must end.

On the surface, it is easy to point to movie portrayals of black men as strong or aggressive. This is not a petition to make films politically correct, which is about the height of dishonesty. Things have happened that should not historically be rewritten to satisfy the latest Orwellian decree from our betters to pretend something didn't happen or does not fit the present narrative of the politically correct. Rather, it is a petition to question the assumption, if the assumption is held. The Chicago Tragedy is a prime example of the vilification of men to the extent that a daily tragedy that occurs for young black men is ignored by our nation because they are male and because they are of color. If scores of young black women were dying a violent death every day, our betters would allow its discussion nationally, but the Democratic National Committee's weekly talking points to their state committees and to the national media on the left, which is to say almost all print, cable, television, and social media, prohibits discussion of "the Chicago Tragedy." The DNC, in my opinion, has a running footnote at the bottom of their weekly talking points: "Do not discuss the Chicago Tragedy." But for this prohibition, we, as a nation, could discuss why, for young black men between the ages of eighteen and twenty-four, murder and manslaughter are the primary cause of death at 54 percent. It is like the death rate for the COVID-19 pandemic in Europe, where two men were dying to the rate of one woman in 2020. In the United States, it was about a 60:40 ratio or men dying to women. Since it was men dying, that was not newsworthy. If the ratio had been reversed, then there would have been claims that structural sexism or a misogynistic society brought that about. It is like the shorter life span for men versus women. Men die sooner. It just is. Don't worry about it. But if the statistics were reversed, there would be many stories again about structural sexism and why women were dying sooner. Likewise, since the Chicago Tragedy is about young black men and boys dying in jurisdictions run by Democrats for the past forty or more years, there could be no political profit made for the Democratic Party; therefore, their deaths don't count.

On the lighter side, there is the comedy set piece where a man is hit in his private area, which brings considerable pain. Granted, men will joke and laugh at it when it happens to others or to themselves, so long as they don't have to go to the hospital. This gag is developed repeatedly in movies for a little levity or "justice." Again, men can laugh at that, but one should not and would not make comedy about a woman being hit in any way that might cause pain. In a home improvement show, the male host would generally oversee the renovation of houses that the married, and then later not-married, couple purchased to make money on. She would make the design recommendations and choices, and they would work together to bring the project to fruition. Almost invariably, he would suggest during the project that they not spend money on a certain element that she recommended but they would go for it and that element would end up being one of the elements that make the house shine and sell, so he is regularly the idiot and she is regularly the genius. It's a formula. In middle school or high school, it is likely that people cheer for the "girls to beat the boys" in some sort of competition, but it would be impolite to cheer for the "boys to beat the girls."

Personally, by age sixty, I understood, after forty years of adult life, that in politics and in society, men are generally bad, particularly white men. So you just accept it and not say anything. That does not mean that I have accepted the proposition that boys or men are generally bad, just as I have not accepted the proposition that girls or women are generally bad. Each hypothesis is wrong. Nonetheless, the pervasive vilification of men does not help men generally and definitely does not help black men and boys at all. For those who revel in saying white men are responsible for most of the things wrong in the world while ignoring all the good works of these selfsame men, it is ignorant to then say, "While white men are bad, black men and other men of color are good." That would be a strange supposition, that the amount of melanin in a boy or man's skin is responsible for a person's inherent goodness or badness. This is not a conundrum for some of the politically correct, as they are able to thread just that needle despite the ignorance of the supposition. In the wake of the killing of George Floyd and your expressed desire to improve our society as it relates to black men and women, it behooves you to not gratuitously vilify men or to sit idly by when men are put down just because they are male.

64. Do you know that black men earn less than white men, white women, and black women? So how does vilifying men help these black men, who are at the bottom of the earnings scale? Until you can justify the gratuitous denigration of men, you should stop vilifying men. When black men and boys have to deal with barriers placed in their way, it makes it even more difficult for them if there is a general narrative that men are bad.

Chapter 18

Rights and Defense of the Accused Should Be Respected

57. **D**O YOU THINK every human being is entitled to a defense in a court of law? Would you want to be defended if the state charged you with a crime, even if you were deemed unpopular? The Sixth Amendment to the United States Constitution confirms that a citizen can "have the assistance of counsel for his [or her] defense." Not to mention the ability to have a summons issued to bring witnesses in favor of the citizen's defense, to confront witnesses against him or her, as well as a jury trial and a speedy and public trial. These rights may be taken for granted as they have been around for our lifetimes, but our lifetimes are insignificant for the time that man and woman began to walk on the face of this earth. Our lifetimes are insignificant to the amount of time that man lived beneath the fist of tribal leaders, kings, queens, khans, and dictators. So many have sacrificed over the evolution of our political systems to arrive at the *rule of law* in 1776, that we must be vigilant, lest these hard-earned freedoms and rights are vitiated. There is a mantra at the NAACP that lies behind its work as the largest civil rights organization in America: "We are just trying to live the rights set forth in the Declaration of Independence, our Constitution and the Bill of Rights." If the rights and freedoms set forth in these constituent documents can be lived out by all Americans, not just black Americans,

but all Americans, then the work of the NAACP will have been done. This is why one's ears should go up when elements accost or seek to lessen the citizens' rights.

58. Do you browbeat, chastise, and shame an attorney who represents an unpopular defendant? To be represented by counsel is a right under the Sixth Amendment. Imagine if a prosecutor brings charges against you, the lonely citizen. The prosecutor will bring you before a judge, who must run the trial of the matter, with or without a jury. The prosecutor has police officers and investigators at his or her discretion. These police officers and witnesses brought in by the police officers and investigators can bring other witnesses and evidence against you. The prosecutor, police, and investigators will still have a job and will still be able to live in their homes and eat whether they win or lose the case. You, on the other hand, face an entirely different scenario. Innocent and your life likely continues on, but with expensive legal defense bills. Guilty and you may be going to jail and losing your liberty and the ability to be with your family and to make a living. That is a big deal. Shall we not forget the presumption of innocence as a backdrop? It is not a right enumerated in our constituent documents, but it is a societal norm of preferring to wait for a conviction after a fair trial as opposed to the verdict of the mob as had been exercised by lynch mobs in our country. The presumption of innocence is even more relevant to those not in the majority, as it is more likely that one in the minority may face charges from the majority. Allow the trial to happen.

Does a mob represent the *rule of law* or the *rule of man*? It represents the *rule of man*, which is customarily steeped in majority rule for the benefit of the majority. Sometimes the minority or an outside power or both are used as a threat to the well-being or future of the majority. This is a handy tool for dictators to drum up domestic support, by pointing to foreign elements that are trying to take over or infringe on the aspirations of that nation. By the same token, a minority in a country can be accused by the dictator as undermining the fabric of society, and only he or she, the dictator, is what stands between the majority and ruin. Think of the lynch mobs in America that came to a black person's home, and even a white person's home, as about two-thirds of the lynching victims in America were black, who represented a much smaller segment of society. The lynch mob comes and demands justice, which neither the victim nor his family can resist. In old Western films, they would show a prisoner locked up, awaiting trial or transfer to another jail for trial, under the watchful eye and care of the sheriff. A lynch mob arrives demanding justice and threatens the sheriff, and the mob prevails and kills the jailed person without the benefit of a speedy and public trial and all the procedural safeguards to ensure a fair trial. We protect the accused so that they avail themselves of the right to due process and uphold the *rule of law* at the same time. Because one day that might be you.

As an attorney, I take great pride in the ability of attorneys to defend the accused against prosecution by the state. The burden is on the state to prove its case. If the state fails to prove its case, then the defendant shall go free. During the War on Terror and efforts to minimize attacks on the United States and her citizens by religious terrorists, foreigners were seized and put into the United States military base at Guantanamo Bay, on the island of Cuba. Yes, the United States had seen two commercial airliners flown into the Twin Towers in Manhattan on September 11, 2001, with the resultant loss of over 3,500 civilians, more than those killed by the Japanese surprise attack on Pearl Harbor on December 7, 1941, the Day of Infamy. The United States had seen planes crashed into the Pentagon in Washington, DC, and another plane crashed into a field in Pennsylvania when the passengers aboard fought back. The United States and others invaded Afghanistan, from whence these attacks had originated by order of Osama bin Laden. During these wars, those enemy combatants who were deemed the highest level or most dangerous were shipped to Guantanamo Bay. Boo, hiss. Yet when it came time to run military trials in front of some military commissions for crimes on the battlefield or such, scores of attorneys in the United States military volunteered to act as defense counsel for these men. Otherwise, it wouldn't be a fair fight. These attorneys, Judge Advocate General's Corps officers, were not looked down upon by their brother and sister attorneys but were handled respectfully as carrying out a sacred duty that everyone deserves a defense. This is no different in our criminal justice system, where judges, prosecutors, and defense counsel work together to try to arrive at the truth and to test the government's ability to prove its case.

What are the rights against self-incrimination, or Miranda warnings, or the right against unreasonable searches and seizures or the right to be secure in your own home worth if you browbeat attorneys who defend unpopular defendants? They are defending you and your rights. What if an attorney had been able to argue against the no-knock warrant to search the home of Ms. Breonna Taylor?[113] Would a judge have signed it? Who stands up to the state to tell them that our lives and homes are supposed to be sacrosanct and that the nature of a search by the state has limits to time of day and what the government is trying to discover? Are you familiar with the adage from law school that it is better if ten guilty men go free than for one innocent man to be jailed? How do you feel about that adage?

When Hollywood mogul Harvey Weinstein was fighting multiple sex-crime charges against him, he added attorney Ronald Sullivan to his defense team. Mr. Sullivan was an African American professor at Harvard's School of Law in Cambridge, Massachusetts. His African American wife, Stephanie Robinson, was also a law professor at Harvard University, no small feat for anyone. Both of them had also been the first African Americans at Harvard to become faculty deans for the Winthrop House, something about breaking down barriers. Much pressure was put on Mr. Robinson to resign from representing Mr. Weinstein by cancel cancer advocates. They succeeded: Mr. Robinson withdrew from Mr. Weinstein's defense team. The mob had won. But the mob was not done. The mob wanted more. Ultimately, Harvard University caved and failed to renew either Attorneys Robinson to their posts as faculty deans at Winthrop House.[114] According to USAToday the two stated in a

---

[113] The police in the Breonna Taylor case said that they did knock and announce themselves before breaking in.

[114] Joey Garrison, "Former Harvard Dean, Removed after Defending Weinstein, Speaks Out for the First Time Since Ouster, Condemns School," *USA Today*, June 14, 2019, accessed November 20, 2020.

video that although they, too, had protested when they were students at Harvard, they "did not demonize the people with whom [they] disagreed. [They] did not, nor would [they] ever attack the character of innocence."[115] Should the US Army JAG officers who have and continue to defend detainees at Guantanamo Bay be ostracized for doing their constitutional duty? To watch Atticus Finch in *To Kill a Mockingbird* defend Tom Robinson, an African American man, which was not a popular thing to do in town, would bring a tear to your eye at some point. Shall the mob silence Atticus Finch or Ronald Sullivan? Do you support the mob? Are you part of the faceless and spineless mob that prefers intimidation to debate?

If George Floyd had lived and had been charged with a crime of disturbing the peace or taking prohibited drugs, should his defense counsel be mocked or canceled even though you *know* that he is guilty? If you believe that he should not have a defense because he is "guilty anyway," then that is the rule of the mob, and one day the mob may come for you, and who will be left to defend you as the mob demands you be destroyed? You should not fire an attorney from his or her other jobs because of the legal defense work they take on. They are merely making our constitutional system work and protecting the rights of the accused, which are your rights.

---

[115] Ibid.

Chapter 19

Who Constructs Barriers to Advancement for the Poor and Destroys High-Needs Communities?

59. WHO ARE THE people responsible for the structural racism that was cited as a rallying cry in protests after the killing of George Floyd, or is it structural statism, or both? Are you responsible for structural racism/statism? Surely, if you knew where some of your past policies have led and how they have made life more difficult for African Americans, you might reconsider them. Where would one find a treasure trove of enablers of structural racism, which may also include structural statism? Whole Foods is a good place to start. What? These are progressives, through and through. They have enough disposable income to pay a premium for necessities and not-so-necessities. Generalizations are apt to be wrong, but there are some traits of some Whole Food Shoppers that identify the forces behind structural statism. For readers who are not familiar with the Whole Foods Market, it is a chain of primarily food stores, with nonfood items that you would find at a Safeway, Stop and Shop, City Market, Price Chopper, Albertsons, and Krogers. Whole Foods Market tend to be smaller than a typical food store chain location. There are many more organic selections. Whole Foods prides itself on the finest natural and organic food available, with strict quality control. For a shopper at regular

discount supermarkets, the prices at Whole Foods Market are significantly higher. In my opinion, it is where you get two for the price of three, versus ShopRite, where you get three for the price of two. Stepping into the stores during the coronavirus pandemic revealed a busy and well-run store, but there was a certain feeling in the air that was palpable. You need to follow the rules. There were arrows that showed the direction in which the shopper should travel, as there were at other supermarkets during the peak of the COVID-19 pandemic. But there was an air that if you went the wrong way or dashed down an aisle without your cart to grab one item and rushed back to your cart, you would be shamed. The other shoppers had a right to expect that the rules be followed for the health protection of all. The difference is, if you went the wrong way at Trader Joe's or at ShopRite, it is likely that few people would have shot you daggers with their eyes or body language. Do not even think of grabbing that bag of salad next to the shopper that has stood there for five minutes, contemplating what lies before that person in the cooler section. If one were to say, "Excuse me," and reach in quickly to grab that salad or pound of butter, the idle shopper might have sprung into action by violently jumping to the side as if assaulted. When it came time to check out your items, there was an organized line. Be sure to follow that system as many eyes were on the alert for those who wandered off course consciously or unconsciously.

Why discuss the Whole Foods shopper? You will find some of the enablers of structural statism there. These shoppers have the disposable income to spend extra for their own food, which is to be commended. But is there a view of their fellow citizens that accompanies it? One thing you will not find at Whole Foods are shoppers who use government assistance to buy their food. It is not a good way to stretch the dollar. You may find more of those at ShopRite, and few shoppers at ShopRite rolled their eyes at you if you went the wrong way or grabbed a product near them after saying, "Excuse me." It's a class thing. The Whole Foods shopper is more likely to be intolerant for their fellow shopper who didn't follow the coronavirus rules inside and outside of the store versus the more egalitarian

ShopRite customer. Query whether the Whole Food shopper has a similar attitude when applied to policies. Less tolerance for others.

We are all individuals, but some of us are more insistent than others that people follow the ideas promoted by our betters.[116] Before the COVID-19 pandemic, it was just harried shoppers overpaying for slightly better-than-average food in a Whole Foods Market. After the onset of the COVID-19 pandemic, it was still harried shoppers overpaying for slightly better-than-average food, but with the added twist of conformity. This is not about conformity in wearing masks but the rest of the etiquette of separation and aisle directions. I surmise that these shoppers have warmly embraced structural statism in the past and will continue to do so in the future. Everything is so much neater that way!

Are you familiar with the incident that occurred in Central Park in New York City on May 25, 2020, between an Amy Cooper, a white woman, and Christian Cooper, a black man? Coincidentally, George Floyd was killed on that same day, May 25. According to video and news reports, Ms. Amy Cooper was in the Ramble part of Central Park without a leash on her dog. A bird-watcher, Mr. Christian Cooper asked her to put her dog on a leash as dogs disturbed the birds that he was hoping to see. Instead of complying, Ms. Cooper called 911 and reported, "There's a man, African American, he has a bicycle helmet… He is recording me and threatening me and my dog."[117] Outrageous behavior, which fortunately came to naught, as when the police finally arrived, Mr. Cooper was no longer there. Nonetheless, in keeping with the time, an author of a story about this incident called her conduct "systematic behavior against people of color." There is that word again, *systematic*, in the same family as *systemic*.

Considering all the affluent and enlightened customers at Whole Foods, would it surprise you if Ms. and Mr. Cooper, no relation, were Whole Foods shoppers? Both appeared to be well-off.

---

116   Those who have higher educational degrees and/or greater net worth than the average citizen.

117   Elvia Diaz, "What's Wrong with Amy Cooper, the White Woman in Central Park? Her Sense of Entitlement," *The Arizona Republic*, May 26, 2020, accessed November 20, 2020.

How each acted on that May 25 is, by one interpretation, a micro-cosm of where we were as a nation but also a possible route to a better future. Ultimately, the prosecuting authorities in Manhattan brought charges against Ms. Cooper for abusing the 911 emergency calling system to level an unwarranted threat against Mr. Cooper that he was an "African American male threatening her life." Mr. Cooper, accord-ing to news reports, later deferred cooperating with the prosecutor as Ms. Cooper had suffered enough for her conduct in terms of being fired from her job and the social shaming on and off the internet.

As soon as you saw the video of Ms. Cooper making a baseless claim to the 911 operator against Mr. Cooper, you could tell it was likely her employer would put her on administrative leave to sort out the implications of leveling such a charge against Mr. Cooper that a black man was threatening a white woman's life. For the target of the accusation, that can mean questioning on a good day or worse on a bad day. Ms. Cooper was sacked by the end of the day or so. Would Mr. Cooper have done the same as her employers? He indicated later that he didn't think she should have lost her job, in view of the many other repercussions against her.

As her employer, what would you have done? In retrospect, are the employers of Ms. Cooper as intolerant as she? If they are of the same political stripe and of the same political correctness, then the firing of Ms. Cooper was as sure as the sun goes down in the west. The internet mob had gathered outside the door of her employer, so to speak. The mob was demanding satisfaction in the sacking of Ms. Cooper. And this is what democracy is supposed to protect us from: the mob and the tyranny of the majority. The politically cor-rect lack humility, compassion, forgiveness, and belief in the power of redemption. Therefore, if they find one fault in your present or past as a human being, the mob condemns you to a purgatory of ignominy. They do not have the human capacity to recognize that they themselves are human and have faults and have made mistakes in their own life. They lack compassion for another human being and demand a sacrifice. The politically correct do not know "there but for the grace of God go I." Who can say that we are better than someone else? Who is without sin should cast the first stone. Is that you? Unlikely. And what of redemption? Once a human being makes a mistake, are they forever condemned to suffer for it or to carry that burden? Do you not believe in the individual's ability to redeem themselves within their community? Can a human being not right their ship and live right? If you don't agree with any of these propositions, then our future together as a nation continues to face a bumpy road.

You should take a cue from Mr. Cooper, the very man whose life and liberty were put at risk by Ms. Cooper leveling a specious but historical charge: "An African American man is threatening me!" How many times have the authorities come to detain or arrest an African American male on spurious charges? And if he is lucky, he is only dishonored in his personal freedom by being questioned, let alone detained and brought to a precinct house. Yet, intolerants, listen to Mr. Cooper, whose first name, coincidentally, is Christian. He did not wish her to lose her job. He did not wish her to be vilified. She had suffered enough, so he chose not to cooperate further with the prosecutor in punishing Ms. Cooper. Mr. Cooper exercised all elements of humility, compassion, forgiveness, and redemption. If only the politically correct could follow his example and exercise those values.

It would appear to the casual observer that her former employer was of the same intolerant political stripe as the mob. They appeared to exhibit neither humility nor compassion, forgiveness, and redemption. Did their political righteousness compel them to act this way, or did the fear of the mob at the door? What of Ms. Cooper's humanity and fallibility? Ms. Cooper's employers could later redeem themselves and give Ms. Cooper her job back. It appears Mr. Cooper would counsel no less. It is conceivable that both Ms. Cooper and Mr. Cooper, as affluent New Yorkers, are both patrons of Whole Foods, but only one, Mr. Cooper, an African American man, exhibited the proper way to act. An insight that I would not have had is that there is another, equally plausible explanation for Mr. Cooper's actions that is not based in compassion and forgiveness. If one were to assume that Mr. Cooper had a decent job with a decent company with a comfortable salary, then this is not something that an African

American male has the luxury to turn his back on in a majority-white country. There is a concept of going along to get along. Out of speculation, if Mr. Cooper had taken a harder line on Ms. Cooper and had continued to cooperate with the prosecutor so that the charges of abusing the 911 system and making false claims were to stick, then it is conceivable that people where he worked might ask at the water cooler or in the elevator, "Why are you still pursuing this matter? Hasn't she suffered enough?" Would that suggest that there could be repercussion on his own salary or annual review or assignments into the future? It is speculation but another plausible explanation of Mr. Cooper's magnanimous attitude toward Ms. Cooper.

Would it surprise you if Ms. Cooper were a liberal? With her as an urban white female, highly-educated and of an upper-socioeconomic status, "it [was] statistically highly probable that Ms. Cooper voted for Hillary Clinton in the 2016 general election," as surmised by writer Musa al-Gharbi in the medium *Public Seminar*.[118] A critique of government policy to aid the black, Hispanic, or other marginalized community, implemented and promoted by white liberals, is that it takes a patronizing view of the black community, that the black community cannot make it without government assistance. This goes beyond compensating for avenues barred in the past, but a patronizing view. It can be exhibited when a white liberal will agree with most everything that a black man or woman says because the liberal does not want to offend the black speaker by disagreeing with him or her. After all, for the white liberal, the black vote is a birthright that can be collected every two or four years just by showing up and asking for the vote. That an age-old stereotype could be hurled at Mr. Cooper by an erstwhile white liberal "ally" might confound some, but it is consistent with the patronizing attitude exhibited by some whites to blacks.

As regards those at Ms. Cooper's former employer, if they felt they had no choice in the face of a politically correct mob, who will

---

[118] Musa al-Gharbi, "Amy Cooper: The Paradox of the Shameless White Liberal: How Pious White Anti-Racism Can Contribute to Racist Behavior," Public Seminar, May 29, 2020, accessed November 20, 2020.

make room for a person's humanity? What of humility, compassion, forgiveness, and redemption? The mob does not have it, but Ms. Cooper's employers are not the mob. The criminal justice system did belatedly take up the false claims made by Ms. Cooper, but how much more punishment should be meted out? There are segments in society that have no consideration of the humanity that is all of us. They demand perfection. Failure to live up to the standards of the intolerant mob results in elimination. An analogy to Pol Pot and the Khmer Rouge is appropriate by way of example. Dictator Pol Pot and his political faction, the Khmer Rouge, ran the Killing Fields of Cambodia from 1975 to 1979. What are the *Killing Fields?* you ask. That is a question not for those who were alive at that time but for those too young then or born after that time. The academy, our colleges and universities, don't want our young people to learn of the Killing Fields, as it casts a negative light on the intolerance practiced by Marxists overseas and in the United States today and yesterday. Sadly, Marxism and its offshoots are taught and sheltered by the academy[119] today.

During the reign of the Khmer Rouge from 1975 to 1979, a genocide of Marxist class-based execution was carried out against 1.7 to 2.5 million Cambodians out of a population of 8 million over four years. This involved the dehumanization of the supposed enemies of the ruling power as not worthy of living. If a citizen wore glasses, then the citizen would be killed with a bullet to the head or a plastic bag over that person's head, as plastic bags were cheaper than bullets. The reason that glasses were a death sentence is, it meant the citizen could most likely read, and that necessarily meant the citizen had read something before the rule of the Khmer Rouge. Things written before the Khmer Rouge were unapproved materials or thoughts. The Khmer Rouge wanted to sanitize the past and eliminate it so that they could establish a "perfect" agrarian society in accordance with their Marxist philosophy. As is typical with intolerants, there was no room for humility, compassion, forgiveness, or redemption, only death. The contaminated citizen could not be retrained or retaught;

---

[119] Our colleges and universities.

they could only be eliminated. Today, the politically correct try to sweep across our own land and eliminate those who have thought, uttered, written, or worn something that the politically correct disapprove of. The unenlightened shall ever be chastised and vilified.

If the citizen under the Khmer Rouge spoke a foreign language, the Khmer Rouge would also kill that citizen with a plastic bag over their head or an executioner's bullet. To speak a foreign language meant that the citizen had learned things that the Khmer Rouge did not approve of. Maybe the citizen had worked with the Colonial French some years before? In the words of a Marxist, that work to earn a living would be characterized as "collaboration." To survive the politically correct terror of Pol Pot and the Khmer Rouge, the citizen had to get rid of their glasses and not let anyone know that they spoke a foreign language. This is not to suggest that Pol Pot and his elite did not speak foreign languages—of course they did. There was one rule for the rulers, their betters, and another rule for everyone else. Pol Pot had been the son of a prosperous farmer in Cambodia and had gone to elite schools in Cambodia and had studied in Paris, France. It was fine for Pol Pot and his cohorts to be educated and prosperous, but not for the rest of the country. They went about mercilessly persecuting their countrymen who did not fit in with Pol Pot's political orthodoxy. Millions executed, starved, and tortured to death.

What of the college-educated, affluent white elite in American institutions today who pursue their fellow citizens with a like-minded zeal to punish, silence, and cancel those who fail to live up to the orthodoxies of these elites, our betters? The Khmer Rouge did not know what humility, compassion, forgiveness, and redemption were. The politically correct in the United States appears to also not know what humility, compassion, forgiveness, and redemption are. Mr. Cooper exhibited humility, compassion, and forgiveness by acknowledging Ms. Cooper's humanity. Would that other white Whole Foods shoppers show the same humility, compassion, and forgiveness that Mr. Cooper showed, or are they convinced of their affluent righteousness?

60. Why would Ms. Cooper's employers not show the same humanity toward Ms. Cooper as Mr. Cooper showed?

61. Do you believe that because of your education and physical comforts, you are better than people who don't have your education or physical comforts? The discussion of the interaction between two affluent citizens in the Amy Cooper and Christian Cooper story in Central Park reflects on how affluence might affect how a Caucasian citizen views the world. It is not a fault but perhaps a blind spot that some of us may have. Among whites, we can get into a lather when discussing what a "liberal" or a "conservative" stands for or whose principles are better for moving our nation forward to a better future, each castigating the other for shortcomings. Conservative and liberal whites may appear before black audiences and genuinely argue why their way is better than the way of the opponent. Little do we realize that for some black observers, white liberals and conservatives are all the same. Nothing has changed, and nothing will change. That is an oversimplification as conditions in America and the race question have improved in our nation and will continue to improve, but the enthusiasm of a white liberal or conservative debating each other may fall on deaf ears as the same noise to some African Americans. Excuse the black audience if they have a hard time trusting what whites have to say on either side of the political divide.

62. Do you believe as a citizen with a decent educational back-ground and financial resources to go with it that you are in a better position to determine policy for those with less of a formal educa-tion and fewer economic resources? That is not necessarily an irra-tional conceit. Your physical comforts are proof that your education and hard work have brought results. Would that mean those with less-formal education and resources should see it the way you do? Since the affluent citizen with a decent formal education is well able to read and cope with ever-greater government rules and regulations in business and at home, it may seem like a small hurdle for them. The financial impact of higher prices due to greater minimums that must be met by businesses, and the increased costs for compliance,

can be afforded by the affluent. In fact, the affluent have been known to seek out the more expensive product as a sign of discerning taste and financial resources. It is at one moment an act of conspicuous consumption, as a BMW, Land Rover, or Tesla is clearly more expensive than a Toyota or Chevrolet. Certainly, there are types of clothing and accessories that are known to be more expensive and thereby better. This is human nature. But do not assume that the vast majority of your fellow citizens have the discretionary income to purchase these more expensive items. They would just like to make it through the week with a roof over their head, gas in their car, and food on their plate, thank you very much.

The elite have no inherent right to legislate how people with less-formal education and resources should live. As mentioned above, although you have a good education and have facility in drafting and reading documents, that does not mean that you should require the same of others to enter into transactions or to be allowed to collect for work done. You may be allied with your local PTA, which is allied with your local teacher's union in opposition to providing more school choice to poor Americans. While you deny school choice to the less fortunate, you require flawless paperwork just to work, just to be paid, just to participate in the economy as an entrepreneur.

Will you accept that college is not for everyone? That it would be inefficient to try to get all high school graduates to go to college? Do you accept that for some people, a better route is a trade learned at a trade school or in an apprenticeship for a company? After all, a college degree does not guarantee a good job. There should be scholarships for trade schools just as there are scholarships for colleges and universities. Will you accept the citizen who has not gone to college as your equal?

63. Do you live in a doorman building? If so, you might have a tendency to support such concepts as "defunding the police," championed by some activists after the killing of George Floyd and Breonna Taylor. Yet there was a disconnect with such a facile demand and the reality on the ground. You cannot exercise your civil rights unless you are secure in your person and property. The people most

susceptible to crime are people in economically disadvantaged communities. These communities suffer great rates of murder, robbery, home invasion, rape, burglary, and sexual assaults. It is one of the disconnects between the elite at the top and those who make up the body. The elites, some of whom live in doorman building and some live out in the country in wealthy communities, gave lip service to defunding the police, while the majority of people, black, white, Hispanic, Asian, and others in poorer communities, want the same amount or greater policing in their neighborhoods. Can you accept that or insist that your view is the right way?

64. Did you go to a top university? Then you may have been taught intolerance there and feel it your duty to impose your intolerant self-righteousness on others. Already, by 1980, American universities had more liberal professors than conservative professors. And students are generally more liberal than conservative at a young age. Thus, liberal positions were more acceptable to be expressed on campus than conservative positions. But conservatives and libertarians were still allowed to express themselves without excessive negative consequences. In 1980, at Middlebury College in Middlebury, Vermont, when Ronald Reagan won the presidential election over Jimmy Carter, we, College Republicans, could not identify a single professor who we thought had or would have voted for President Reagan. Not a single professor! There were a few we thought might have voted for John Anderson, independent, for president. That is pretty monolithic. The difference from then to today is that while some liberal professors at Middlebury were busy teaching their biases in 1980, they did not go out of their way to squelch the views of those that they didn't agree with.

Today is a whole different situation with cancel cancer, political correctness, and identity politics. This is not the place to examine the illiberal environment that Marxist-inspired professors and their fellow travelers have imposed on the academy[120] by 2022, but it is chilling. That professors, administrators, and our own student chil-

---

[120] The *academy* are our colleges and universities.

dren are so intimidated by the intolerance of the intolerants that they fear retribution for expressing ideas or discussing topics that the intolerants have deemed off-limits is chilling. You are not in college now, so it is not pressing for you, but you have seen the cancel cancer seep into the world outside of the academy as the intolerants trained by the academy graduate and spread their intolerance throughout the land. Do you approve of this? Are you concerned by it? Are you concerned that the intolerants may have made your institution of higher learning less open to discussion and the pursuit of truth? It behooves the citizen to be open to debate and differences of opinion and to respect differences in perspective and proposed solutions for us to move forward as a united nation.

65. Do you read newspapers in print and online that promote the expansion of the power of the state over the citizen, structural statism? At the beginning of these one hundred questions, the question was posed on what the reader thought *structural racism* was. One of the theses of these one hundred questions is that structural racism and structural statism are often one and the same. All the structural racism that was referred to after the killing of George Floyd had made it through the administration of President Barack Obama from when his term began in January 2009 to when it ended in January 2017, as well as his attorney general, Eric Holder, from January 2009 to 2015. But if structural racism and structural statism are in fact often the same thing, that should not surprise you as we continue to build up the state through more and more laws, rules, and regulations. While well-intended to ameliorate the social condition, and sometimes not well-intended when the insiders and connected game the economy and government to put themselves in a preferred position to profit financially by carving out parts of the economy to return favors to their insiders and with rules to make it harder for newcomers to compete, this makes structural statism even more all-encompassing. The friends and allies of the statists are ready to swoop in and take advantage of new government rules to receive government subsidies, grants, or concessions. An example are rules to battle climate change, which, in fact, do little to effectively affect climate change but do

reward the insiders generously. The rest of the citizenry is left out as they are not on the inside.

To counter the game of these factions to increase the money in their pocket and to secure their economic interests, you should question whether more government rules and regulations actually help the poor generally, or blacks specifically. Since blacks have fewer economic resources, participation in the economy is made harder by increased hurdles, burdens, and barriers. Just passing more laws to make something legal or illegal is not necessarily going to help the poor. The simple concept of the poor litigating themselves into the middle class is an oxymoron. The most time-proven method to get into the middle class is work and thrift. Certainly, the attorneys who bring various lawsuits will make money in fees, and individuals may benefit here and there from such lawsuits, but the overall population will not see their economic condition improve through litigation coupled with thicker statute books. The way should be made clear so that all can participate in the economy and increase their ownership of licenses, equipment, machinery, commercial real estate, franchises, trucks, residential real estate, etc. The expansion of the state is not how citizens have worked forward to realize the American dream, or at least aspire to do so. You have to be in it to win it! The longer one spends on disability, the longer one stays out of employment. The longer one stays out on unemployment, the longer one stays out of working. The longer one is not in it to win it. The only way that citizens are going to improve their lot is by participating in the economy as an employee or as an owner of a business.

Increasing the cost to build a home, for example, is not helping anyone achieve the American dream. Increasing restrictions on building decreases the number of houses and apartments built and the number of affordable housing that we have. None of this helps the poor. Will you continue to default to the candidate that promises more laws and regulations? How does that reduce structural statism?

66. Do you fancy yourself woke? As an adjective, *woke* is "having or marked by an active awareness of systemic injustices and prej-

udices, especially those related to civil and human rights."[121] Used in a sentence: "In light of incidents of police brutality, it's important to stay woke." This would be right up the alley of the protests after the killing of George Floyd, a black man, under the knee of a police officer. "He took one African American history class and now he thinks he's woke."[122] *Merriam-Webster* offers a variation on the definition when used in a slang sense: "aware of and actively attentive to important facts and issues (especially issues of racial and social justice.)"[123] If in fact you are woke, do you believe that your opinions have more weight than those you deem not to be woke? Will you allow any space for the opinions of those you feel are not woke? Do you believe that you have a special ability to divine the truth and that is why you will not give space to others to discuss and challenge your views? If you do not give room to others to discuss the issues of the day, you have a propensity for intolerance and are a threat to our democracy.

67. Do you know who the Wide Awakes were? They were before the Civil War. If you are confident in your wokeness, would you entertain the possibility that somebody was more woke than you over one hundred years ago? One of the original woke political parties was the Republican Party. Our nation had an imperfect beginning at the making of our Declaration of Independence in 1776, and later in the drafting of our Constitution in 1787, in that slavery existed in the United States and continued to exist. Slavery existed and was legal on these shores. Prior to the formation of the Republican Party in the 1850s, the Whig and Free-Soil Parties had opposed slavery and the Democratic Party, the party of slavery. The Whigs and Free Soilers could be referred to as the first "woke" parties in the United States. The opposition to slavery and its extension was not limited to one geographic area of the United States. There were opponents spread out across the Northern states. In fact, the Whigs and Free

---

[121] Dictionary.com, s.v. "woke," accessed December 1, 2020.
[122] Ibid.
[123] *Merriam-Webster's Dictionary*, s.v. "woke," accessed December 1, 2020.

Soil Party members combined with other Americans, including former Democrats, and formed the Republican Party in the 1850s to campaign against the extension of slavery and the Democratic Party. Using the term *woke* is not to give any deference to the politically correct who today cast about demanding that people be woke, and that they fancy themselves woke, but rather for these self-satisfied citizens to reconsider their conceit as they exhibit intolerant tendencies vis-à-vis people different from themselves or their political views.

Early Republicans before the Civil War included the Wide Awakes, who provided a modicum of protection for Republican candidates to present their antislavery positions without being silenced by Democrat mobs that would try to prevent their speeches. The Democratic Party was strong in the District of Columbia and harassed Republicans and even invaded and vandalized the local Republican club headquarters, which had been established in 1855, which same club worked diligently until the election of President Lincoln in 1860 to elect Republicans.[124]

"In political struggles in the 1850s proslavery forces took actions that northerners regarded as lawless and coercive. Congressional gag rules, the mobbing of abolitionist speakers, interference with the mails and denial of free speech in the South, fugitive slave recaptures which abrogated free states' due process of law, the reliance on fraud and violence in the attempt to establish slavery in Kansas [and] *the caning of* [Republican] *Massachusetts Senator Charles Sumner in the Senate chamber.*"[125] It was these types of tactics of intolerance that Republican speakers around Washington, DC, needed the protection of the Wide Awakes for in order to be heard.

Ultimately, it took the formation of the Republican Party and the election of their candidate, Abraham Lincoln, into the presidency in 1860 to bring the struggle between the Slave Power and the rest of the nation to a head and to ultimately defeat slavery. Hundreds of thousands of soldiers fell in that epic struggle. Today, the self-de-

---

[124] At a reunion in January 1899 for members of the 1855–1860 Republican Club, Lewis Clephane gave "a hearty welcome to all the surviving members of the Republican Association of 1855–1860, and the Wide Awakes also."

[125] Herman Belz, *Emancipation and Equal Rights* (New York: Norton, 1978), 3.

scribed woke exhibit intolerance to those not sufficiently woke, but the tactics of the woke today would not have been recognized by the Wide Awakes as democratic or woke!

68. Are you a fascist Antifa participant? In a stroke of good marketing, these are ruffians who are less interested in debate, discourse, and the pursuit of truth and more interested in physically accosting political opponents and damaging property. They have named themselves "antifascists." Opposing fascism is a good thing. *Fascism* is "a political philosophy, movement, or regime (such as that of the Fascisti) that exalts nation above the individual and that stands for a centralized autocratic government headed by a dictatorial leader… *and forcible suppression of opposition.*"[126] But what if your tactics are just like those of the fascists that you claim to oppose? What if you are not really interested in the free exchange of ideas and viewpoints, but instead your tactics and methods are to suppress and silence those with whom you disagree? That would make you a fascist in your own right.

69. Before the COVID-19 coronavirus outbreak in 2020, did you wear a black helmet and a black cloth to hide your face at public demonstrations? This was sometimes the uniform of antifascists, also known as Antifa? What is the purpose of going to a demonstration wearing a motorcycle helmet or other helmet like a solider? When civil rights pioneers like Martin Luther King Jr. exercised their civil right to petition the government for redress of grievances, they were not wearing helmets and covering their faces with black cloths. Antifa participants often also wore cloths over their faces to hide their identity. Studies have shown that people are more likely to commit violence if part of the anonymity of a crowd versus on their own. The anonymity of the crowd can also encourage aggressive behavior that the person might not otherwise engage in if he or she were on their own. To then wrap a cloth around the person's face to shield their identity would only encourage more aggressive behavior with

---

[126] *Merriam-Webster's Dictionary*, s.v. "fascism," accessed December 1, 2020.

an even greater promise of anonymity. To beat up political opponents in the street or to shout them down so that they cannot exercise their civil right of free speech and assembly is thuggish behavior more in keeping with fascists and Marxists. Both forcibly attempt to suppress those they disagree with.

Another group also used violence and intimidation in the past to deny the civil rights of American citizens. That was the Ku Klux Klan. They wore white robes with white hoods that also had veils over their faces to shield their identity. With their face veiled, their victim would not know whether it was a neighbor, the mayor, or some other community member physically accosting them or intimidating them. The veil promised anonymity to the KKK adherent and allowed the KKK to intimidate blacks and whites in America in the North and in the South. These tactics are inimical to democracy. Antifa and the KKK both use, and used, masks and hoods/helmets over their faces and heads in order to deny the civil rights of American citizens through violence and intimidation.

70. If you are not an Antifa adherent and activist, perhaps you are an anarchist who took advantage of the nationwide protests after the killing of George Floyd to take to the streets to protest but to also break things and set things on fire. Anarchy is where society lacks an organized government and there is an absence of governmental control. Coincidentally, anarchists' sartorial tastes tend to be black for everything. That overlapped with the preferred color of the Antifa protesters, which was also black, made it harder to distinguish between an Antifa protester/rioter or an anarchist protester/rioter. Where Rahm Emmanuel, the first chief of staff of President Barack Obama, observed that no emergency should go unused to push an agenda forward, so, too, did the Antifa protesters/rioters and anarchist protesters/rioters use the protests after the killing of George Floyd to foment further unrest and destruction. This was a hijacking of a legitimate protest petitioning the government for redress of grievances into one trying to create anarchy or giving license to Antifa adherents to break things or encourage other protesters to

break things, loot things, or burn things. It was a distraction from the original message.

How does burning a business of an African American man or woman, which business has likely been built up over decades, help the African American community? How does burning or looting a business of a nonblack person who is providing jobs, goods, food, and services to the black community benefit the black community? The chances are that many of the people who work in the African American-owned store, or those not owned by African Americans, that were destroyed by the Antifa and anarchists in the George Floyd protests were also African American. How does looting and defacing a Walmart in a primarily African American community help the local residents? When a Walmart is eliminated, it means scores of local jobs are destroyed and a food desert might be re-established, which can make it more difficult to have access to fresh fruits and vegetables, to the detriment of the African American community. Why are these fascists lauded by the academy and the politically correct? Why do numerous media outlets turn a blind eye to the destruction inflicted on African American communities by these Antifa and anarchist protesters/rioters? It is nonsensical that a person can put on a "Black Lives Matter" T-shirt, march under a "Black Lives Matter" banner, or wear a "Black Lives Matter" button and then literally burn down buildings in a black neighborhood or smash windows there and a media outlet will credit it to "peaceful protesting." Are you willing to sweep such conduct under the rug and ignore it?

Chapter 20

10 Percent Set-Aside Islands to Further Buttress Structural Racism

71.   H AVE YOU HEARD of statutory schemes where 10 percent of business opportunities, funding, or slots are reserved for minorities and women or minority- or women-owned businesses? It seems like a meritorious effort to right past wrongs. It allows politicians to go back to their constituencies and say that they were able to get a 10 percent set-aside for their community. And to the lucky few who get the set-asides, it sure seems like a great deal. Those who receive them are the fortunate ones. The rest can just stay on a list. A list is, after all, where the government would like most of us to be. Instead of being allowed to earn, learn, save what is rightfully ours under the Declaration of Independence and our Constitution, we have been told by the statists that we must get in line and hope that the state will issue us permits to build things or licenses to earn our living or to create a business. Maybe they will give us a grant or government loan for our education if the citizen waits patiently enough at the government's doorstep. That is the posture that the statist wants the citizen to take.

Perhaps the state will deign to allow us to have a license so that we can work to put food on our plate. How generous! Maybe one day they will give us a permit so that we can renovate our apartment. All these things rightfully belong to the citizen. The state, however, in its carefully crafted structural statism, makes us wait and get on lists. "Oh, will I be fortunate today to get permission to work or to renovate my own home?" Perhaps we can ask a politician to see what he or she can do to speed the process along or break the log-jam. How grateful we would be to such an all-powerful politician for helping us get what we are trying to get to pursue our happiness under our God-given rights! This system of making the citizen stand before the statist-erected barriers to beg, wait, and plead for what we are entitled to under our constituent documents of the Declaration of Independence, Constitution, and Bill of Rights is structural stat-ism writ large as applied to the entire nation and structural racism as applied to the African American community.

The 10 percent set-asides are part and parcel of the problem. They can also be referred to as "10 percent islands." By taking a closer look at the 10 percent set-asides, it may appear to be an eco-nomic opportunity or concession or ability to participate in projects; it turns out that the rules on the other 90 percent of that part of the economy have been tightened up to make it harder for outsiders to compete or participate. The insiders are getting their political pay-offs for having financially supported the party or parties in power. Banking regulations are increased, for example. That imposes an additional cost on existing banks, which they try to work into their business model. Someone else, however, who had thought of charter-ing a new bank now has even more regulations, burdens, and costs to contend with. The net effect of layering more regulations and costs on top of the existing regulatory and taxing regimen makes it harder and less likely that any newcomers will appear and set up a compet-ing bank. If you are black or a woman and you believe that the rules have been tilted against your advancement, the ability to break into the banking sector will have been made more difficult by these new rules, fees, and regulations.

This is a variation of the traditional concern that regulatory agencies will customarily be peopled at the top by individuals who work in the business being regulated. That is a rational choice. One would not want a lobsterman overseeing the regulation of our forest-land. Normally, you would get people with experience with forests to do that, and that could be people from the timber industry. Banking regulators would naturally be bankers themselves, as they know how the business works. A sociology professor is probably not a good fit to regulate banks. Agencies overseeing the mining industry will probably have people from mining companies on them or even leading those agencies. This is as it should be. But the problem arises as the government agency is supposed to be looking out for the public weal, yet at the same time they are also working to make sure that America has a strong timber industry, fishing industry, banking sector, and mining. By having strong timber, fishing, banking, and mining industries, for example, America may be selling more to other countries, which helps our balance of trade. Strong industries hire people and pay them money, which is basic to the existence of our citizenry. Strong industries also pay taxes in their localities, and their workers support local businesses. Strong industries pay taxes to the state and federal governments. Our society is better off when timber, fishing, mining, and banking are doing well. So how to balance the need and desire for strong industries with regulation of these same industries? The beauty of the democratic system is that the people may push back if they deem that a business is doing more damage than good. If lumbering practices are denuding mountainsides so that there is more erosion and sedimentation washed into our watersheds, then the people will have them adjust their lumbering practices to mitigate that impact or to protect our environment and not unnecessarily affect our wildlife. If mining dams become unstable or toxic chemicals run off mining operations, democracy allows the people to push back and curtail deleterious impacts of mining, while still allowing the industry. A large country like the United States needs to have the ability to mine for some basic raw materials to be able to employ and defend herself, lest someone cut off supplies of raw materials for our nation.

If banks are using unscrupulous methods to chisel their customers or open bank accounts in their names without their consent, the people will raise a hand through democracy and say, "Enough!" The balance between who regulates and what they regulate is a delicate dance. The top regulators have also been accused from time to time of installing regulations that make it harder for others to enter their business. That is a barrier to entry. And 10 percent set-asides should be closely examined to see whether they have created barriers to entry for the other 90 percent of a project or economy.

Oftentimes, when the statists wish to inflict more regulations on the economy, education, and opportunity, they may offer a 10 percent set-aside to try to win votes from African American, Hispanic American, Asian American, and women citizens, for example. The problem is that these communities are being relegated to a 10 percent island. These are the scraps that the statists throw to gather votes as they further bind up our economy and wall off opportunity for all citizens. What about the other 90 percent of the economy or project? It is being divided and conquered by the friends of the statists. The powerful and the connected divide the 90 percent among themselves. Is it a coincidence that blacks have only one-eighth the net worth of white Americans under this conventional regimen? The focus should not be on 10 percent set-asides; it should be on the 90 percent. The politicians who come back to their communities touting the fact that they brought back 10 percent should not be lauded. Instead, they should be asked, "What about the other 90 percent? I want the 90 percent." The 10 percent set-aside leaves a few lucky winners, like a lottery winner. These are the insiders. This has not changed since there has been government. But a government by, for, and of the people is theoretically in control. The friends of the statists keep their insider status going by contributing to the existing politicians to keep the gravy train flowing. And what happens to the rest of us? The 90 percent is put further off-limits to minority communities.

Consider that in 2020, the Nasdaq, formerly known as the National Association of Securities Dealers Automated Quotations, and which had the stocks of about three thousand publicly traded companies in it, requested approval of a rule that companies listed on it have at least two "diverse" members. They then defined what was *diverse* as "one director who self-identifies as female and one who

self-identifies as with an underrepresented minority or LGBTQ+."[127]
An "underrepresented minority" is an individual who self-identifies
in one or more of the following groups: Black or African American,
Hispanic or Latinx, Asian, Native American or Alaskan native, Native
Hawaiian or Pacific Islander, or two or more races or ethnicities.[128]
But if you are gay or have only one parent who is of the groups listed
and you don't declare it to the world, then you don't qualify. Leaving
aside that anyone who is already at this director level is doing better than the average American, one should ask whether there is any
self-interest sprinkled into this proposed quota system for companies that are supposed to be making money for their owners, which
include citizens, senior citizens, and pension funds. Why does one
prefer one set of elites over another by overt rules? The difference
that we can see on the surface of people represents only 0.04 percent
of our DNA. That is correct. Ninety-nine point six percent of our
DNA is identical. All we see is 0.04 percent. Is that what society is
to judge directors of a public corporation by versus the individual's
background and life's experience? What about the best for the job? So
now these corporations can hire a company like Equilar or Nasdaq's
own Center for Board Excellence. Is it that simple? You cannot regulate what is in a person's head any more than you can regulate what
is in a person's heart. It would seem that you should treat people
for who they are and not by some quality that is not susceptible to
change, like the color of your skin. Everybody is an individual.

---

[127] Nasdaq, "Nasdaq to Advance Diversity through New Proposed Listing Requirements," Nasdaq.
com, December 1, 2020.
[128] Ibid.

Chapter 21

What Is a Racist?
How It's Used to Stifle Debate
and How We Can Discuss Race

72. OES THE FIRST person to accuse someone else of being a racist win the argument? Is it the skin tone of the speaker that makes something racist versus if a person with a different skin tone had said it? Of all the negative epithets that can be ascribed to an individual, to be called a racist is about the worst. Yet it is freely thrown about on major news networks and by politicians. What is *racist*? "The belief that race accounts for difference in human character or ability and that a particular race is superior to others." It is also "discrimination or prejudice based on race."[129] That would be the dictionary meaning and could be applied to anyone who believes that they are better than another person because of their race or the color of their skin. But there is also a definition that ties racism into the economic power of actually being able to do something about it. In other words, if a person has zero economic power in terms of owning property or running a business or determining who gets hired or what jobs people do at a government or private sector job, then that person has little ability to make that racism affect others. On the other hand, if one is able to deny

---

129   The Free Dictionary, s.v. "racism," accessed December 11, 2020.

housing choices, employment, or credit availability, then such person has the ability to have their racism affect others in their lives. The maximum position on the other side is that if a person has no economic power, then they cannot be racist, since they cannot negatively affect the economic success of another individual. Focusing on economics is central, as with better economics, the citizen can afford better housing, schooling, clothing, food, and medical care. Better economics helps to ameliorate the rough edges of life. Too much wealth can also work the other way by introducing temptations and excess that can degrade the quality of a person's life. Most of us would probably embrace the challenge of too much wealth. That might be a good problem to have. Nonetheless, calling someone a racial epithet still qualifies as racist in and of itself if the color of the speaker was used to make the charge.

If a citizen is of a group that is customarily considered a minority, the word *racist* may be heard and used more often than for a member of the majority. For example, in the United States, blacks were originally brought here by the transatlantic slave trade and died on the journey, or some died under the harsh conditions of slavery. The Civil War and the Emancipation Proclamation did not end prejudice against blacks. Jim Crow laws of "separate but equal" and the Ku Klux Klan came after the Civil War. Prejudice against blacks has existed in America for centuries. Therefore, it is not surprising that within the African American community, something might be described as racist, or that a person might be described as racist may be referenced more frequently. On the other hand, for a white person to call a black person racist might be laughed off, as there was historically little economic or political power for a black person to effectuate any perceived racism into a negative consequence for a white person. This is to say that the word *racist* may be used and perceived differently within the white community versus the black community.

A more nuanced method of designating something or someone as racist is not by looking at one incident but rather by looking for a repeated pattern. Is it fair to call someone racist if they misspoke on one occasion or used a politically inappropriate word or phrase? That would seem to be a pretty hard standard to label someone as racist. On the other hand, if there was a pattern over a long period of trying to subvert another group, then the term *racist* might apply if the actions were intentional. That could occur in housing or employment.

Is racism or calling someone racist a problem particular to the United States? Is the United States the only place where there is a majority and a minority? No. The competition between majority and minority plays out the world over. Who is the majority and who is the minority differs on where you are. There are Christian-majority nations as well as Muslim- or Buddhist-majority nations. If one is a Muslim in a Buddhist country, such as Thailand or Burma, the Muslim person will not get what the majority Buddhists get from the government. If one is not Han Chinese in China, that person will not get what the Han Chinese get in housing, jobs, or social stature. China is over 90 percent Han Chinese. If you are Tibetan or a Muslim Uygur in China, you are under repression by the government. In 2020, the communist government even had detention camps for over one million Muslim Uighurs, mostly men, in the far western region of China, to imprison and denigrate the Muslim faith and to re-educate these men to honor China and their Communist system. In January 2021, Secretary of State Mike Pompeo designated the persecution of Muslim Uighurs by China genocide with forced sterilizations, forced marriages to non-Muslims, political re-education camps, torture, and imprisonment.

If you are Christian in a Muslim nation such as Syria, Iraq, or Saudi Arabia, you will not get what the majority gets. If you are of Korean descent in Japan, you will not get what the majority Japanese get. If you are anything other than Korean in North Korea, you will not get what the majority gets. This is a story of history since time immemorial. In the United States, Puritans and Quakers fled Europe where they were vilified and sought a new life in America and succeeded. Consider the Amish, who live a simpler life in states like Pennsylvania and Ohio. Some Amish intentionally do without electricity and some comforts of modern life. They do not get what the majority gets, but they persevere.

In America, sometimes for an African American to get a job or to get a promotion, they have to actually be better than their peers, due to prejudice. A racial quota system, on the other hand, feeds the narrative that a person has the job due to their skin color and not the quality of their work. In 1903, W. E. B. Du Bois wrote about the color line between whites and blacks, where life in the United States for a black person was much more difficult with the Jim Crow laws of the South, the overt racism in the North and South, and the denial of equal opportunity than for a white person. To step over the color line and be on the other side as a black person was to be behind the Veil. Since a white person could not be behind the Veil, that person could also not really imagine the experience or view from behind the Veil. But W. E. B. Du Bois, the first African American PhD from Harvard University, was not totally without hope. "Surely, there shall yet dawn some mighty morning to lift the Veil and set the prisoned free. Not for me—I shall die in my bonds—but for fresh young souls who have not known the night and waken to the morning; a morning when men can ask the workman, not 'Is he white?' but 'Can he work?' When men ask artists, not 'Are they black?' but 'Do they know?' Some morning this may be, long, long years to come." That is the direction that the United States is heading: "Can he work?" "Is she good?"

73. Do ideas have a race? Or is the pursuit of truth open to all so that all ideas may participate? Unfortunately, the charge of "racist" is sometimes used as a tool to silence debate. It seems that the first person to call another person racist "wins" the debate. We assume that the one who uses the word knows that it is a bad thing and would avoid consciously doing racist things or acting in a racist way. This gives the first user of the word a presumption of righteousness, and with that comes moral authority. The error is that when this word of last resort is used as the first resort, it is overused and loses its necessary sting. The allegory is to the story of the boy who was asked to watch out for the sheep. The shepherd was key to the economics of the town, as the sheep provided milk to drink. The sheep provided wool not only to make clothes with but also to sell. The sheep

also provided meat to eat once they were slaughtered, or when the sheep made more sheep, sheep could be sold to other buyers. Thus, watching over the sheep to make sure that they didn't wander away or that they weren't attacked by a wolf was an important job. "Young man, if a wolf comes, cry 'Wolf!' and we will come from the village to chase off the wolf." Watching sheep at night and during the day, in sunshine and in rain, can become tedious. To break up that tedium and to exert some power of a young person making numerous adults come running, wouldn't that be something to make a tedious job more interesting? Even if there were no wolf. And that was what the young shepherd did. He cried "Wolf!" when there was no wolf. The men and women from the village came running only to find that there was no wolf. By the fourth false alarm over many days, the villagers came more slowly, until at last, when a wolf did appear, nobody came from the village when the young shepherd cried, "Wolf!" This allowed the wolf to kill many sheep without consequences. That allegory is similar to what happens when the word *racist* is overused or used too easily; it has less impact or urgency when there is a real racist incident or crime.

The discussions in this book may be called racist by some as a method of silencing the discussion. It is with some risk to discuss race as a white man in the politically correct atmosphere that informs parts of the academy and our country. For some opponents of uncomfortable discussions, *racist* can be used to silence and shut off discussion. Our betters make ample use of it to end discussion. Mistakes will be made in this book, but it is hoped that some value can be added to the discussions attempted here to a better social contract. It is a risk to black, white, and other voices to discuss race as the ultimate negative epithet of "racist" may be leveled vociferously at the speaker. Who will stand by the speaker, even if you don't agree with the speaker? Because if we allow the intolerants to curtail debate, then you will be the next speaker silenced. There is a thing called safetyism. One's eyes will roll with yet another "ism," but this is of deep concern for the mental well-being of our young people as well as adults. With social media such as Instagram, Tik Tok, Facebook, and other platforms, young people have to gather followers and likes.

What a young person, and adults for that matter, doesn't want to collect are dislikes or negative comments. The nightmare is to have some post interpreted as racist, sexist, colonialist, classist, xenophobic, etc. The shaming of a young person can be spread far and wide if the negative comments or trolling goes viral, where it reaches thousands of people. The next thing the person knows is that a negative news story is run locally or, worse, nationally, which puts that young person in a bad light. Decades ago, one did not have to live with the possibility that a misstep at a young age could bring disrepute onto that individual overnight.

How to avoid such a fate? The easiest way is to say nothing. That is safetyism. It doesn't just apply to a person's social media presence but to the questions asked in high school or college as well. Papers written for school. Participation in the discussion of political topics. If you say nothing and do nothing other than what the czars of political correctness approve, then there is little likelihood that that young person, or adult, for that matter, will be called out, vilified, ostracized, or canceled. This is exactly what the intolerants[130] want. They want to silence their fellow Americans to remove them from the stage so that only the intolerants may speak and set the agenda.

Under Mao Zedong, who led the Chinese Communist Party to victory in China in 1949, the Communist system instituted a public shaming system that was called a "struggle session," where a citizen accused of being a landlord, rich peasant, counterrevolutionary, or bad character would be humiliated on a public stage before tens, hundreds, and even thousands of fellow citizens. The object of the

---

[130] *Intolerants* are the politically correct. If you ask the general citizen the following question, you will usually get agreement with the statement: "Do you agree that the more politically correct a person is, the more intolerant they are?" This is a variation on the experiment where if you asked one hundred professors of Yale University to design an ideal society and you took the first hundred people out of the phone book and asked them to design an ideal society, the professors of Yale University would design such an all-encompassing regime that the normal citizen would flee from. There would be so many demands on what a person would have to become, what they would have to believe, and how they would have to treat others that those who did not conform would be ostracized and formally punished for failing to live up to the aspirations of the professors. That is a variation on tyranny. The one hundred citizens, on the other hand, would design a society that would respect their neighbors and allow them to live their lives as they saw fit, so long as they did not adversely affect the lives of their other neighbors.

struggle session might be accused of being a rich landlord or the son of a rich landlord or a corrupt government official. The person or persons would have to stand on a stage for hours with head bowed or stand on a chair for hours in front of their fellow citizens. A sign might be hung around their neck categorizing the nature of their alleged offense. They might have a dunce cap made of paper put on their head. Maybe their hair would be cut off onstage and black ink smeared on their faces. For the lucky ones, they leave with their lives. For the unlucky ones, they might be loaded onto a truck to be paraded around town, with the sign still around their neck, for the residents of the town or city to see and then driven to a field on the outskirts of the city or town to be shot dead and buried. Another method to end a struggle session was to have another citizen, maybe a poor relative, beat the person who was the subject of the struggle session to death with a farm implement, such as a garden hoe. The poor cousin had to finish the job, for which there can be no training. Refusal to kill could mean that you were next.[131]

The point of doing all this persecution publicly is to send a message to all other citizens that if they are not careful, they could be next onstage. If they were lucky, they could escape with their lives. This is a variation of what has brought about safetyism for our children. It is not a coincidence but rather a method. It has worked in the past for intolerants to silence their opponents, and the intolerants seek to apply it here today in the United States. Adults are now apprehensive at their place of employment or in their own community if the wrong social post or comment might get them fired or ostracized for not being politically correct.

This is a method by which Marxists define political enemies and seek to eliminate them. This is not to say that someone who calls someone racist is doing what a Marxist would like them to do to silence debate. But there are actors in the political realm that use the word *racist* just to silence others and to control the discussion. This does not mean that you are to come running to defend Trogladyk

---

[131] Yang Su, *Collective Killings in Rural China during the Cultural Revolution* (New York: Cambridge University Press, 2011), 217–218.

dinosaurs, but we need to recognize that the purpose of struggle session tactics are to shape public opinion and to humiliate and persecute those deemed to be political enemies.[132] The word *racist* will come from some corners to criticize parts or all of this book, and yet I hope you will be able to read on in the hope of a better understanding of where we are and to re-evaluate current efforts and, in so doing, to make this a better nation for all.

One would hope that societal issues can be discussed openly without silencing voices or ideas legitimately trying to address society's challenges. This, of course, does not mean that white supremacists or race-baiting participants have a seat at the table. Does calling something racist mean that you are right? Who determines what is racist? Is it the person that can get the most people to "trend" on the internet or who can assemble the largest mob to denounce someone else in the absence of a debate who gets to determine what racist is? That would seem to be more intimidation than debate.

74. Are the words *racist* and *racism* so overused that they have lost their sting? The valid point has been made that if you are African American and in the United States, you will have experienced racist comments and actions in your life that a person who considers themselves part of the majority will not have experienced. As such, it may be easier to discuss racist episodes that affect the everyday life of a black citizen, whereas for a Caucasian citizen, it rarely happens. And statistically, since the white citizen has a higher net worth than nonwhite citizens, it may be less likely to happen where it can have a negative economic impact on him or her. This is not to say that in terms of employment and in social situations, a white citizen cannot also be the subject of racial animus or bias. So when a nonblack citizen who tries to treat all equally and avoid being biased against others based on their skin color hears the charge of "racist" or "racism," that citizen may be more skeptical. The challenge is to keep the conversation going, and efforts at unity to make ours a better nation. The overuse of the words *racists* and *racism* can dull the conversation and

---

[132] Wikipedia, s.v. "struggle session," accessed December 12, 2020.

good-faith efforts to ameliorate barriers put in the way of blacks and other citizens. A closer look at the amorphous term *structural racism* has revealed that much of what passes for structural racism is, in fact, structural statism, one and the same!

75. Do you characterize your political opponents as racist, and almost any proposal or idea of theirs as racist, versus meeting the argument? That is intellectually lazy. To merely brush off other ideas that challenge core assumptions prevents us from arriving at a better solution. In 2020 in Connecticut, for example, there was a push to increase spending on public schools for poorer communities, which tended to be black, Hispanic, and other people of color. One of the groups leading the effort called Public Action for Education Equity was FaithActs for Education. This is a group of about seventy to eighty separate churches, mostly African American churches. FaithActs for Education was founded in 2014 in Connecticut. Their site says they were "people of faith building power to get our children the education they deserve."[133] In December 2020, they were pushing for changes in school funding as city schools in Connecticut rely on local property taxes and funds from the state to run their schools. FaithActs was using a funding figure of about $18,000 per student per year for cities such as Bridgeport and New Haven and about $22,000 per student per year for a wealthy town such as Westport. In the constrained financial times of the COVID-19 pandemic, which was affecting state and local government finances, they were working to change the funding formula to get more funds for the schools that served primarily black, Hispanic, and other students of color—a laudable goal. This effort was done in coordination with public teachers' unions, who are always asking for more money and employees from which to draw union dues and exert their political muscle, which is one of the strongest in Connecticut as well as in other states.

But FaithActs was ignoring the elephant in the room, which has been the campaign by the public teachers' unions, their erstwhile

---

[133] FaithActs for Education, "About," FaithActs.org, accessed December 12, 2020.

allies, to curtail and kill public charter schools in Connecticut that serve primarily high-need black, Hispanic, white, Asian, and other students. The public education unions have used their ample strength to suppress these public charter schools to only 2 percent of the Connecticut student population in grades K–12, with the result that thousands of high-need black, Hispanic, white, and Asian students are on waiting lists to get into the few public charters schools that have been allowed to exist. The public education unions and their statist allies in Hartford have used their muscle to keep the per-student state contribution for public charter school students artificially low at $11,000 to $11,250 per student per year. Compare that to the $18,000+ spent per student in New Haven and Bridgeport. Yet public charter schools in Connecticut consistently outperform their conventional public school rivals academically. Stamford Charter School for Excellence, which was only opened in Stamford, Connecticut, in 2015 over public teachers' union opposition, is already one of the highest-performing public schools in the entire state, with 95 percent proficiency in math for third and fourth graders and 85 percent proficiency for English arts. If public charter schools in Connecticut were offered $16,000 per year per student, they would be doing backflips with joy. Have you any idea what a public charter school in Connecticut could do with $16,000 per year in student funding? Considerably more than the public school monopoly. Just ask the parents and guardians of current public charter school students. Don't ask public teachers' union representatives, because they are trying to finish off public charter schools in Connecticut for high-need black, Hispanic, white, Asian, and other students.

If the state of Connecticut were offering $12,000 vouchers per high-need student per year to attend private schools, such as Protestant, Catholic, Muslim, or nonsecular day schools, high-need black, Hispanic, white, Asian, and other students would be rushing for such vouchers. Instead, FaithActs for Education ignores this inequity and exercise of sheer political power by their erstwhile allies. FaithActs for Education, on the other hand, puts their good-faith effort to improve education for our children and works with and for the statists who have no love for their faith tradition. Would opposi-

234   100 QUESTIONS *after the* KILLING *of* GEORGE FLOYD

tion to the Public Action for Education Equity bring accusations of racism? Is one even allowed to point out the hypocrisy of the statists and public education unions, who claim to be working for education equity while blocking school choice for high-need black, Hispanic, white, Asian, and other students? How would the proponents of school choice be treated?

76. Do you avoid discussing possible solutions to the inequity in education, housing, income, assets, and safety of person and property of African Americans because you are concerned that any alternative offered will be labeled racists? Or if you do, you use the threat of calling someone racist in order to squelch discussions of how to change the existing system to improve outcomes in education, housing, income, assets, and safety in person and property for African Americans? Shouldn't one be able to talk about it and not be called racist?

Chapter 22

All Black Lives Should and Do Matter, and the Chicago Tragedy

77. $\quad$I N THE BEGINNING of this book, the silence of America on the Chicago Tragedy was discussed. Were you aware of the Chicago Tragedy before reading this book? Some years ago, two young men of color died a violent death every day in Chicago, and the media elite and their enlightened followers said absolutely nothing. Our betters could not be bothered. Somehow, those who describe themselves as woke seemed to have missed the Chicago Tragedy. Prior to the killing of George Floyd and Breonna Taylor, the daily death rate for young black men and boys in Chicago had declined by about 25 percent down to about 1.5 young men dying every day in Chicago.

Subsequent to the killing of George Floyd and Breonna Taylor, the death rate has increased, as there were demonstrations against the police along with calls to defund them. At the same time, it has been postulated that the police may have felt that there was less support in the community for their policing, so they have become less involved in enforcing the laws. Over the weekend of June 8, 2020, twenty-four people were killed in Chicago and sixty-one people were injured by gun violence. That was less than two weeks after the killing of George Floyd. According to police superintendent David Brown, seventeen of those deaths occurred on a Sunday. On the Memorial Day weekend before, ten people were fatally shot and thirty-nine injured by gunfire. During the previous year, on the first June weekend, eight had died of gunfire and fifty-two had been injured. Twenty-four killed and sixty-one people injured by gun violence on that June 8, 2020, weekend are significant. That is three times more people killed from the previous year's weekend! The victims were primarily African American males who died of their injuries. That is a lot of young men and boys who were living on Friday but were no longer able to wake up to embrace the daily gift of life on Monday morning as they had been killed. That is a big problem, but the politically correct will not speak of it.

78. This is not limited to specific neighborhoods in Chicago, Illinois. Are you aware that young men of color die a violent death every day across America? The Chicago Tragedy plays out in Philadelphia, Baltimore, St. Louis, and Flint, for example, but the leading newspapers, media outlets, Silicon Valley blowhards, soap-box, self-promoters are silent day in and day out! If you knew about the extent of the Chicago Tragedy, did you share that with your friends, neighbors, and work colleagues? If not, why not? Why do we ignore the Chicago Tragedy? Do the solutions seem to be too hard to get to or contain too many levels? Or do the solutions involve questioning the efficacy of the Welfare-Industrial Complex and its facilitation of the Chicago Tragedy? What is known in some communities as urban trauma is also a product of the Welfare-Industrial Complex and the War on the Family, also known as the War on Poverty.

79. Do you know that if two young black women were dying a violent death every day in Chicago, we would hear about it, but as the Chicago Tragedy involves primarily young men of color, their lives don't matter to the elites and our betters? Do they matter to you? All these young men's lives should matter. It is a tragedy when the cause of death for young black males between the ages of eighteen and twenty-five is gun violence for about 50 percent of deaths, followed by accidents for about 30 percent of deaths, and only then do illnesses and diseases appear at about 10 percent. For anybody but

people approaching old age, the assumption is that people die from medical conditions with something wrong with their organs or cancer rearing its ugly head. There are common morbidities from lung disease, skin cancer, leukemia, breast cancer, then the COVID-19 virus, that we would expect to show up in women or men as they age. It is not the normal expectation to see that a violent death makes up half of the death rate for a particular category of citizen! You might think that professional soldiers or police officers might have violent deaths in their measure of morbidity, but neither soldiers nor police officers have half their deaths coming from violence, and then followed closely by accident at around 30 percent.

80. Is silence on the Chicago Tragedy complicity? The quote by Senator Cory Booker that "silence is complicity" should give our nation pause. When we don't discuss this tragedy for our young men, that is wrong.

81. If the lives of young black men in cities such as Chicago and Baltimore don't matter to our nation, is that racist? Is that sexist? Would the politically correct be more concerned if young women of color were to die at this rate? What if young black women between the ages of eighteen and twenty-five had as their cause of death gun violence half the time? That would be alarming, and our nation would mobilize to talk about it and see whether there is something that we could do about it. But when it is boys and men, we do very little. This is part and parcel of the vilification of men and why we should not gratuitously vilify men or boys.

Chapter 23

How the War on Poverty
Should Be Changed

82.   **D**O YOU KNOW or even care that the War on the Family, a.k.a. War on Poverty, has decimated family formation in poor urban and rural communities, whether white, black, Hispanic, Asian, or other communities? If you are poor and the government came to help your community, the number of single-parent families has increased under the watchful eye and hand of the Welfare-Industrial Complex. Single-parent families have a higher rate of living below the poverty line than two-parent families. Four percent of married couples were below the poverty line in 2019 versus 22.2 percent for female householder, no spouse present. That is a five times greater poverty rate versus the married couple (see Appendix B, Table B-2, "Families and People in Poverty by Type of Family: 2018 and 2019"). The mental, educational, and physical health of children in two-parent households is better than the mental, educational, and physical health of children from single-parent households. This is not to disparage the many single parents, the vast majority of whom are women, who work valiantly to make a home and to provide for their children, but two parents end up delivering better results for our children. Since blacks have historically had less economic assets than whites, the efforts and disincentives of the Welfare-Industrial Complex have had a disproportionate impact on

poor urban black families. Poverty rates are higher. Education levels are lower, and physical health levels are lower. With that record in mind, do you support the same approach to poverty and the Welfare-Industrial Complex that you have supported for the past fifty years and expect anything will change for the better in the future? That would seem like the definition of insanity, doing the same thing over and over and expecting a different result. The government never has enough money for all the programs statists wish to run, so increasing the budgets for these welfare-industrial programs will not change the dismal results of the Welfare-Industrial Complex.

83. Do you think the Welfare-Industrial Complex of wages, benefits, health-care benefits, pensions, disability, sick pay, vacation days for the well-meaning public workers that make up the Welfare-Industrial Complex wants to change one single element of the policies of the past fifty years except the application of more state? Is there any motivation by the Welfare-Industrial Complex to increasingly cooperate with privately based organizations, such as senior centers run by a church or homes for abused young women run by a local nonprofit? There is zero motivation for the Welfare-Industrial Complex to change anything. What's in it for them? The Welfare-Industrial Complex does not want its staffing reduced! The complex does not want their wages or pensions reduced. The complex, naturally, doesn't want to see fewer employees and consultants on its roster of personnel. They do not want poverty solved. That would shrink their universe. Organizations are organic beings, and they want to grow and prosper. The possibility of shrinking the size of the federal and state workforce that is employed by the Welfare-Industrial Complex is not in its game plan. But if the citizens demand a different and better way to address the social contract that the least and last are not left behind, that the least and last do have a chance to elevate themselves and have adequate housing, food, and medical care, then the Welfare-Industrial Complex must change. To improve the existing social contract would require churches, synagogues, mosques, and nonsecular, private nonprofits to expand their role in the War on Poverty by founding separate nonprofit agencies to take over some of

the roles of the Welfare-Industrial Complex. Otherwise, the War on the Family will not change. How many more generations of government dependence must a family endure?

A reimagined War on Poverty would bring the effort closer to the local level. Before the Great Depression and the introduction of the New Deal efforts of the Roosevelt administration in the 1930s, there were thousands more private eleemosynary institutions across America to help succor the poor and less-fortunate. When Alexis de Tocqueville, a French aristocrat and social scientist, traveled across the United States in the early 1800s, Mr. Tocqueville was impressed by the voluntary nature of American institutions to be brought together by the citizens, independent of the central government, to go about solving their problems. This might make sense for a country that was expanding westward and with new communities arising far removed from centralized authority. In Europe, on the other hand, one looked to the king or queen to solve the problems in the community. That is why the Americans are the highest givers to charitable causes the world over.

When government takes over a role and displaces private institutions, that is referred to by economists as "crowding out." As the government stepped in to take on more and more roles, the citizen was less inclined to give to charitable efforts to do the same thing when the government was taking taxes and fees away from the citizen in the first place. This is a natural result and is to be expected. But what is American society getting for the dollars given to the state? For all the dollars spent on wages, salaries, pensions, health-care plans, disability coverage, sick days, and office buildings, to name a few, what have we gotten? The drop in family formation of two parents is one of the most alarming side effects of the policies of the Welfare-Industrial Complex. While marriage has waned in all strata of society, it is still a strong institution among the well-to-do and among the elite. This is part of the success formula of graduating from school, getting a job, getting married and only then having children. And if the success formula works, then it is rational to pursue it.

There is a tension between those who say that the social safety net is a last resort and that it is incumbent on the individual to provide for themselves and those on the other side who say that structural inequities prevent many from climbing out of poverty; plus, the randomness of life events such as death, addiction, incarceration of parents, and economic dislocations requires a strong, state-run welfare program. This book will not resolve those competing positions. The proposal, however, is to rethink the present Welfare-Industrial Complex to make it more responsive and humane.

84. Do you know that the state cannot love a human being? Yet there are politicians that speak as though the state can love their wards. The politician may love those who are in need, but that does not mean that the state can love those in need. There is no question that many of the individuals who work valiantly in the War on Poverty care deeply about those that they tend to and are devoted to the people and families that they are trying to help, but that does not alter the fact that the state cannot love a human being. Yet this misconception is at the core of why the Welfare-Industrial Complex will continue to fail its intended beneficiaries and will not change the cycles of generational poverty among the poor in rural and urban America. The Welfare-Industrial Complex must change to bring in more locally created and locally run charitable organizations to take over and replace programs run by the Welfare-Industrial Complex.

85. Do you know that only you can elevate you? If I come over and pick you off the ground and set you on your feet but, after I leave, you sit down again, there is little that I can do for you. Only you can elevate you. Social policy needs to recognize this truth. It is not necessary to provide quality appliances, windows, cabinets, and accoutrements at publicly assisted housing, for example. It is not supposed to be a permanent location for any citizen. If the citizen wants better appliances, countertops, windows, and cabinets, the citizen is supposed to be motivated to go out and earn themselves better housing, appliances, cabinets, and accoutrements. This small vignette on housing is but an example of what the social contract should be based on a broader scale. A policy that steers clear of the need for there to be an incentive for the individual to strive for themselves will continue to do a great disservice to those it was dedicated

to help. And how can a distant bureaucracy effectively respond to the needs of the community? How can the Welfare-Industrial Complex, which is located in our nation's capital of Washington, DC, respond adroitly to the needs of our communities throughout our country? That is so challenging that the Welfare-Industrial Complex has recognized some of its shortcomings and instead has tried to give grants of money or infusions of funds to the fifty states to implement the policies of the Welfare-Industrial Complex. These grants of money or infusion of funds come with conditions attached. If the states or the private institutions do not use the funds as instructed and limited by the Welfare-Industrial Complex, then that state or private institution will have to reimburse the federal government. But how can state government bureaucracies adeptly manage these social welfare funds and programs from the state capital when the majority of people to be helped and the majority of funds are spent outside of the state capital and in towns, cities, and villages?

It is a hard road to follow. As expected, there are rules to follow for the disbursement of the federal and state Welfare-Industrial Complex dollars. This is as it should be, but it is still distant and impersonal to the intended beneficiary. Already at this level, accusations of favoritism can be leveled at the promotion of public employees within the bureaucracy or the giving of grants to politically connected private organizations. Or in the case of home health care, the private home health-care agencies must hue closely to the state's rules or risk being eliminated from the list of participants and put out of business.

We saw such conduct during the 2020 coronavirus pandemic, where certain states like New York or California had stricter shutdown orders for private businesses, such as restaurants and churches, than states like Florida or Texas, their economic nemesis. Recall that the Speaker of the House of Representatives was able to go in for a hair appointment in San Francisco during the COVID-19 shutdowns in 2020, sometimes wearing a mask and sometimes not wearing a mask, all the while the normal burgher was prohibited from going to a hair salon in San Francisco. Imagine if a normal person had been caught in a hair salon at that time, whether that hair salon or the licensed hair-person would lose their licenses to operate. It is risky to challenge the government. "Do as

I say and not as I do," said the ruler to his or her subjects. December 9, 2020, three bars in Yonkers, New York, lost their license for violating COVID-19-related rules, Margarita's Restaurant and Lounge, Uptown Bar and Grill, and Sahara Café, for having too many patrons in the bar. This is understandable, and according to lohud.com, 279 bar and restaurant businesses lost their licenses in New York State during the COVID-19 pandemic. While you may be happy that these businesses had their licenses pulled, [134] it is an example of how easily the administrative state can stop an enterprise dead in their tracks. The administrator in the government suffers no side effects. Their salary is paid every two weeks, their office is open, their pension benefits continue to accrue, and their health-care insurance is still in effect.

The for-profit or not-for-profit enterprise, however, has had its *raison d'être* stopped cold. If the enterprise cannot serve their customers, then they have nothing to do. If a not-for-profit enterprise that is in charge of home health care has its funding interrupted, it cannot continue providing home health care. This is the power of the state to silence critics and competition from outside of the administrative state.

In Los Angeles, Grace Community Church held indoor church services during the 2020 pandemic, contrary to Los Angeles County rules, so "the county's Department of Public Works unilaterally decided to cancel the church's lease agreement for a large portion of the church's parking lot."[135] Is it appropriate that the administrative state use a parking lot lease to try to gain leverage to make a private entity do what the administrative state wanted it to do? There was no mention that the church was storing things improperly on the leased parking lot or that they had converted the parking lot to a use that was not contemplated by the lease, nor was there any allegation that lease payments had not been made. It is just an example of the bare-knuckle tactics that the state can use to make individuals and entities bend to the will of the state. A reader can readily agree that in view of the threats that the coronavirus posed in 2020, the county

---

[134] David Propper, "Three Yonkers Bars Lose Liquor Licenses over COVID Rules; One Owner Wants 'Second Chance,'" *The Journal News*, December 9, 2020.

[135] Tyler O'Neil, "Retaliation: LA County Cancels Church's Lease as John MacArthur's Congregation Continues to Worship God," PJ Media, August 31, 2020.

was right to pull the lease to get the church to stop meeting inside and the state should use its many levers of power against the citizen. Or is this bullying and abridging our freedom of religion?

But what is the response when the state feels that its territory is being threatened with replacement or obsolescence? To remake the Welfare-Industrial Complex to bring the delivery of services down to the lowest level to the citizen as possible will require locally run initiatives by churches and nonchurches alike. This is to change what the Welfare-Industrial Complex has done by bringing the decision-makers closer to the people that they serve. Instead of a large bureaucracy that issues rules from Washington or state capitals, the power to pursue a healing social policy should be at the level closest to the people. Local organizations and 501(c)(3) entities should be empowered with funds and statutory authority to run housing assistance, food banks, substance abuse treatment, job counseling, job training, domestic abuse shelters, nutrition and health-care counseling, and psychological counseling. A church can build and run a senior center to be subsidized by the state. A synagogue can run a meals program. A mosque can run a jobs training program. The most important element is that people of the community with standards of conduct and expectations for the potential of their fellow citizens would be right there next to the citizens that need it most. There is value in setting an example for conduct, but also for community disapproval if an individual flouts the community's norms. It is not a one-way street. The individual cannot just expect for resources to flow one way. There needs to be expectations of the individual. If an individual is not expected to live to standards, then that individual is less likely to live up to those standards, which means that individual may continue to be a burden to the community, and the quality of life for the community suffers.

To change the Welfare-Industrial Complex with a reallocation of resources away from the Welfare-Industrial Complex and to small privately run agencies is a direct challenge to the existence of the complex. The natural reaction of the complex will be to maintain the status quo and not give quarter to any newcomers. That means that the complex must pressure politicians. "Scandals" regarding these new, privately run entities must be reported. The Welfare-Industrial Complex is an organic being and wants to grow, regardless of its inefficiencies and malfeasance in executing its mission. Even if one were able to realign many of the programs to help the poor, the Welfare-Industrial Complex would work nonstop to undermine the work of the newly created local organizations to pull these services back into the complex. By withholding funds or claiming improprieties, the complex could freeze the operations of newly formed programs to run housing assistance, food banks, substance abuse treatment, job counseling and job training, nutrition and health-care counseling, and psychological counseling, maybe a senior center or meals program. Those within the administrative state can claim to be acting for the benefit of the taxpayer by "investigating" a government subcontractor. A "temporary" hold can be put on any more funds to run the subcontractor's program, all the while that the people within the administration keep getting paid. As shown during the 2020 pandemic, the administrative state has many tools to bring nongovernment agencies to heel. How to counterbalance that will be a challenge in designing the replacement for the Welfare-Industrial Complex.

We already have community development corporations that have sometimes been used to develop real estate within economically challenged neighborhoods to build more affordable housing. The Welfare-Industrial Complex encompasses so much more than housing, but community development corporations might serve as a starting point along with faith-chartered organizations.

By having members of the same community that the high-need citizens live among run the local shelter, substance abuse clinic, food pantry, job training, or domestic violence home, the beneficiaries are more likely to act accountably since they see these people regularly in the same community, versus a faceless bureaucracy. We, as citizens, know instinctively what we are supposed to do in terms of educating ourselves, working, saving, and getting along with our neighbors, but we may not do it if we are only answerable to a faceless bureaucracy. This is not to say that the people who people the bureaucracy are faceless. They are not, but the success of the mission is not tied as well to keeping one's job. If a private organization is consistently missing realistic targets that other peer organizations in other like-situated communities hit, then such private organization may find itself terminated from running one of the programs of the Welfare-Industrial Complex.

This is analogous to how public charter schools only get a limited charter in terms of years until they must show what their effectiveness is. Maybe the charter is for five years. If the public charter school cannot demonstrate to the state education committee that they have at least met their objectives or close to it, then that public charter school may be put on a probation of a year or two, but if things don't turn around, then that public charter school would see its charter expire and the school would close. The assumption is that their students would do better in the local public school or in another competing public charter school, or perhaps they are lucky enough to qualify for a tuition voucher for part of the tuition at a private day school, such as a Protestant or Catholic day school. Likewise, a privately run home for single mothers with children would need to meet various targets relevant to its mission, similar to the targets that government programs are supposed to be meeting, but for which there are few consequences if targets are not met for the government agency. The irony is that a failing government agency might be rewarded with *increased* funding. By requiring accountability for private organizations that are running on public funds to do work that the Welfare-Industrial Complex had been doing, should give some incentive to perform well. If goals are not met, then the government has the flexibility to try a different not-for-profit agency. Under the present system, the Welfare-Industrial Complex just labors on, with little consequences to those that work for the state. If there is no incentive to change, such as termination, reduced salary, or reduced civil servant status, then how can the citizen expect a responsive administrative state? They cannot. The free market is responsive to the needs and desires of the customer. If a free market enterprise does not successfully fill the needs of its customers in curing their addictions, healing families, preventing domestic abuse, improving nutrition, improving job training, then that free market enterprise goes out of business. The government does not go out of business.

If an individual is encouraged by the local community to do right, that individual may choose to do right. "I may not be what I ought to be, but I am not what I used to be." That is what local organizations are better able to push for than large bureaucracies. It is an act of self-preservation by the community to take care of what is in front of its own door, and it doesn't matter what somebody else does in Washington, DC, or in Hartford and any other state capital. That is why the power and resources need to be filtered to the lowest level possible. That is why the large Welfare-Industrial Complex must be taken apart and rebuilt with resources and power applied at the lowest local level possible to privately formed entities. Within a community, there is a shared value. We cannot allow family to be an endangered species at the altar of the secular state, which shows little affinity for faith or family.

Let the secular statists who are indifferent to faith and family raise their objections and their hand. Let these statists state clearly and succinctly why faith and family should not have an equal seat at the table to design and implement a reworked social welfare contract that brings more resources to the local level. Privately run organizations that value family as a core institution of society would be funded to run shelters for single mothers or foster children. Let family and faith organizations run substance abuse treatment facilities. The secular state may also run programs to keep a fair competition of ideas and methods in the process to learn how to achieve better outcomes for our brothers and sisters. The secular state should be measured by the same yardstick as any family-, faith-, or secular-oriented agency in adoption, home care, substance abuse, and shelters for battered women, for example.

For the statists who are dead set against sharing the stage with anyone other than other statists, let them prove their worth in results. The free market rewards those who supply goods and services that people want. The free market rewards those who meet the needs of our citizens. If a business does not do a good job or does not satisfy its customers repeatedly, that business will go out of service. Unfortunately, the state has not had to operate by free market standards. If the product or service is bad, tough luck for the citizen.

What motivation is there for the state to do better? Jobs are guaranteed. Salaries are guaranteed. Pensions are guaranteed. Subsidized health care is guaranteed. Sick days are guaranteed. There are no such guarantees in the free market system.

This brings to mind the signs at the Department of Motor Vehicles in Wethersfield, Connecticut. While I was waiting with my daughter to get her driver's license test, we had to stand and/or sit and wait. That was all fair enough. But while we waited, there was a message on a sign that the Department of Motor Vehicles had taken steps to reduce your wait times and provide better services. This is an obvious objective for a motor vehicle department. The irony is that you get to read the sign while you wait in line about how they are working to make the line shorter. This does not mean that we would be privatizing the Department of Motor Vehicles, but it is a good example. For a time, Connecticut allowed AAA, the American Automobile Association, to execute some DMV functions at AAA offices, such as replacing licenses or paying for your registration. The menu of things that you could do at the AAA office was short, but what a treat! It was fast and painless. For years it has been painful to go to the Department of Motor Vehicles in Connecticut just to give the state the money it wanted for sales tax and registering a used car or boat that one had purchased. Does spending four to six hours seem like a fair amount of time to have to wait just to register a car or boat, just to wait in line to give the state money? Add to this the time to get to the Department of Motor Vehicle near you, and that ends up being an entire workday. So you ended up paying not just the sales tax and registration and title fee but also lost an entire day of wages! Luckily for Connecticut, with the election of Governor Ned Lamont in 2018, changes were made at the DMV and more staff were sitting at the DMV registration windows, and now a citizen could be out the door with a registered car or boat within the hour, the way it is supposed to be. As of 2020, however, AAA was still not allowed to provide limited DMV services. One can be confident that the state has a good reason not to farm out some of its work—i.e., job security.

The Welfare-Industrial Complex will fight tooth and nail to defend its territory and keep as much of the complex as it can to reward the insiders: the well-meaning public employees themselves and their public employee unions. That is the raw power and politics of the complex. The best interest of our brother and sister citizen adults and children is secondary. Whether a young single mother would be better served by a private organization matters little to the complex. That ten-step recovery programs based on religious values are more effective than secular programs will not sway the complex. That foster children often suffer because their parents are dealing with the disability of drug dependency and abuse will not interest the statists, who are trying to push recreational marijuana on our children, adolescents, and adults. Think how much money the state could make for education by getting our children addicted to pot. Count the tax revenue from legalized recreational marijuana while paranoia and anxiety spread and murder and violent crime increase in states that have adopted recreational marijuana. Oh. This is news? Perhaps it is because the major media doesn't care about our children and adolescents. Nor does it care about paranoia and anxiety if it relates to the ill effects of pot.

The complex is all about the state. The complex has a complicated and meritorious assignment ameliorating the many hardships and obstacles presented in life for the less fortunate. A worthy and necessary undertaking. The complex, however, has put its own interest ahead of that of the citizen. This is repugnant to our constitutions nationally and at every state level. Good government was to be for the happiness of the citizen and not the state and how best to achieve that happiness. Serving the state *qua* state has nothing to do with "good government." But it is where the complex has left us in the early twenty-first century. The citizen is first asked to assure the complex of their employment terms, duration, and number of employees. Only after these guarantees are met can the actual work of the War on Poverty be done. This is backward. All free governments are instituted for the benefit of the citizen. If our governments are indeed free, then the first inquiry is what is best for our brother and sister citizens and not what is best for the complex!

Science shows us that children raised with a father and mother in the home, or a mother and mother, or a father and father, do better emotionally, physically, and educationally than those with one parent or guardian. This is not to disparage the many of us who were raised by a strong single parent. Nonetheless, why fight this science in order to pursue a political agenda of antipathy to a family with two parents? Science counsels us to buttress the covenant of marriage and family.

There are statists who do not lament the destruction of marriage in poor urban and rural communities. For some, they see it as a revolutionary condition to break with the rules of the past and forge a Marxist-inspired way. But the data does not support this revolutionary path. Instead, it is one littered with physical, mental, and education shortcomings. Let the statists or modernists identify themselves and state their reasons for devaluing the family of two parents. That is the better way to arrive at the truth through debate.

Family should not be an endangered species. When it actually began to change in Connecticut is hard to say, but fathers are starting to experience a renaissance and recognition of their worth, in spite of the pastime of many to vilify men just because it is easy to do so, with little to no negative repercussions. Would you be deemed "woke" if you postulated that men are inherently bad? That would be a mistake. That would be ignorant. Consider that a father is a provider. Consider that a daddy and father are not the same things. A *father* is a protector of his children, physically, spiritually, and educationally. One of the most important things a father can do is to show up in his children's lives. He is a superman to his children. A *daddy* might just be the male who was there at conception and might be referred to as a "baby daddy." And that is about where the responsibility and involvement of a baby daddy end, at conception. A father, on the other hand, is there throughout. A father lives near his children and tries to shape their education and character as they grow up, by being around them. A father might be called Daddy by his children, but a man who has a child or children and does not stay involved with them and try to raise them is not a father. This is part of what it means to have two parents.

The mother must teach essential morals and values to her children; otherwise, they cannot reach their potential. She is a superwoman to her children. A person without the proper morals and values is at a severe disadvantage throughout life. What would proper morals and values be? They could be doing what a person said they were going to do. Showing up on time for an appointment. Showing up at work at the right time and place. Being courteous to others that you work for or who are in your employ. Give honest labor for the time that you work. Delivering honest value for the goods or services that you sell. Being honest. When in a situation of learning or school, to study in good faith to add to your knowledge so that you may be better able to serve yourself, your family, and the society. Respect women if you are a man. Respect men if you are a woman. Respect men and women. One does not highlight the infirmities of others. Appearing in a neat and orderly fashion. Dressing appropriately for the situation. Helping those who are less fortunate than oneself. Avoiding excess in food and drink. Considering moderation as a guide to conduct with others and in one's own life. Respect the right of others to disagree or have different opinions. Carry yourself with humility before others. Exercise forgiveness as a gift, not just to the person receiving your forgiveness, but to yourself. Be compassionate to those less fortunate than you. Don't needlessly expose the infirmities of others. Avoid using derogatory language when speaking to others. Don't spend all that you have earned; save some for a rainy day. Practice deferred gratification. These morals and values are a mere sampling and may vary to your own. But without the value to show up for work at the right time and place and to be willing to give good service for the pay we will receive, it is hard to excel at our work. If we don't deliver fair value in the things we sell, then our business model may not last that long, as customers may not return. These values are not universal and might overlap with some of your values. But if a person has few of these morals and values, then that person will have a tough time getting his or her first job and keeping it. That person may not study and learn at school or trade school. Once in a job, if a person does not give value for the time the person is paid for, then it is harder to be promoted or to keep that job. If we spend every dollar that we earn immediately, then it will be hard to have something socked away for a rainy day. If we spend every dollar that we earn, then it may be harder to reinvest in your own business or your own clothes and training for work.

Since the New Deal of the 1930s, and particularly since the introduction of the Great Society programs of the 1960s, the Welfare-Industrial Complex has increasingly made the raising of our children the work of overworked mothers. Single mothers with their children are a growing number for those below the poverty line. That is the opposite direction that society wants those numbers to trend. This metric needs to be bent the other way. There are ways to encourage men to be fathers in the lives of their children so that the single women are not carrying the load on their own to raise their children with the aid of their family, friends, community, and the state. This does not mean that they have to get married or even live together. Although marriage has been proven time and again an elevator out of poverty.

To discuss more men participating in the lives of their children and to support their children is not a plea but rather an expectation of what it means to be a father. To support fathers and mothers fulfilling their sacred duty of being fathers and mothers requires working through special interests within the complex to satisfy the needs of full employment by those that work within the complex and to make sure the salaries, retirement promises, and health-care options for workers for the complex are met before one can tinker with the assumptions of how the complex goes about its work. That is a lot of power to push against to put the interest of the citizens, whom we are trying to aid, before that of the well-meaning people working for the Welfare-Industrial Complex. Disincentives to a mother and father to fulfill their roles and obligations as parents must be removed.

A person can sit for years waiting to be healed by the intervention of the state or to have his or her life improved by some action of the state. Sitting and waiting. That could be on a waiting list for affordable housing. That could be a waiting list for entering into a work training program. That citizen can draw comfort from the people around him or her who are also waiting for his or her life to be improved by getting off a list or for that "right" opportunity. He or she is sometimes crippled by their language of "I can't" or "I don't have the will to get up." If society asks back, "Will you get up?" or "When will you take up your bed and rise and be better?" how long should society wait for an affirmative answer? Has the complex made it too comfortable or easy to remain seated or lying down, to wait for the next best thing to come around, which may actually never come around, as in the perfect job or apartment? The social contract was not designed to be a permanent caretaker except for the most extreme cases of mental or physical disability. We do not question the efficacy of social security helping a parent with a child that has significant, permanent mental or physical disabilities that prevent their child from living independently. But the easy example of a single adult person without any dependent children is a citizen the complex was never designed to take care of for a lifetime. That is neither good for the person nor fair to the state and the citizens who pay taxes to the state to maintain such ward of the state.

We also know of the satisfaction derived by any citizen for working and, in some manner, giving back to the community by doing their job. It can be a ticket checker at a sports arena or a maintenance worker at a public park, an assistant for autistic patients, or a clerical worker at a public agency. This is a good that society wants to share with those who are not already working, caring for someone else, or contributing to society. It is patronizing to each able-bodied citizen to pretend that they do not need to contribute in some way to society. Having one standard for oneself of needing to do at least something to be productive and yet having a separate standard for others that they don't need to give back so as to avoid being "judgmental" is patronizing. Making work and/or service a goal as well as self-sufficiency for all able-bodied adults is not condescending; it is honesty. It is not cruel to reduce certain government programs with the goal of pushing able-bodied individuals out of the nest, so to speak, and into the economy or the service of others. It is the opposite. It is humane. If you are not in the game, you cannot succeed. And the game is working in the economy. We do it for our own children, as much as we may wish to spoil and protect them. As parents, we know that it is good if our children have to fly on their own, make their own money, rent or own their own apartment or house, and provide for their own transportation and sustenance. Some of us parents are a little better, and some are a little worse than others in trying to make our children independent. To want less than that for the children of other people is a double standard. You are willing to push your own children and have standards for them, but in the interest of being "nice" or "nonjudgmental," you don't require the same of other people's children. After all, we all started in the same place as we came into the world. And everybody is somebody's child. The same principles may be applied to other people's children as you apply to your own children.

"What would you do?" is a question that highlights a double standard of some of us on how the Welfare-Industrial Complex should operate. If you had to decide which between two families you would place your own child with underscores our double standard. You must place your child in one of two homes. In the first home, there is a mother and father with some of their own children. The mother and father are struggling valiantly to put food on the table and to have a place for their family to live. If you decide to place your child with these two parents, there may be some nights that your child goes to bed hungry, as there is occasionally not enough food. Or your child might wear some hand-me-down clothes that are well-worn. Some days in the winter, their apartment or house might be cold, as there is insufficient heat. On the other hand, you could place your child in the home with a single parent, which, more often than not, is led by a single mother who is struggling valiantly to make things work for her children. Your child will not go to bed hungry on any evening, as government assistance assures that there will always be some food on the plate. Your child will not go to bed in a cold home in the winter, as the government-provided housing keeps the heat going. And your child will not wear hand-me-down clothing. Where would you want to place your child? More often than not, the citizen will choose the family with two parents together struggling to make it work, even if there will be some missed meals, cold evenings, and ill-fitting clothes. The empirical evidence supports the first choice for their own child. Children who grow up in two-parent households do better educationally, physically, and emotionally. So why do we have a double standard for the children of others than what we do our own children?

Why is the instinct of tough love characterized as cruel and inhumane by some? There are numerous reasons, but one of them is the self-preservation mode of the complex itself! Any threat of shrinking the complex is a threat to the jobs, health care, pensions and wages of the people who people the Welfare-Industrial Complex. The complex is a living and breathing organism. It will do all in its power to continue living and, if possible, to expand. That is what all living organisms try to do. Thus, the complex will trot out numerous social workers, social scientists, bureaucrats, and statists to testify and exhort against any such "inhumane" policies that would shrink the size and reach of the complex. Independent of the need of the complex to live, statists, who place the power and strength of the state above the citizen, will react instinctively to push back any effort to freeze or shrink the size of the state! National Public Radio, also known as NPR, will be one of the first in line to document the "cruel" cuts to the length or amount of welfare payments, disability payments, unemployment benefits, rental assistance payments, etc. NPR will have wards of the state testify to the impact that these cuts will have on their lives and trying to build a budget for their family. Or if it is aimed at only able-bodied single adults, how cruel it is to curtail their benefits entirely after a set amount of time! Perhaps NPR would interview the adult child that is finally given the ultimatum by his or her parents, or parent, of moving out of the family's basement at age twenty-four. These stories will be interesting to hear, but the rush to defend the breadth and scope of the failed Welfare-Industrial Complex is not part of the solution to accelerating the independence of our brother and sister citizens.

NPR was one of the most reactionary forces in American political life in the early twenty-first century. If anyone threatened to touch one hair on the hide of the administrative state, NPR would be there to document each and every cruel "cut" and "parsimonious" budget crafted by "unfeeling" politicians! Oh, if only we could all be as humane and caring as the reporters and editors of the reactionary NPR!

For a state like Connecticut, with the fourth or fifth worst fiscal condition of its state government with over sixty billion dollars in debt and unfunded pension and health-care obligations to people who no longer work for the state to right its fiscal ship and hope to one day grow at the same rate as the rest of the nation, Connecticut will have to cut the size and scope of its public workforce and public spending. It has been a downward spiral of increased taxes, fees, "revenues," and "investments" that the statists have demanded there to balance the state's budget every year, only to learn that obligations have been pushed further down the road on future generations for those who might still be in the state, or that another sea of red ink has arisen yet again. We cannot get away from the truism that the statists never have enough money and that the statists always have something that they are willing to spend your money on. NPR has been there all along, exhorting and championing the expansion of the size of the government of Connecticut specifically as an example, but generally for the Welfare-Industrial Complex of our nation. Would that we could all sleep as well at night as the reporters and editors of NPR, knowing that we have not cut a single program of the complex. Since the intentions behind all the programs that make up the complex are assumed to be good, that should mean that voting to fund them is good. And who would be against something that is good, even if the results of the complex in areas such as the Chicago Tragedy, rising poverty for families led by single women, and multigenerational dependence on the welfare state for poor urban and rural families have been disastrous? You can feel good about voting for more funding of the complex and then look the other way when these negative products of the complex keep persisting.

Then there are those who want to undermine the basic institution of family of mother, father, son, and daughter to be replaced with anything other than the core institution of family.[136] The opponents of family are encouraged by the low marriage rate that the complex

---

[136] The use of the traditional family of mother, father, son, and daughter does include for purposes of this discussion mother, mother, son, and daughter and father, father, son, and daughter. The latter are less prevalent than mother, father, son, and daughter, so it is easier to use the traditional description, which does not exclude other two-parent households.

has incentivized for urban and rural poor communities "saved" by the complex. Consider the rate at which recent Hispanic and Asian American immigrants, legal and illegal, are climbing the social ladder through work, saving, education, entrepreneurial efforts, and family. A supporting element for these successful first- and second-generation immigrants in buying their first house or apartment and sending their children to the local school to learn English is the family unit of mother, father, son and daughter. These immigrants and daughters and sons of immigrants have brought with them the respect and value of family. Those who practice it and are able to avoid being enveloped by the complex are more likely to surge ahead and start to realize the American dream versus the allure of multigenerational dependence on the complex. But don't suggest to the statists and NPR that there is a way to improve the complex that involves shifting as much of the complex that can be shifted to neighborhood-based and organized not-for-profit institutions. Some would be run by run-of-the-mill charitable organizations, and some would be run by faith-based, chartered organizations.

The prospect that a Catholic-, Protestant-, Muslim-, or Buddhist-organized institution would run parts of the complex can make statists as well as the reporters and editors of NPR apoplectic. A few are motivated by bigotry, and some of the statists and NPR reporters and editors believe that faith has no seat at the table. They are both wrong and need to accept a more inclusive and diverse array of methods to improve the social contract. The First Amendment guarantees freedom *of* religion and not freedom *from* religion, as the committed statists would have us believe.

Right off the bat, good things can happen when a person associates with the right people. If a citizen finds herself or himself in a counseling center or housing facility run by a church, synagogue, mosque, or temple, the citizen may find herself or himself among good people with good values. Something happens when you spend time with the right people. Could it be that people working for a faith-chartered organization may go the extra mile to share positive messages and encouragement to the citizen? Sometimes, advice has to be given to a citizen to be careful whom they chose for their friends. When a citizen surrounds himself or herself with people who make bad choices, then it is more likely that that person will make bad choices.

That a citizen, at one time or another, needs the temporary help of the complex or a neighborhood eleemosynary institution does not define that person's future. Each citizen has the power within herself or himself to alter their course. If any of us think the road forward will be smooth, then we are probably on the wrong road. Through no fault of our own, we may need or rely on the help of others to make it through a rough patch.

In redesigning the complex, the standards of the community should be adhered to and not lowered due to the demands of the intolerants, the politically correct; otherwise, the community is no longer a community in the absence of its standards and expectations. Included in this is the lesson that the individual must have a commitment to herself or himself. That commitment can make the difference. This commitment can be exhibited by simply eating properly and avoiding substances that can incapacitate the person in altered states. The commitment can be to their schooling or trades. At the same time, procrastination can be the number 1 dream killer. Quitting is also not an option. Quitters never win. How could they? They quit! What about having a plan for the future? If you don't have a plan, then you have a plan to fail.

But failure is nobody's destiny, as failing is not failure if the person gets up and tries again. Don't many businesspeople have a few stories of failed enterprises before they came back and were successful? It is not an exaggeration that we learn more from our defeats than our victories. In order to succeed, you have to have failed before. The only people who are successful are those who failed at something. This failure and perseverance will mature you into a capable adult, for failure is not permanent. You must look to *when* you overcome a failure, not *whether* you overcome a failure. It is a matter of when and not if when you commit yourself to prevailing. It is a commitment to keep showing up even when the odds are against you that increase your likelihood of success. Perseverance builds character, and character creates hope for a better future.

Some people need to get off the figurative porch and get something done and stop waiting for someone to put them in a healing pool. How hard are you willing to work? Do not diminish your personal victory with negative words. There will always be someone in front of you, but there will always be someone behind you. Have you advanced yourself in that line? One year later, are you still in the same position in line? The policy of these privately created charitable organizations, as well as secular local charitable organizations that would be funded by the federal and state governments in lieu of existing programs run by the complex, can help instill these values.

We should cease focusing on what the complex used to be but rather embrace the future of how the complex can be amended to pass the work to local organizations standing right next to our brother and sister citizens who need some help and then to learn what they can make of themselves. Obviously, the complex public unions will fight doubly hard to keep the complex unscathed and under the public union roof so that the public unions may continue to prosper and that the union dues continue to flow, regardless of the best interests of our brother and sister citizens whom we, as a nation, are trying to help with a better and more humane social contract.

When we help people work toward a better education, perhaps a GED, graduation equivalency diploma for high school or other formal schooling, we should not overlook the value of trade schools and practical skills. The road to economic prosperity does not run just through a college diploma. That would be overpromising and underdelivering. Economic self-sufficiency has run countless times through the trades. These trades can be that of a plumber, electrician, heating and air-conditioning contractor, framer, excavator, truck driver, mason, finish carpenter, painter, food cart entrepreneur, restauranteur, landscaper, etc. Each of these trades is needed and is not at risk of being replaced by artificial intelligence or computers at any time in the future decades. Computers don't know how to excavate for a house. They don't know how to pour a foundation or frame a house. They don't know how to wire a house for electricity or high-definition entertainment systems. A robot cannot paint windows or a room. Neither can a robot install hardwood floor in a house, sand it, stain it, and polyurethane it. The installation of granite, marble, or man-made stone countertops for kitchens and bathrooms needs the personal touch of tradespeople. A robot cannot come into an existing house and apartment and do demo work to prepare for renovated bathrooms and kitchens. Nor can artificial intelligence make you a lunch or dinner that looks and tastes good.

To become a tradesperson does not even require a high school diploma, although it is highly beneficial as the need to read instructions and be proficient in paperwork is imperative for running a business in the trades. For recent immigrants, it sometimes does not even mean great proficiency with the written English language, as their children in school or their friends may help them through the paperwork, all the while that they deliver A-1 goods and services. There are no devastating student loans that need to be taken out to work as an apprentice plumber for years, all the while learning about plumbing and then striking out on one's own. When advocates for erasing student debt speak, it is almost a class-based push to have tradespeople work and pay taxes so that white-collar workers can have their student debt load lightened for a decision they made themselves. If you don't like working with your hands, that is your choice, but don't ask others to subsidize your choice of lighter work.

Starting and owning one's business, trucks, equipment, real estate is just as likely to bring economic independence through working in a trade as you are likely to achieve economic independence by getting a degree and being a counselor, accountant, or engineer. The tradesperson doesn't generally need much help from anyone to start their business. There is also a consideration that is relevant in the light of the killing of George Floyd and Breonna Taylor. The risk for a black American is that prejudice can reduce their chances to succeed some of the time. When you are in the employ of someone else, there is always the possibility that the person with power within the company could use their prejudice to hinder the elevation of a qualified worker who happens to be black.

When you work for someone else, whether it be in the private or public sectors, you have entrusted your economic advancement to someone else. Let's hope the person above you advances people based on ability. When you run your own business as a tradesperson, on the other hand, others could decide to buy your product or not buy your product or use your service or services or not, but a better product or service has a chance in the marketplace. The route of "long hours and low pay" to economic independence should not be slighted or discounted. Countless Americans have realized the American dream by owning and running their own enterprises. The reason one can refer to this as "long hours and low wages for the possibility of economic independence" is the nature of being a business owner. The business owner of a barbershop or a food concession stand will put extra hours in just to make more money. Then the business owner will take extra time in the evening to prep quotes, equipment, or food for the next day. These are hours of business that the customer does not even see. When the business makes some profit, the owner might decide to invest profits into a new stove or printer or truck or employee instead of going out to dinner on Friday or Saturday evenings or taking a vacation two states over or overseas. The businessperson might put off new appliance or new clothes to reinvest in their business. This means that for a while the business owner is reinvesting whatever they can into their business. It may be that after the owner has paid rent for five years, a bank sees the steady rental payments and is willing to lend them a mortgage to buy the same building. Then for twenty years, the businessperson pays their mortgage, taxes, and insurance on the land and building. In the meantime, the value of the land and building might have increased beyond the rate of inflation. That going concern, land, and building might provide a decent nest egg for retirement and economic independence. This is why it is "long hours and low pay for possible economic independence!"

86. In analyzing the social contract that America has tried to buttress with the Welfare-Industrial Complex, do you oppose the "success sequence" of graduating from school or college first, then getting a job, then getting married, and then having children? For many Americans, the success sequence is not a controversial topic. For some supporters of the existing complex, the success sequence is not realistic or contains too many values. These same opponents of the success sequence are

also opposed to decentralizing the complex. Isn't a young American allowed to be exposed to the success sequence and then decide for himself or herself how they would like to live their lives? What is the harm of publicizing the success sequence to our young people in school? Do you oppose the success sequence in your politics?

Science shows that people who follow the success sequence have better economic, social, and physical health outcomes for their children and themselves. Just as two-parent families are less likely to be in poverty than one-parent families, why oppose the science of the success sequence? Some are ambivalent about the family of mother and father, daughter, and son or father and father or mother and mother, son, and daughter. For the ambivalent and opponents of family, family is merely bourgeois claptrap about the hallowed correlation of parent and child. The ambivalent and opponents of family would destroy the most hallowed of relations, family as the core institution of our society. These interests wish to abolish the family, which is why they do not lament the declining portion of poor in rural and urban communities with two parents at home. They don't see it as a problem, disregarding the fact that marriage is strongest among the economically successful.

When Assistant Labor Secretary Patrick Moynihan published *The Negro Family: The Case for National Action* more than fifty years ago in 1965, he had posited that the increasing number of families headed by single mothers was hindering progress for blacks in America. This certain political interests could not abide. Criticisms of the work came from many quarters, but their objections did not vitiate the correlation between family and avoiding poverty for people of any skin color or ethnic background. The results are better for our children with two parents versus one. That does not mean that all children of two parent families are better off mentally, physically, and academically than the children from one-parent households. There are plenty of children from one-parent families that are doing well and are in good shape, but the point of the data is to see what happens when you add all the numbers together. And when you add all the numbers together for families that are black, Asian, white, Hispanic, and other families, a two-parent family will perform better economically and their children will be further ahead. Since that is what the data shows, it is rational to have the complex support two-parent families as the preferred unit. It does not mean that it is the only one.

Nonetheless, if it is determined that the complex has rules or incentives that dissuade people from forming two-parent families, then those rules should be changed so that they do not discourage two-parent families. When in our tax structure it was found that there was a tax penalty for two married people to file jointly versus two adults filing separately, then that was seen as a "marriage penalty." A rational policy would eliminate marriage penalties and disincentives to marriage. While you may not want the state to encourage marriage for whatever reason, you may not object to the elimination of rules or programs that discourage marriage and/or two-parent households. Such a position would be neutral on families as opposed to against families. We should seek to highlight the benefit of two-parent households and to eliminate disincentives to two-person households.

While Marxists lambast family as an oppressive bourgeois institution, few citizens or politicians have assigned family to the ash heap of history, as communism was relegated to the ash heap of history at the end of the twentieth century as one communist country after another folded, the most significant being the Union of Soviet Socialist Republics, a.k.a. the USSR. If you believe that family should be assigned to the ash heap of history, then please say so openly. The latter would be opposed by politicians who support family as well as those who are indifferent but not antithetical to family! That makes up a strong majority of voters to at least give family room to recover and prosper.

Let the opponents of family show themselves. They may well be the same people who would oppose allowing faith institutions to create entities using funding that would have gone to the complex to fight poverty. Where does that leave you in reforming the complex?

One of the natural concerns in giving antipoverty work to locally formed entities is the proper administration of a government agency and its programs. How would these locally chartered and locally run antipoverty agencies be funded? One assumes that the administrative state is inherently inefficient as there is little incentive to carefully administer the people's money today. There is no competition for the Welfare-Industrial Complex to uncover waste and fraud. In the interest of effectiveness of having local organizations run various functions of the complex and achieving fiscal savings, the locally chartered organizations would be funded at 80 percent of what it cost the complex to do the same job. To expect a locally chartered organization to do the same job as the complex and to do it better at 50 percent is unfair. That could be setting programs up for failure. The 80 percent funding rate saves the taxpayer 20 percent, which would translate into billions of dollars annually, not something to sneeze at in tighter economic times. With leaner and more responsive local groups, it would not be unheard of to learn that functions of the complex can be done for less. The locally responsive groups may also have the untapped resource of volunteer workers who are able to do some small part of the group's job.

The expectation is that the 80 percent would be improved upon by doing a better job than the complex. If policies are run more effectively, then you start to chip away at a generational cycle of poverty enabled by the complex; that means fewer customers as a percentage of the population. Just as some public charter schools are doing better by their children and adolescent students than the local public school monopoly for less dollars, the graduates of public charter schools are also learning values that are more likely to steer them away from using the services of the complex. That means more students are taken out of the school-to-prison pipeline run by the public school monopoly.[137]

In addition, by having many faith-based and secular groups running housing programs, nutritional aid, health services, substance abuse counseling, domestic violence shelters, disability services, and foster care, there would be some programs that work better than others and some that don't work at all. The programs that don't work at all would be terminated. That is one of the criticisms of the administrative state: once you start a department, it tends to just keep living,

---

[137] Peter Thalheim, *The School-to-Prison Pipeline: How the Public School Monopoly and the Teachers' Unions Deny School Choice to High Needs Black, Hispanic, White, Asian, and Other Students* (Fulton Publishing, 2022).

even if it doesn't do its job well. A place is made for it in a budget. People work in the department that you like and are nice people. Why eliminate it when it is supposed to be doing well? The department ends up with perpetual life disconnected from the metric of whether it actually does a good job efficiently. A privately run group that is being funded in part by dollars from the complex has to show more positive than negative results. If the privately run group has more negative than positive results, then it would be cut off from further government funding. On the other hand, groups that were doing above average might have their methods duplicated by other privately run groups. Imagine that. Best practices being spread around to the complex itself. One should not get one's hopes up that this is a panacea. It is not. We will not know until we get there. Proponents of the complex will already call the shift a failure before it has even begun. They will call it "cruel" and "heartless," regardless of the results. Anything to get the dollars back into the complex. Every fiscal quarter the proponents of the complex will declare the shift to privately run groups a failure. For them it will not be a success until as much of the functions of the complex can be brought back into the bureaucracy of the complex, which is then shielded by the politicians to whom the complex pays donations and contributes man-hours for campaigning.

The citizen, on the other hand, may be a bit more fair-minded and give these privately run groups a chance over years to do a better job of mending our social contract and delivering help to the least and the last and those who fall on hard times at different times in their lives.

87. In reimagining the Welfare-Industrial Complex as set forth above, do you think faith institutions should have a role?

88. If you are opposed to Protestant-, Catholic-, Muslim-, or Buddhist-chartered organizations using direct government financial support to address hunger, housing, medical care, disability, addiction, domestic abuse, foster care, etc. for urban and rural poor, are you a bigot?

89. Do you know that the state cannot love a human being? Will you continue to assume that the complex can replace the love of a human being with the cold embrace of the state? Is the state an adequate substitute for the love of a family member? It is not, and to support policies that weaken the bonds of family or that prevent the bonds of family from even being developed is inhumane. Are you familiar with the science that human beings need to be held when they are young? Do you know the stories of adoptive parents who travel to Russia, China, or Africa to adopt the perfect child out of an orphanage? What joy to bring home this bundle of joy, only to learn later that because this child was not held by his or her mother or father, aunt or uncle, grandmother or grandfather, sister or brother, cousin or babysitter while they were babies and toddlers, this child will have difficulty developing attachment to other human beings as a young person and adult!

Of equal value to the value of food and shelter to a human being is to be held by another human being. Putting our children into pre-schools and away from their parents, guardians, brothers and sisters, grandparents, or babysitter is not necessarily best for our children's emotional health. If you choose as a social policy to usher young children into preschools versus facilitating mothers and fathers, grand-mothers and grandfathers, to be the ones caring and holding their child or grandchild, you are making it more likely that the child will lack the ability to attach to other human beings later in life, like the babies in orphanages that were not held sufficiently. That is the science. The ushering of preschool children into state-sponsored schools sounds like a nice feature for working parents, but what is the impact on a young child? Instead, father and mother or another family member should be encouraged to spend more time with their child, as they are more likely to simply hold their child. The state cannot love your child, but a family member can.

90. In redesigning the Welfare-Industrial Complex, are you willing to promote policies that support family formation versus fur-ther aggrandizement of the state?

Chapter 24

Accountability and Public Union Binding Arbitration: An Oxymoron

91. HAVE YOU USED the word *accountability* since the killing of George Floyd and Breonna Taylor? Did you use it along the lines of requiring accountability for police officers in the line of duty? The assumption with any job is that the person doing it is accountable for their actions if they fall far outside of the realm of what is required to do the job. When a police officer is required to work at a protest, their job is to protect the people protesting as well as the onlookers. The peace officer's duty also includes protecting property, both public and private. Public property would be public parks, town halls, courthouses, government vehicles, streets, and anything else in the public domain. The police officer is also charged with protecting the property of our citizens, such as their houses, cars, commercial buildings, and businesses. Clearly, if the police officers are so outnumbered that they cannot reasonably execute their duties without putting their own well-being on the line, it is understandable for them to tactically retreat to a position that allows them to do as much of their job as the circumstances allow. If protesters are peaceful and if the public watching the protest or simply passing by in the conduct of their everyday affairs are peaceful, then the job of the police officer is not as difficult versus the opposite condition of a riot. If protesters are seeking confrontation and stick-

ing their fingers, fists, and faces into the faces of police officers, at some time those actions go from protest to provocation or physical assault on the officers. The law does allow a police officer to defend himself or herself and to try to maintain public order. The calls for accountability come when people get beaten or beaten up or killed, whether the conduct of the police was excessive or whether it was necessary in light of the conditions that occurred at the protest or riot.

Accountability for excess force is easier to imagine in the quiet of typing a report or story on a protest or riot as opposed to being in the fog of a riot and which actors are benign and which are aggressive on either side. After the killing of George Floyd and Breonna Taylor, much was written about accountability and how it should be improved. It was learned in some communities around the United States that a few police officers who had had more than their share of citizen complaints for excessive force were still police officers in the same or other jurisdictions. Police and nonpolice alike have lamented the fact that there are a few bad apples among the ranks of police officers, but collective bargaining agreements have made effective accountability difficult, if not impossible. How have your past political choices made accountability out of reach for citizens as you have structurally placed the state above the citizen? Did you, and do you still, support the ability of collective bargaining to place public servants beyond accountability to the citizenry? If you do, then you should not lament the lack of accountability or pretend that you support accountability.

It is the bad apples that distort the picture of the police and peace officers who come to keep our communities safe. In Minneapolis, Minnesota, where Mr. Floyd was killed, it was learned that the public union protocols were so effective to protect "bad apple" police so as to make them effectively out of reach. From a citizen's perspective, this is unacceptable. Good government, as recounted by James Madison in *The Federalist Paper* no. 62, "implies two things: first, fidelity to the object of government, which is the happiness of the people; secondly, a knowledge of the means by which that object can be best attained." Therefore, the happiness of the people demands accountability by "bad apple" police officers to the people. Public union binding arbitration has made that relatively impossible, as there are so many procedural safeguards that it is hard to discipline and remove a problem officer. A low percentage of citizen complaints ever get results or see the light of day. Even if a police chief were to fire a problem officer, that does not mean that the discharged officer will not be back in the department three years later after years of arbitration and lawsuits. Is that good government?

Theoretically, all civil servants are answerable to the citizenry. But not all citizens are made alike. A public union is under a duty to put their well-meaning employees first, the union second, and the public third. Otherwise, they would not be doing their job to get the best terms for their members. Yet that puts good government on its head and suggests that public unions for public servants may be anathema to good government since barriers to transparency and public access to records on public employees are restricted and will continue to be restricted in the interest of the public servant as opposed to the citizen, for whom they work. And that is where it will remain, despite all the self-righteous demands for accountability. Nothing will change.

So spare your high talk of accountability if you are not willing to dismantle public union binding arbitration. The stronger the binding arbitration laws in your state, the less accountability to the public in your state. How could you fix that and still be fair to the police officers as well as all other public servants? These jobs are vital to running our federal, state, and local governments and must remain a place where people want to work and faithfully perform the duties of the individual jobs of the state, from police officer to schoolteacher to landscaper to registrar of voters. The policy fix is that terms of employment are to be set by the elected representatives of the people. At the state and federal level, that would be the state legislatures and Congress approving the terms proposed by the executive branches of governors and presidents. At the local level, mayors, boards, or commissions elected by the local populace would set the terms and salaries of employment. The pay, benefits, sick days, disability, 401(k), and health insurance terms should be at a level sufficient to staff the needs of the federal, state, or local government. If the pay, benefits, sick days, disability, 401(k), and health insurance terms are not high enough, then the federal, state, and/or local government would have to increase them as the market conditions would require, as opposed to the political muscle of public unions, which are well-adept at getting politicians elected to increase pay and benefits above the free market level, an unfair result to the rest of the citizenry who do not have such privileges.

By having the state legislatures, Congress, governors, the president, mayors, local committees set the terms of employment, which includes employee standards of conduct and transparency in the service of the public, the public will have re-established accountability by our well-meaning public servants generally, and police officers specifically, to the people. That is accountability.

92. Are you aware of *supersedence*, whereby terms in public union contracts and binding arbitration settlements can take precedence over the duly enacted laws of a state? That means the laws enacted by the legislators and governor, elected by the people of that state, can be overridden by public union contracts. How can laws enacted by the representatives of the people for accountability be set aside by negotiators and arbitrators elected by no one? Something is seriously wrong. Perhaps you thought that what a state legislature and governor signed and passed as laws under your state's constitution was the law of the state? Well, under supersedence, you would be wrong. In Connecticut, a collective bargaining agreement takes precedence over a state statute. That's right. So if the people's representatives make a law, unelected collective bargaining agents can change that as it applies to state workers! That is unconstitutional.

But if there is no one to bring an action against this abuse of our constitutions, and if the jurists who sit as judges and Supreme Court Justices of our states favor the state nine times out of ten over the citizen, then our courts will uphold these unconstitutional acts. The statists treat the citizen as subjects to be ruled and not as the sovereign power, the ultimate wellspring of legitimacy and the power of the state. When you wager at a gambling house, there is a rule about who wins when both lose or tie. Since the gambling house runs the place and wants to stay in business, they have enacted rules to give the house an edge over time to win all your money. If the house and the player tie in blackjack, then nobody wins, but if the player goes over twenty-one, the house wins. That is how many of our statist jurists see it: if the citizen does not clearly win, then the state wins. With supersedence, the statists win and the citizens lose as the laws enacted by their duly elected representatives are overruled by the specific terms of a labor agreement.

If there were a conflict between a state statute on accountability for police misconduct and a collective bargaining agreement, the collective bargaining agreement would take precedence. Many demonstrated in the summer of 2020, but their attention span did not last long enough to correct this imbalance. Supersedence is alive and well in states like Connecticut. Supersedence can apply to pension payments, employee overtime, complaints against the police, freedom of information requests, and grievance processes. How about a state worker being placed on paid administrative leave? The Connecticut State statute says administrative leave can only be for fifteen days. Yet the state worker was on administrative leave for sixty-nine weeks. To understand the grossness of the disparity, fifteen days is one day over two weeks. Sixty-nine weeks is four weeks more than one year and three months![138] Or how about a university professor who was accused of sexual harassment by multiple students, but those accusations were kept secret for years, despite freedom of information laws, "FOI," concerning personnel records, yet the university contract provision superseded the state FOI laws.

Or how about for Connecticut's corrections unions term that grievance hearings against their officers were closed to the public?[139] Is this the accountability that you were demanding after the killing of

---

[138] Suzanne Bates, "Supersedence: The Consequences of Government Unions' Special Privileges," Yankee Instituted Policy Paper, Series of 2019, vol. 4, citing Marc Fitch, "Connecticut Law Requires Full Funding of Pensions, SEBAC Overrode It," Yankee Institute, September 26, 2018.

[139] Ibid., citing Corrections (NP-4) Bargaining Unit Contract Between the State of Connecticut and Council 4 of the American Federation of the State, County and Municipal Employees, effective July 2, 2016, to June 30, 2021, 19.

George Floyd? You may even have hung a "Black Lives Matter" banner out of the window of your house or placed a "Black Lives Matter" sign in your yard. But will you reassess your reflexive support of all things government? Will you question the wisdom of granting ever more powers to the state and allowing the public unions to further cordon our public servants off to public scrutiny and accountability? This is not a retrograde effort to revamp public service; instead, it is to return accountability and fiscal authority back to our elected representatives, unencumbered by the actions of unelected collective bargaining officials to overrule the will of the people. Accountability demands public oversight of all things that our representative democracy does. The chances are that after the banner outside your window fades or the wind blows the sign in your yard over or the car wash blemishes the bumper sticker on your car, your commitment to Black Lives Matter and accountability will fade and disappear with it and you will not change anything. Instead, you will leave supersedence in place and maybe even redouble your support for the statists who put supersedence in force in the first place. The public unions are stronger than your professed will to change things for more accountability.

93. Are you aware that *accountability* and *public union binding arbitration* are oxymorons, as they cannot be used in the same sentence? By law, public unions promote first their members, second their union, and third the public for which they serve. Where does that leave you? In third place. Any request that you make to change things for service to the people first will be rebuffed and overcome by the muscular public unions that had also professed publicly for greater accountability after the killing of George Floyd. The public union allies are many. The politicians who owe their election to public unions dare not raise a hand for greater accountability, lest they be shown the door. The public union political action spending is robust. You will change nothing because you will move on to the next topic that makes you feel good about yourself and even give your electoral support to statists who erect even more barriers of accountability of the state to the people.

94. Are you aware that you cannot "fire" a public employee, as they can come back via arbitration and civil litigation should the arbitration be unsuccessful? Even if the disciplinary procedures for overseeing our well-meaning public servants allow on its surface for the removal of bad apples or incompetent state workers, that is not the end of the story. An administrator can fire the worker, but then there is a whole procedural process for the employee to challenge the firing, first at the administrative level within the department, and then later in the court system outside of the department. Nurses were fired for abusing mentally ill patients at a public hospital. They were rehired. Then later they were arrested again for abusing patients.[140]

A police officer who used profanity on camera, threatened violence, and told an immigrant to leave the country was fired. But that was not the end of it, as the city of Danbury, Connecticut, was ordered to rehire the officer. The behavior was "outrageous and disturbing," but not enough to fire him.[141] This is another example of the difficulty for a police department to fire a public employee that they determine is no longer appropriate for their department. Whose interest is being protected here? Is that the accountability that your public persona has demanded?

---

[140] Ibid., citing Marc Fitch, "The Fitch Files: Whiting Hospital Was Forced to Rehire Employees Terminated for Abuse," Yankee Institute, March 28, 2018.

[141] Associated Press, "City Ordered to Rehire Cop Fired for Berating Immigrant," NEWS8, April 11, 2018, accessed December 21, 2020.

Chapter 25

The Hypocrisy of "Science Is Real" Dogmatists

95. WHY DO YOU say that science and data are real, yet you silence the science and data you disagree with? Science is "1. Originally, state or fact of knowing; knowledge, often as opposed to intuition, belief, etc. 2. Systematized knowledge derived from observation, study, and experimentation carried on in order to determine the nature or principles of what is being studied. 3. Especially one concerned with establishing and systematizing facts, principles, and methods, as by experiments and hypotheses. 4. A systematized knowledge of nature and the physical world..."[142] Data is "things known or assumed; facts or figures from which conclusions can be inferred."[143]

The science and data of faith and family is that economically successful people are married and economically unsuccessful people are not married. People who go to church, synagogue, mosque, and temple are more successful than those who do not. This is the science. That is the data. To refer to the single, successful woman who is fabulously wealthy or preeminent in her field or both is not

---

[142] Webster's New World Dictionary of the American Language, College Edition, The World Publishing Company, Cleveland, 1957, science, p. 1305.
[143] "Id.," data, p. 374.

counterfactual. She is a data point, a person whom women and men should emulate and respect. It is, however, by adding up all of the data points together that you come up with empirical evidence. This is how science works. Adding up the data.

Digits, numbers, do not desire to be politically correct. Digits are ambivalent and are available to be used objectively every day. Just because you are a bigot or a Marxist or fellow traveler or useful idiot for Marxists or bigots does not mean that you can ignore the science and the data. The "inevitable" revolution of a Marxist dictatorship as posited by Karl Marx and Friedrich Engels in their 1848 *The Communist Manifesto* for advanced industrial countries never happened and never will happen because it was never inevitable or based on science or data. It was a totally, artificial construct to give power to an elite, the dictatorship of the proletariat. In the 1848, words of Marx and Engels "a small section of the ruling class cuts itself adrift, and joins the revolutionary class, [the proletariat]…now a portion of the bourgeoisie goes over to the proletariat, and in particular, a portion of the bourgeois ideologists [soft hands people], who have raised themselves to the level of comprehending theoretically the historical movement as a whole."[144] This Marx clarified as the dictatorship of the proletariat in 1850. As mentioned above, Marxism has been the most deadly political ideology to those unfortunate to fall into its totalitarian grip in the twentieth and twenty-first centuries, all led by soft-hand elitists: Lenin, Stalin, Mao, Castro, Pol Pot, Kim, and Xi, to name a few.

China has been run by an elite since 1949, and the elite there has never asked for the consent of the governed through free elections. Marxism is just another rationale for the rule of man of kings, queens, khans, tsars, dictators, and tribal leaders. It is elite thought. The billionaires and millionaires of the Chinese Politburo determine every five years what the course will be for the other 1.4 billion Chinese for the following five years based on the Politburo members' consciousness of the proletariat that allows the few to rule over the

---

[144] "The Communist Manifesto," translated by Samuel Moore, The Merlin Press, Wellington, 1998, p. 11.

276   100 QUESTIONS *after the* KILLING *of* GEORGE FLOYD

many as the elite has done since prehistory. These millionaires and billionaires of the Chinese Politburo maintain that their decisions are based on the science and data of Marxism and socialism that allows them to rule over their people.

Witness for a moment the suppression on the island prison of Cuba, citizen protestors were again beaten with metal rods and truncheons[145] in 2021, followed by arrest, torture, summary trials, imprisonment, and in some cases death. That is where the science and data of Marxism inevitably leads.

Science politicized for political ends ceases to be science as competing theses of how things work are squelched to serve the interests of the state or elite. Peer review within the scientific community to mimic trial experiments of other scientists to examine the reliability of what is being postulated to vet ideas for scientific rigor is eliminated in favor of the politically correct hypothesis *du jour*. Science ceases to be an element for the advancement of humanity and atrophies yet another casualty in the drive of the elite to govern their brother and sister citizens. Yes, you with the sign that states, that "science is real," are the biggest threat to science. Data ceases to be apolitical digits but rather propaganda to support the rule by our elites whom you support. The masking of children in grades K-6 after the distribution of the Pfizer and Moderna vaccines to the adult population was the poster child of control of the populace despite the data at the time that the threat of death for an older citizen was one thousand times more likely than that for a youth in grades K-6. The psychological damage to our children to study and play with masks on for years to satisfy the political control of the elites is inexcusable. Science and data is withering away under the onslaught of the intolerants, the politically correct and statists.

The signs in your yard, the banner hanging out of your window, the bumper sticker on your car claiming your allegiance to "science is real" is an indicator of the opposite, that you will not allow there to be science which requires competing ideas to be vetted by

---

[145] *Truncheon* "a short, thick staff; cudgel; club; now used chiefly on a policeman's baton." "Id.", Webster's New World Dictionary, p. 1564.

numbers and data and not by political komisars. The chances that you are an intolerant, the politically correct, and use your influence in social circles, business power, and the ballot box to punish those whose contribution to science and data you disagree with politically are great. Your sign, banner, and sticker advertise you as intolerant, the opposite of what you fancy yourself to be. Perhaps you also have a Black Lives Matter sign, banner, or bumper sticker posted on your house, apartment, or automobile and yet you will not discuss the Chicago Tragedy, its causes, and how best to ameliorate the tragedy. To discuss the Chicago Tragedy challenges your political preferences, past, and present and forces you to deal with the science and data of faith and family and what happens when we ignore the science and data of the proper morals and values for all our citizens!

Chapter 26

The Empty Platitudes of Some Faith Leaders: Re-examining Your Political Default to Empowering the State and Our Betters

96. WHY DID FAITH leaders and ministers recite empty platitudes and promises after the death of George Floyd and Breonna Taylor? Is it so that we may know how pure their hearts are, and yet they continue to support statist solutions over the citizenry? Minister, why do you counsel "giving up power" when your very politics before and after the killing of George Floyd accentuates the "power" of the state? In the previous paragraph we examined how the statists have erected barriers to public accountability, yet faith leaders and ministers will exhort support of these statists since they say the right things. Following a crime by the state, why do you default to granting more power to that same state over the citizen, the same state that ended the lives of Mr. Floyd and Ms. Taylor? Isn't the response to be less power to the state? Yet from your pulpits you encourage your flocks to support growing the state. It may be that you either don't know that you keep handing more power to the state or you wish to ignore that your politics have consistently added to the ability of the state to rule over the lives of your congregants, your flocks, and your sister and brother citizens. In the face of your obliviousness to the nature of cause and effect, why should I heed your exhortations?

This reminds me of one of the numerous Catholic Masses that I listened to on Fordham University's radio station, WFUV. Though I am not a Catholic, their services have a pleasing cadence and message. One Sunday, the priest leading the service gave a message wherein he set up a straw man of somebody who supports "small government." In his message, that was not a good thing, so once setting up the straw man, he easily swatted it down. How naive. Was he at all aware who big-government proponents are? Does he want his flock and those outside his Catholic flock to support big-government types? Examples of big governments are Marxist, communist, fascist, and totalitarian governments. A totalitarian government has only one political party, and that political party rules all aspects of a country's life. Had this minister not heard of Adolf Hitler, who was a big-government proponent, as were Mussolini, Lenin, Stalin, Mao, Castro, and Pol Pot. The government has the first and last say in everything. Was this minister ignorant of the millions of Christians, Jews, Catholics, and Protestants that have been persecuted and killed by these apostles of big government? His straw man verged on pathetic and was conceived in naiveté. Would he have counseled more big government after the killing of George Floyd?

97. Why do you support and continue to promote ever more regulation and control of the citizen by the state? You seem content if the amount of money extracted from the citizenry is increased. You seem content when more government programs are instituted, yet you say little of the virtual elimination of marriage among poor rural and urban Americans facilitated by these very government programs. That silence has particularly negative consequences for our most vulnerable citizens. As a faith leader, it is assumed that you support the covenant of marriage.

98. Why do you correctly preach that "we must give up the power so that they can all have the God-given rights of a human being," and yet you say "they" and not "we" when we are all brothers and sisters? By pushing and advocating for the rights of all citizens to our God-given rights as a human being, all strata of society will

benefit. Consider that your exhortation that "we must give up the power" is that we must give up the power of the state over the citizen so that we "can all have the God-given rights of a human being." The ways in which the state prevents the least and last to take on a job through licensing requirements; to work with their hands and back to put food on their plate; to make housing less affordable with ever-greater layers of minimums and permitting requirements; to increase the cost of living for the least and last through taxes, fees, revenues, tolls, licensing, permitting, etc.; to deny school choice by fortifying the public school monopoly's power; to addle our children and adolescents on marijuana so that the state can have more money; and to increase the cost of having a car and utilities for the poor by subsidizing millionaires and property owners at the expense of the least and last. All these are manifest through the state exercising its power over the citizenry in ever-widening circles. The minister counsels giving up power but will reflexively pull the lever and elect more statists to power, who will grow the power of the state over the citizen even more.

99. Don't you know that the "God-given rights of a human being" are recited in the Bill of Rights of the first ten amendments to the Constitution, as well as the subsequent seventeen amendments? The purpose of our revolution was to combat tyranny, not only of an unaccountable monarch, but also of the majority. The design of our Constitution was limited government so that the citizen could enjoy life, liberty, and the pursuit of happiness.

100. Were you not taught that the *rule of law* is based on an observed Constitution and Bill of Rights, that the citizen is sovereign and not the state of king, queen, khan, czar, or dictator?

101. Why do you constantly seek to trade a bit of our freedom for more security and thereby diminish our freedom and aggrandize the state?

102. Isn't this struggle after the deaths of Mr. Floyd and Ms. Taylor for all true Americans, for our ideals encompassed in the Declaration of Independence, the Constitution, and its amendments and in the *rule of law*?

103. Isn't what we all seek to have the Constitution, the Bill of Rights, and its amendments enforced so that we can live the rights and privileges set forth therein?

104. Why don't you embrace the positivity of life, love, liberty that every day is a gift; that we are all brothers and sisters, children of God; and that the liberties in our constituent documents are for all Americans?

105. Why aren't you watching the Sunday-service sermons of African American ministers Dr. Boise Kimber at First Calvary Baptist Church, Reverend Tommie Jackson at Rehoboth Fellowship Church, Dr. Joseph Ford at Faith Tabernacle Missionary Baptist Church, and Reverend James Hinton at Rose of Sharon Church? Why don't you have the time to *listen and learn* from their positive messages for our entire nation that these ministers extoll every week? You will not know exactly what you learn the first, second, or third time, but learn you will. Give life, love, liberty, and our nation a chance!

Appendix A: Center for Disease Control and Prevention, "Leading Causes of Death by Age Group, Black Males -United States, 2015

Ages 1-44 by Age Group – Black Males

Rank	Age 1-4	Age 5-9	Age 10-14	Age 15-19	Age 20-24	Age 25-34	Age
1	Unintentional injuries 29.4%	Unintentional injuries 31.2%	Unintentional injuries 22.1%	Homicide 49.5%	Homicide 49.7%	Homicide 35.5%	Hear disea 21.09
2	Homicide 14.9%	Cancer 10.7%	Homicide 15.3%	Unintentional injuries 23.0%	Unintentional injuries 22.3%	Unintentional injuries 22.3%	Unin injuri 17.59
3	Birth defects 8.4%	Chronic lower respiratory diseases 9.5%	Cancer 9.0%	Suicide 8.8%	Suicide 8.5%	Heart disease 8.3%	Hom 14.29
4	Cancer 4.6% **(tie rank 4)**	Birth defects 7.3%	Chronic lower respiratory diseases 8.5%	Heart disease 3.0%	Heart disease 3.8%	Suicide 6.8%	Canc

5	Heart disease 4.6% (tie rank 4)	Homicide 7.0%	Suicide 8.3%	Cancer 2.7%	Cancer 2.4%	Cancer 3.8%	Suici
6	Perinatal conditions 3.0%	Heart disease 4.6%	Heart disease 4.3% (tie rank 6)	Birth defects 1.3%	HIV disease 1.1%	HIV disease 3.0%	HIV d 3.9%
7	Influenza & pneumonia 2.8%	Septicemia 1.5% (tie rank 7)	Birth defects (tie rank 6) 4.3%	Chronic lower respiratory diseases 1.1%	Chronic lower respiratory diseases 1.1%	Diabetes 1.9%	Diab 3.7%
8	Chronic lower respiratory diseases 2.4%	Anemias 1.5% (tie rank 7)	Stroke 2.0%	Diabetes 0.8%	Anemias 0.7%	Stroke 1.1%	Strok
9	Stroke 1.9%	Stroke 1.5% (tie rank 7)	Diabetes 1.5%	Legal intervention 0.5%	Diabetes 0.7%	Chronic lower respiratory diseases 0.9%	Kidne disea
10	Medical & surgical	Benign neoplasms	Influenza & pneumonia	Anemias 0.4%	Legal intervention	Influenza & pneumonia 1.5%	Hype 1.5%

Cancer 3.8%	Suici

Appendix B: Income and Poverty in the United States: 2019 US Census Bureau, September, 2020, Tables B-2, B-5 and B-6

Table B-2.

Families and People in Poverty by Type of Family: 2018 and 2019

(Populations in thousands. Margins of error in thousands or percentage points as appropriate. Population as of March of the following year. For information on confidentiality protection, sampling error, nonsampling error, and definitions, see <https://www2.census.gov/programs-surveys/cps/techdocs/cpsmar20.pdf>)

Characteristic	2018					2019					Change in poverty (2019 less 2018)*	
		Below poverty					Below poverty					
	Total	Number	Margin of error[1] (±)	Percent	Margin of error[1] (±)	Total	Number	Margin of error[1] (±)	Percent	Margin of error[1] (±)	Number	Percent
FAMILIES												
Primary families[2]	**83,508**	**7,504**	**208**	**9.0**	**0.2**	**83,698**	**6,554**	**226**	**7.8**	**0.3**	***-951**	***-1.2**
Married-couple	61,971	2,938	119	4.7	0.2	62,355	2,507	135	4.0	0.2	-431	-0.7
Female householder, no spouse present	15,052	3,742	153	24.9	0.9	14,838	3,300	148	22.2	0.9	*-442	*-2.6
Male householder, no spouse present	6,485	824	79	12.7	1.1	6,506	746	82	11.5	1.2	-77	-1.2
Unrelated subfamilies[3]	**467**	**156**	**31**	**33.3**	**4.8**	**399**	**111**	**29**	**27.9**	**6.3**	***-44**	**-5.4**
PEOPLE												
Persons in Families												
In primary families[2]	262,010	25,489	699	9.7	0.3	263,696	22,431	697	8.5	0.3	*-3,058	*-1.2
Related children under age 18	72,425	11,491	410	15.9	0.6	71,854	10,165	360	14.1	0.5	*-1,327	*-1.7
Related children under age 6	23,395	4,016	194	17.2	0.8	23,144	3,579	174	15.5	0.8	-437	*-1.7
In married-couple families	196,418	10,518	446	5.4	0.2	198,495	9,036	499	4.6	0.2	*-1,481	*-0.8
Related children under age 18	49,983	3,820	246	7.6	0.5	49,959	3,220	237	6.4	0.5	*-600	*-1.2
Related children under age 6	16,680	1,296	107	7.8	0.6	16,697	1,059	100	6.3	0.6	-237	-1.4
In families with a female householder, no spouse present	46,660	12,491	519	26.8	1.0	46,255	11,262	473	24.3	1.0	*-1,230	*-2.4
Related children under age 18	17,058	6,664	315	39.1	1.5	16,716	6,099	288	36.5	1.5	*-565	*-2.6
Related children under age 6	4,995	2,381	154	47.7	2.4	4,890	2,235	151	45.7	2.3	-146	-2.0
In families with a male householder, no spouse present	18,932	2,480	227	13.1	1.1	18,946	2,133	234	11.3	1.2	*-347	*-1.8

	2018 Number	MOE	2018 Percent	MOE	2019 Number	MOE	2019 Percent	MOE	Change Number	Change Percent
Related children under age 18	5,384	113	18.7	1.9	5,178	116	16.3	2.0	*-161	-2.4
Related children under age 6	1,719	58	19.7	3.1	1,558	60	18.4	3.4	-53	-1.4
In unrelated subfamilies[3]	1,069	73	34.6	5.0	941	65	26.9	6.3	*-116	*-7.7
Children under age 18	539	41	37.5	5.8	476	38	29.9	7.1	*-60	-7.6
Persons Not in Families										
Unrelated individuals	60,768	338	20.2	0.5	60,117	346	18.8	0.5	*-987	*-1.4
Male	29,887	232	17.7	0.7	29,318	236	16.6	0.7	*-443	*-1.2
Female	30,881	219	22.6	0.6	30,799	236	20.9	0.7	*-544	*-1.7

* An asterisk preceding an estimate indicates change is statistically different from zero at the 90 percent confidence level.

[1] A margin of error (MOE) is a measure of an estimate's variability. The larger the MOE in relation to the size of the estimate, the less reliable the estimate. This number, when added to and subtracted from the estimate, forms the 90 percent confidence interval. MOEs shown in this table are based on standard errors calculated using replicate weights.

[2] A primary family is a group of two or more people, one of whom is the householder, related by birth, marriage, or adoption and residing together. All such people (including related subfamily members) are considered as members of one family.

[3] An unrelated subfamily is defined as a married couple with or without children or a single parent with one or more own, never-married, children under the age of 18 living in a household and not related by birth, marriage, or adoption to the householder.

Note: Details may not sum to totals because of rounding.

Source: U.S. Census Bureau, Current Population Survey, 2019 and 2020 Annual Social and Economic Supplements (CPS ASEC).

Table B-5.

Poverty Status of People by Family Relationship, Race, and Hispanic Origin: 1959 to 2019

(Populations in thousands. Population as of March of the following year. For information on confidentiality protection, sampling error, nonsampling error, and definitions, see <https://www2.census.gov/programs-surveys/cps/techdocs/cpsmar20.pdf>)

Race, Hispanic origin, and year	All people			People in families						Unrelated individuals		
				All families			Families with female householder, no spouse present					
	Total	Below poverty		Total	Below poverty		Total	Below poverty		Total	Below poverty	
		Number	Percent		Number	Percent		Number	Percent		Number	Percent
ALL RACES												
2019	324,754	33,984	10.5	263,696	22,431	8.5	46,255	11,262	24.3	60,117	11,300	18.8
2018	323,847	38,146	11.8	262,010	25,489	9.7	46,660	12,491	26.8	60,768	12,287	20.2
2017[1]	322,548	39,564	12.3	261,599	26,720	10.2	47,517	13,525	28.5	59,835	12,465	20.8
2017	322,549	39,698	12.3	260,709	26,766	10.3	47,999	13,378	27.9	60,786	12,593	20.7
2016	319,911	40,616	12.7	259,863	27,762	10.7	48,243	13,914	28.8	58,839	12,336	21.0
2015	318,454	43,123	13.5	258,121	29,893	11.6	48,019	14,719	30.4	58,988	12,671	21.5
2014	315,804	46,657	14.8	256,308	32,615	12.7	48,019	15,905	33.1	57,937	13,374	23.1
2013[2]	313,096	46,269	14.8	256,070	32,786	12.8	49,951	17,170	34.4	55,400	12,707	22.9
2013[3]	312,965	45,318	14.5	254,988	31,530	12.4	47,007	15,606	33.2	56,564	13,181	23.3
2012	310,648	46,496	15.0	252,863	33,198	13.1	47,085	15,957	33.9	56,185	12,558	22.4
2011	308,456	46,247	15.0	252,316	33,126	13.1	48,103	16,451	34.2	54,517	12,416	22.8
2010[4]	306,130	46,343	15.1	250,200	33,120	13.2	46,454	15,911	34.3	54,250	12,449	22.9
2009	303,820	43,569	14.3	249,384	31,197	12.5	45,315	14,746	32.5	53,079	11,678	22.0
2008	301,041	39,829	13.2	248,301	28,564	11.5	44,027	13,812	31.4	51,534	10,710	20.8
2007	298,699	37,276	12.5	245,443	26,509	10.8	43,961	13,478	30.7	51,740	10,189	19.7
2006	296,450	36,460	12.3	245,199	25,915	10.6	43,223	13,199	30.5	49,884	9,977	20.0
2005	293,135	36,950	12.6	242,389	26,068	10.8	42,244	13,153	31.1	49,526	10,425	21.1
2004[5]	290,617	37,040	12.7	240,754	26,544	11.0	42,053	12,832	30.5	48,609	9,926	20.4
2003	287,699	35,861	12.5	238,903	25,684	10.8	41,311	12,413	30.0	47,594	9,713	20.4
2002	285,317	34,570	12.1	236,921	24,534	10.4	40,529	11,657	28.8	47,156	9,618	20.4
2001	281,475	32,907	11.7	233,911	23,215	9.9	39,261	11,223	28.6	46,392	9,226	19.9
2000[6]	278,944	31,581	11.3	231,909	22,347	9.6	38,375	10,926	28.5	45,624	8,653	19.0
1999[7]	276,208	32,791	11.9	230,789	23,830	10.3	38,580	11,764	30.5	43,977	8,400	19.1
1998	271,059	34,476	12.7	227,229	25,370	11.2	39,000	12,907	33.1	42,539	8,478	19.9
1997	268,480	35,574	13.3	225,369	26,217	11.6	38,412	13,494	35.1	41,672	8,687	20.8
1996	266,218	36,529	13.7	223,955	27,376	12.2	38,584	13,796	35.8	40,727	8,452	20.8
1995[8]	263,733	36,425	13.8	222,792	27,501	12.3	38,908	14,205	36.5	39,484	8,247	20.9
1994[9]	261,616	38,059	14.5	221,430	28,985	13.1	37,253	14,380	38.6	38,538	8,287	21.5
1993[10]	259,278	39,265	15.1	219,489	29,927	13.6	37,861	14,636	38.7	38,038	8,388	22.1
1992[11]	256,549	38,014	14.8	217,936	28,961	13.3	36,446	14,205	39.0	36,842	8,075	21.9

Year												
1991[12]	251,192	35,708	14.2	212,723	27,143	12.8	34,795	13,824	39.7	36,845	7,773	21.1
1990	248,644	33,585	13.5	210,967	25,232	12.0	33,795	12,578	37.2	36,056	7,446	20.7
1989	245,992	31,528	12.8	209,515	24,066	11.5	32,525	11,668	35.9	35,185	6,760	19.2
1988[13]	243,530	31,745	13.0	208,056	24,048	11.6	32,164	11,972	37.2	34,340	7,070	20.6
1987[13]	240,982	32,221	13.4	206,877	24,725	12.0	31,893	12,148	38.1	32,992	6,857	20.8
1986	238,554	32,370	13.6	205,459	24,754	12.0	31,152	11,944	38.3	31,679	6,846	21.6
1985[14]	236,594	33,064	14.0	203,963	25,729	12.6	30,878	11,600	37.6	31,351	6,725	21.5
1984[15]	233,816	33,700	14.4	202,288	26,458	13.1	30,844	11,831	38.4	30,268	6,609	21.8
1983	231,700	35,303	15.2	201,338	27,933	13.9	30,049	12,072	40.2	29,158	6,740	23.1
1982	229,412	34,398	15.0	200,385	27,349	13.6	28,834	11,701	40.6	27,908	6,458	23.1
1981[16]	227,157	31,822	14.0	198,541	24,850	12.5	28,587	11,051	38.7	27,714	6,490	23.4
1980	225,027	29,272	13.0	196,963	22,601	11.5	27,565	10,120	36.7	27,133	6,227	22.9
1979[17]	222,903	26,072	11.7	195,860	19,964	10.2	26,927	9,400	34.9	26,170	5,743	21.9
1978	215,656	24,497	11.4	191,071	19,062	10.0	26,032	9,269	35.6	24,585	5,435	22.1
1977	213,867	24,720	11.6	190,757	19,505	10.2	25,404	9,205	36.2	23,110	5,216	22.6
1976	212,303	24,975	11.8	190,844	19,632	10.3	24,204	9,029	37.3	21,459	5,344	24.9
1975	210,864	25,877	12.3	190,630	20,789	10.9	23,580	8,846	37.5	20,234	5,088	25.1
1974[18]	209,362	23,370	11.2	190,436	18,817	9.9	23,165	8,462	36.5	18,926	4,553	24.1
1973	207,621	22,973	11.1	189,361	18,299	9.7	21,823	8,178	37.5	18,260	4,674	25.6
1972[19]	206,004	24,460	11.9	189,193	19,577	10.3	21,264	8,114	38.2	16,811	4,883	29.0
1971[20]	204,554	25,559	12.5	188,242	20,405	10.8	20,153	7,797	38.2	16,311	5,154	31.6
1970	202,183	25,420	12.6	186,692	20,330	10.9	19,673	7,503	38.1	15,491	5,090	32.9
1969	199,517	24,147	12.1	184,891	19,175	10.4	17,995	6,879	38.2	14,626	4,972	34.0
1968	197,628	25,389	12.8	183,825	20,695	11.3	18,048	6,990	38.7	13,803	4,694	34.0
1967[21]	195,672	27,769	14.7	182,558	22,771	12.5	17,788	6,898	38.8	13,114	4,998	38.1
1966	193,388	28,510	14.7	181,117	23,809	13.1	17,240	6,861	39.8	12,271	4,701	38.3
1965	191,413	33,185	17.3	179,281	28,358	15.8	16,371	7,524	44.0	12,132	4,827	39.8
1964	189,710	36,055	19.0	177,653	30,912	17.4	N	7,297	44.4	12,057	5,143	42.7
1963	187,258	36,436	19.5	176,076	31,498	17.9	N	7,646	47.7	11,182	4,938	44.2
1962	184,276	38,625	21.0	173,263	33,623	19.4	N	7,781	50.3	11,013	5,002	45.4
1961	181,277	39,628	21.9	170,131	34,509	20.3	N	7,252	48.1	11,146	5,119	45.9
1960	179,503	39,851	22.2	168,615	34,925	20.7	N	7,247	48.9	10,888	4,926	45.2
1959	176,557	39,490	22.4	165,858	34,562	20.8	N	7,014	49.4	10,699	4,928	46.1
WHITE ALONE[22]												
2019	248,086	22,512	9.1	200,954	14,295	7.1	27,848	6,007	21.6	46,332	7,998	17.3
2018	247,634	24,945	10.1	200,479	16,240	8.1	28,375	6,972	24.6	46,338	8,429	18.2
2017[3]	247,255	26,026	10.5	200,267	17,022	8.5	28,671	7,399	25.8	46,147	8,731	18.9
2017	247,272	26,436	10.7	199,462	17,386	8.7	29,019	7,473	25.8	47,005	8,779	18.7
2016	245,985	27,113	11.0	199,330	18,022	9.0	29,420	7,793	26.5	45,643	8,661	19.0
2015	245,536	28,566	11.6	198,571	19,444	9.8	29,396	8,205	27.9	45,963	8,717	19.0
2014	244,253	31,089	12.7	197,607	21,072	10.7	29,134	8,680	29.8	45,409	9,476	20.9
2013[2]	243,346	31,287	12.9	198,041	21,486	10.8	30,428	9,796	32.2	43,924	9,132	20.8

See footnotes at end of table.

Table B-5.

Poverty Status of People by Family Relationship, Race, and Hispanic Origin: 1959 to 2019—Con.

(Populations in thousands. Population as of March of the following year. For information on confidentiality protection, sampling error, nonsampling error, and definitions, see <https://www2.census.gov/programs-surveys/cps/techdocs/cpsmar20.pdf>)

Race, Hispanic origin, and year	All people			People in families						Unrelated individuals		
		Below poverty		All families			Families with female householder, no spouse present				Below poverty	
	Total	Number	Percent	Total	Below poverty		Total	Below poverty		Total	Number	Percent
					Number	Percent		Number	Percent			
2013[3]	243,085	29,936	12.3	197,001	19,944	10.1	28,795	8,404	29.2	44,998	9,544	21.2
2012	242,147	30,816	12.7	196,378	21,328	10.9	28,707	8,691	30.3	44,509	8,940	20.1
2011	241,334	30,849	12.8	196,709	21,456	10.9	29,636	8,999	30.4	43,295	8,809	20.3
2010[4]	239,982	31,083	13.0	195,441	21,543	11.0	28,032	8,721	31.1	43,324	8,971	20.7
2009	242,047	29,830	12.3	197,938	20,701	10.5	28,163	8,283	29.4	43,010	8,580	19.9
2008	240,548	26,990	11.2	197,763	18,558	9.4	27,010	7,340	27.2	41,810	7,982	19.1
2007	239,133	25,120	10.5	195,944	17,141	8.7	27,159	7,188	26.5	41,931	7,505	17.9
2006	237,619	24,416	10.3	196,061	16,644	8.5	27,057	7,160	26.5	40,461	7,334	18.1
2005	235,430	24,872	10.6	194,277	16,782	8.6	25,943	7,021	27.1	40,164	7,718	19.2
2004[5]	233,741	25,327	10.8	193,024	17,445	9.0	26,139	6,892	26.4	39,712	7,416	18.7
2003	231,866	24,272	10.5	192,074	16,740	8.7	25,536	6,530	25.6	38,913	7,225	18.6
2002	230,376	23,466	10.2	190,823	16,043	8.4	24,903	5,992	24.1	38,575	7,105	18.4
WHITE[23]												
2001	229,675	22,739	9.9	190,413	15,369	8.1	24,619	5,972	24.3	38,294	6,996	18.3
2000[6]	227,846	21,645	9.5	188,966	14,692	7.8	24,166	5,609	23.2	37,699	6,454	17.1
1999[7]	225,361	22,169	9.8	187,833	15,353	8.2	23,913	5,947	24.9	36,441	6,411	17.6
1998	222,837	23,454	10.5	186,184	16,549	8.9	24,211	6,674	27.6	35,563	6,386	18.0
1997	221,200	24,396	11.0	185,147	17,258	9.3	23,773	7,296	30.7	34,858	6,593	18.9
1996	219,656	24,650	11.2	184,119	17,621	9.6	23,744	7,073	29.8	34,247	6,463	18.9
1995[8]	218,028	24,423	11.2	183,450	17,593	9.6	23,732	7,047	29.7	33,399	6,336	19.0
1994[9]	216,460	25,379	11.7	182,546	18,474	10.1	22,713	7,228	31.8	32,569	6,292	19.3
1993[10]	214,899	26,226	12.2	181,330	18,968	10.5	23,224	7,199	31.0	32,112	6,443	20.1
1992[11]	213,060	25,259	11.9	180,409	18,294	10.1	22,453	6,907	30.8	31,170	6,147	19.7
1991[12]	210,133	23,747	11.3	177,619	17,268	9.7	21,608	6,806	31.5	31,207	5,872	18.8
1990	208,611	22,326	10.7	176,504	15,916	9.0	20,845	6,210	29.8	30,833	5,739	18.6
1989	206,853	20,785	10.0	175,857	15,179	8.6	20,362	5,723	28.1	29,993	5,063	16.9
1988[13]	205,235	20,715	10.1	175,111	15,001	8.6	20,396	5,950	29.2	29,315	5,314	18.1
1987[13]	203,605	21,195	10.4	174,488	15,593	8.9	20,244	5,989	29.6	28,290	5,174	18.3
1986	202,282	22,183	11.0	174,024	16,393	9.4	20,163	6,171	30.6	27,143	5,198	19.2

Year												
1985[14]	200,918	22,860	11.4	172,863	17,125	9.9	20,105	5,990	29.8	27,067	5,299	19.6
1985[15]	198,941	22,955	11.5	171,839	17,299	10.1	19,727	5,866	29.7	26,094	5,181	19.9
1983	197,496	23,984	12.1	171,407	18,377	10.7	19,256	6,017	31.2	25,206	5,189	20.6
1982	195,919	23,517	12.0	170,748	18,015	10.6	18,374	5,686	30.9	24,300	5,041	20.7
1981[16]	194,504	21,553	11.1	169,868	16,127	9.5	18,795	5,600	29.8	23,913	5,061	21.2
1980	192,912	19,699	10.2	168,756	14,587	8.6	17,642	4,940	28.0	23,370	4,760	20.4
1979[17]	191,742	17,214	9.0	168,461	12,495	7.4	17,349	4,375	25.2	22,587	4,452	19.7
1978	186,450	16,259	8.7	165,193	12,050	7.3	16,877	4,371	25.9	21,257	4,209	19.8
1977	185,254	16,416	8.9	165,385	12,364	7.5	16,721	4,474	26.8	19,869	4,051	20.4
1976	184,165	16,713	9.1	165,571	12,500	7.5	15,941	4,463	28.0	18,594	4,213	22.7
1975	183,164	17,770	9.7	165,661	13,799	8.3	15,577	4,577	29.4	17,503	3,972	22.7
1974[18]	182,376	15,736	8.6	166,081	12,181	7.3	15,433	4,278	27.7	16,295	3,555	21.8
1973	181,185	15,142	8.4	165,424	11,412	6.9	14,303	4,003	28.0	15,761	3,730	23.7
1972[19]	180,125	16,203	9.0	165,630	12,268	7.4	13,739	3,770	27.4	14,495	3,935	27.1
1971[20]	179,398	17,780	9.9	165,184	13,566	8.2	13,502	4,099	30.4	14,214	4,214	29.6
1970	177,376	17,484	9.9	163,875	13,323	8.1	13,226	3,761	28.4	13,500	4,161	30.8
1969	175,349	16,659	9.5	162,779	12,623	7.8	12,285	3,577	29.1	12,570	4,036	32.1
1968	173,732	17,395	10.0	161,777	13,546	8.4	12,190	3,551	29.1	11,955	3,849	32.2
1967[21]	172,038	18,983	11.0	160,720	14,851	9.2	12,131	3,453	28.5	11,318	4,132	36.5
1966	170,247	19,290	11.3	159,561	15,430	9.7	11,573	3,646	29.7	10,686	3,860	36.1
1965	168,732	22,496	13.3	158,255	18,508	11.7	N	4,092	33.4	10,477	3,988	38.1
1964	167,313	24,957	14.9	156,898	20,716	13.2	N	3,911	35.4	10,415	4,241	40.7
1963	165,309	25,238	15.3	155,584	21,149	13.6	N	4,051	35.6	9,725	4,089	42.0
1962	162,842	26,672	16.4	153,348	22,613	14.7	N	4,089	37.9	9,494	4,059	42.7
1961	160,306	27,890	17.4	150,717	23,747	15.8	N	4,062	37.6	9,589	4,143	43.2
1960	158,863	28,309	17.8	149,458	24,262	16.2	N	4,296	39.0	9,405	4,047	43.0
1959	156,956	28,484	18.1	147,802	24,443	16.5	N	4,232	40.2	9,154	4,041	44.1
WHITE ALONE, NOT HISPANIC[22]												
2019	194,643	14,152	7.3	154,328	7,608	4.9	17,528	3,064	17.5	39,747	6,406	16.1
2018	194,815	15,725	8.1	154,545	8,883	5.7	18,179	3,740	20.6	39,694	6,664	16.8
2017[1]	195,218	16,619	8.5	154,636	9,343	6.0	18,334	3,800	20.7	40,012	7,090	17.7
2017	195,256	16,993	8.7	153,956	9,732	6.3	18,597	3,893	20.9	40,760	7,096	17.4
2016	195,221	17,263	8.8	154,627	9,853	6.4	19,390	4,252	21.9	39,875	7,108	17.8
2015	195,450	17,786	9.1	154,713	10,373	6.7	19,339	4,404	22.8	40,043	7,122	17.8
2014	195,208	19,652	10.1	154,734	11,566	7.5	19,015	4,630	24.4	39,603	7,779	19.6
2013[2]	195,118	19,552	10.0	155,965	11,688	7.5	19,141	5,123	26.8	38,256	7,492	19.6
2013[3]	195,167	18,796	9.6	155,119	10,710	6.9	18,889	4,325	22.9	39,245	7,758	19.8
2012	195,112	18,940	9.7	155,395	11,387	7.3	19,180	4,655	24.3	38,822	7,202	18.6
2011	194,960	19,171	9.8	155,982	11,562	7.4	19,909	4,746	23.8	38,003	7,222	19.0
2010[4]	194,783	19,251	9.9	155,723	11,509	7.4	18,914	4,689	24.8	38,211	7,351	19.2

See footnotes at end of table.

Table B-5.

Poverty Status of People by Family Relationship, Race, and Hispanic Origin: 1959 to 2019—Con.

(Populations in thousands. Population as of March of the following year. For information on confidentiality protection, sampling error, nonsampling error, and definitions, see <https://www2.census.gov/programs-surveys/cps/techdocs/cpsmar20.pdf>)

Race, Hispanic origin, and year	All people			People in families						Unrelated individuals		
	Total	Below poverty		All families			Families with female householder, no spouse present			Total	Below poverty	
		Number	Percent	Total	Below poverty		Total	Below poverty			Number	Percent
					Number	Percent		Number	Percent			
2009	197,164	18,530	9.4	158,646	11,211	7.1	19,033	4,532	23.8	37,757	6,946	18.4
2008	196,940	17,024	8.6	159,344	10,138	6.4	18,799	4,046	21.5	36,848	6,539	17.7
2007	196,583	16,032	8.2	158,703	9,553	6.0	19,179	4,099	21.4	36,909	6,155	16.7
2006	196,049	16,013	8.2	159,572	9,676	6.1	19,349	4,353	22.5	35,642	6,021	16.9
2005	195,553	16,227	8.3	159,204	9,604	6.0	18,899	4,278	22.6	35,626	6,393	17.9
2004[5]	195,098	16,908	8.7	159,221	10,323	6.5	19,009	4,116	21.7	35,141	6,237	17.7
2003	194,595	15,902	8.2	159,215	9,658	6.1	18,792	3,959	21.1	34,683	6,015	17.3
2002	194,144	15,567	8.0	158,764	9,389	5.9	18,664	3,733	20.0	34,614	5,947	17.2
WHITE, NOT HISPANIC[23]												
2001	194,538	15,271	7.8	159,178	9,122	5.7	18,365	3,661	19.9	34,603	5,882	17.0
2000[6]	193,691	14,366	7.4	158,838	8,664	5.5	18,196	3,412	18.8	33,943	5,356	15.8
1999[7]	192,565	14,735	7.7	158,550	9,013	5.7	17,892	3,545	19.8	33,189	5,412	16.3
1998	192,754	15,799	8.2	159,301	10,061	6.3	18,547	4,074	22.0	32,573	5,352	16.4
1997	191,859	16,491	8.6	158,796	10,401	6.5	18,474	4,604	24.9	32,049	5,632	17.6
1996	191,459	16,462	8.6	159,044	10,553	6.6	18,597	4,339	23.3	31,410	5,455	17.4
1995[8]	190,951	16,267	8.5	159,402	10,599	6.6	18,340	4,183	22.8	30,586	5,303	17.3
1994[9]	192,543	18,110	9.4	161,254	12,118	7.5	18,186	4,743	26.1	30,157	5,500	18.2
1993[10]	190,843	18,882	9.9	160,062	12,756	8.0	18,508	4,724	25.5	29,681	5,570	18.8
1992[11]	189,001	18,202	9.6	159,102	12,277	7.7	18,016	4,640	25.8	28,775	5,350	18.6
1991[12]	189,116	17,741	9.4	158,850	11,998	7.6	17,609	4,710	26.7	29,215	5,261	18.0
1990	188,129	16,622	8.8	158,394	11,086	7.0	17,160	4,284	25.0	28,688	5,002	17.4
1989	186,979	15,599	8.3	158,127	10,723	6.8	16,827	3,922	23.3	28,055	4,466	15.9
1988[13]	185,961	15,565	8.4	157,687	10,467	6.6	16,828	3,988	23.7	27,552	4,746	17.2
1987[13]	184,936	16,029	8.7	157,785	11,051	7.0	16,787	4,075	24.3	26,439	4,613	17.4
1986	184,119	17,244	9.4	157,665	12,078	7.7	16,739	4,350	26.0	25,525	4,668	18.3
1985[14]	183,455	17,839	9.7	157,106	12,706	8.1	16,742	4,136	24.7	25,544	4,789	18.7
1984[15]	182,469	18,300	10.0	156,930	13,234	8.4	16,742	4,193	25.0	24,671	4,659	18.9
1983	181,393	19,538	10.8	156,719	14,437	9.2	16,369	4,448	27.2	23,894	4,746	19.9
1982	181,903	19,362	10.6	157,818	14,271	9.0	15,830	4,161	26.3	23,329	4,701	20.2
1981[16]	180,909	17,987	9.9	157,330	12,903	8.2	16,323	4,222	25.9	22,950	4,769	20.8

Year												
1980	179,798	16,365	9.1	156,633	11,568	7.4	15,358	3,699	24.1	22,455	4,474	19.9
1979[37]	178,814	14,419	8.1	156,567	10,009	6.4	15,410	3,371	21.9	21,638	4,179	19.3
1978	174,731	13,755	7.9	154,321	9,798	6.3	15,132	3,390	22.4	20,410	3,957	19.4
1977	173,563	13,802	8.0	154,449	9,977	6.5	14,888	3,429	23.0	19,114	3,825	20.0
1976	173,235	14,025	8.1	155,324	10,066	6.5	14,261	3,516	24.7	17,912	3,959	22.1
1975	172,417	14,883	8.6	155,539	11,137	7.2	13,809	3,570	25.9	16,879	3,746	22.2
1974[18]	171,463	13,217	7.7	155,764	9,854	6.3	13,763	3,379	24.6	15,699	3,364	21.4
1973	170,488	12,864	7.5	155,330	9,262	6.0	12,731	3,185	25.0	15,158	3,602	23.8

BLACK ALONE OR IN COMBINATION

Year												
2019	47,260	8,836	18.7	37,689	6,374	16.9	15,323	4,571	29.8	9,492	2,433	25.6
2018	46,825	9,695	20.7	36,729	6,910	18.8	14,820	4,692	31.7	9,942	2,726	27.4
2017[1]	46,337	10,050	21.7	36,675	7,290	19.9	15,201	5,258	34.6	9,480	2,688	28.4
2017	46,391	9,820	21.2	36,702	7,013	19.1	15,297	5,089	33.3	9,535	2,758	28.9
2016	45,683	9,965	21.8	36,028	7,353	20.2	15,315	5,231	34.2	9,105	2,563	28.2
2015	45,227	10,797	23.9	36,463	7,965	22.1	15,809	5,642	35.7	8,999	2,744	30.5
2014	44,566	11,581	26.0	35,545	8,711	24.5	15,304	6,179	40.4	8,836	2,793	31.6
2013[2]	44,154	11,162	25.3	35,958	8,533	23.7	16,188	6,277	38.8	8,045	2,588	32.2
2013[3]	44,112	11,959	27.1	35,657	9,174	25.7	16,906	6,319	42.4	8,199	2,657	32.4
2012	43,583	11,809	27.1	35,205	9,016	25.6	15,113	6,220	41.2	8,179	2,663	32.6
2011	42,648	11,730	27.5	34,495	9,012	26.1	15,282	6,500	42.5	7,986	2,635	33.0
2010[4]	42,385	11,597	27.4	34,347	8,891	25.9	15,362	6,269	40.8	7,730	2,587	33.5
2009	40,876	10,575	25.9	33,330	8,184	24.6	14,463	5,755	39.8	7,368	2,285	31.0
2008	40,097	9,882	24.6	32,818	7,768	23.7	14,332	5,782	40.3	7,123	2,042	28.7
2007	39,564	9,668	24.4	32,427	7,668	23.6	14,396	5,702	39.6	7,036	1,968	28.0
2006	39,013	9,447	24.2	32,130	7,411	23.1	13,848	5,422	39.2	6,715	1,935	28.8
2005[5]	38,551	9,517	24.7	31,663	7,459	23.6	14,080	5,524	39.2	6,754	2,003	29.7
2004[5]	38,037	9,411	24.7	31,468	7,495	23.8	13,830	5,484	39.7	6,418	1,840	28.7
2003	37,503	9,108	24.3	31,059	7,162	23.1	13,664	5,312	38.9	6,194	1,814	29.3
2002	37,207	8,884	23.9	31,008	6,985	22.5	13,551	5,145	38.0	6,034	1,851	30.7

BLACK ALONE[24]

Year												
2019	42,965	8,073	18.8	34,033	5,777	17.0	13,939	4,118	29.5	8,863	2,271	25.6
2018	42,773	8,884	20.8	33,237	6,242	18.8	13,500	4,277	31.7	9,388	2,584	27.5
2017[1]	42,477	9,224	21.7	33,261	6,594	19.8	13,986	4,811	34.4	9,064	2,573	28.4
2017	42,474	8,993	21.2	33,250	6,315	19.0	14,066	4,628	32.9	9,101	2,644	29.1
2016	41,962	9,234	22.0	33,199	6,709	20.2	13,964	4,777	34.2	8,679	2,484	28.6
2015	41,625	10,020	24.1	32,890	7,305	22.2	14,549	5,198	35.7	8,549	2,635	30.8
2014	41,112	10,755	26.2	32,546	8,013	24.6	14,091	5,670	40.2	8,419	2,685	31.9
2013[2]	40,498	10,186	25.2	32,658	7,665	23.5	14,838	5,759	38.8	7,717	2,483	32.2
2013[3]	40,615	11,041	27.2	32,564	8,390	25.8	13,816	5,871	42.5	7,842	2,536	32.3
2012	40,125	10,911	27.2	32,122	8,251	25.7	13,931	5,735	41.2	7,841	2,549	32.5
2011	39,609	10,929	27.6	31,800	8,334	26.2	14,145	5,980	42.3	7,659	2,524	33.0
2010[4]	39,283	10,746	27.4	31,596	8,181	25.9	14,236	5,831	41.0	7,419	2,479	33.4

See footnotes at end of table.

Table B-5.

Poverty Status of People by Family Relationship, Race, and Hispanic Origin: 1959 to 2019—Con.

(Populations in thousands. Population as of March of the following year. For information on confidentiality protection, sampling error, nonsampling error, and definitions, see <https://www2.census.gov/programs-surveys/cps/techdocs/cpsmar20.pdf>)

Race, Hispanic origin, and year	All people			People in families								Unrelated individuals		
				All families			Families with female householder, no spouse present							
	Total	Below poverty		Total	Below poverty		Total	Below poverty				Total	Below poverty	
		Number	Percent		Number	Percent		Number	Percent					Number	Percent
2009	38,556	9,944	25.8	31,306	7,642	24.4	13,680	5,427	39.7			7,102	2,209	31.1
2008	37,966	9,379	24.7	30,986	7,339	23.7	13,648	5,533	40.5			6,835	1,970	28.8
2007	37,665	9,237	24.5	30,778	7,312	23.8	13,741	5,459	39.7			6,807	1,898	27.9
2006	37,306	9,048	24.3	30,621	7,072	23.1	13,244	5,180	39.1			6,545	1,897	29.0
2005	36,802	9,168	24.9	30,154	7,164	23.8	13,481	5,303	39.3			6,521	1,949	29.9
2004[5]	36,426	9,014	24.7	30,065	7,153	23.8	13,244	5,247	39.6			6,217	1,792	28.8
2003	35,989	8,781	24.4	29,727	6,870	23.1	13,118	5,115	39.0			6,034	1,781	29.5
2002	35,678	8,602	24.1	29,671	6,761	22.8	13,030	4,980	38.2			5,858	1,800	30.7
BLACK[23]														
2001	35,871	8,136	22.7	29,869	6,389	21.4	12,550	4,694	37.4			5,873	1,692	28.8
2000[6]	35,425	7,982	22.5	29,378	6,221	21.2	12,383	4,774	38.6			5,885	1,702	28.9
1999[7]	35,756	8,441	23.6	29,819	6,758	22.7	12,823	5,232	40.8			5,668	1,562	27.5
1998	34,877	9,091	26.1	29,333	7,259	24.7	13,156	5,629	42.8			5,390	1,752	32.5
1997	34,458	9,116	26.5	28,962	7,386	25.5	13,218	5,654	42.8			5,316	1,645	31.0
1996	34,110	9,694	28.4	28,933	7,993	27.6	13,193	6,123	46.4			4,989	1,606	32.2
1995[8]	33,740	9,872	29.3	28,777	8,189	28.5	13,604	6,553	48.2			4,756	1,551	32.6
1994[9]	33,353	10,196	30.6	28,499	8,447	29.6	12,926	6,489	50.2			4,649	1,617	34.8
1993[10]	32,910	10,877	33.1	28,106	9,242	32.9	13,132	6,955	53.0			4,608	1,541	33.4
1992[11]	32,411	10,827	33.4	27,790	9,134	32.9	12,591	6,799	54.0			4,410	1,569	35.6
1991[12]	31,313	10,242	32.7	26,565	8,504	32.0	11,960	6,557	54.8			4,505	1,590	35.3
1990	30,806	9,837	31.9	26,296	8,160	31.0	11,866	6,005	50.6			4,244	1,491	35.1
1989	30,332	9,302	30.7	25,931	7,704	29.7	11,190	5,530	49.4			4,180	1,471	35.2
1988[13]	29,849	9,356	31.3	25,484	7,650	30.0	10,794	5,601	51.9			4,095	1,509	36.8
1987[13]	29,362	9,520	32.4	25,128	7,848	31.2	10,701	5,789	54.1			3,977	1,471	37.0
1986	28,871	8,983	31.1	24,910	7,410	29.7	10,175	5,473	53.8			3,714	1,431	38.5
1985[14]	28,485	8,926	31.3	24,620	7,504	30.5	10,041	5,342	53.2			3,641	1,264	34.7
1984[15]	28,087	9,490	33.8	24,387	8,104	33.2	10,384	5,666	54.6			3,501	1,255	35.8
1983	27,678	9,882	35.7	24,138	8,376	34.7	10,059	5,736	57.0			3,287	1,338	40.7
1982	27,216	9,697	35.6	23,948	8,355	34.9	9,699	5,698	58.8			3,051	1,229	40.3
1981[16]	26,834	9,173	34.2	23,423	7,780	33.2	9,214	5,222	56.7			3,277	1,296	39.6
1980	26,408	8,579	32.5	23,084	7,190	31.1	9,338	4,984	53.4			3,208	1,314	41.0

1979[17]	25,944	8,050	31.0	22,666	6,800	30.0	9,065	4,816	53.1	3,127	1,168	37.3
1978	24,956	7,625	30.6	22,027	6,493	29.5	8,689	4,712	54.2	2,929	1,132	38.6
1977	24,710	7,726	31.3	21,850	6,667	30.5	8,315	4,595	55.3	2,860	1,059	38.0
1976	24,399	7,595	31.1	21,840	6,576	30.1	7,926	4,415	55.7	2,559	1,019	39.8
1975	24,089	7,545	31.3	21,687	6,533	30.1	7,679	4,168	54.3	2,402	1,011	42.1
1974[18]	23,699	7,182	30.3	21,341	6,255	29.3	7,483	4,116	55.0	2,359	927	39.3
1973	23,512	7,388	31.4	21,328	6,560	30.8	7,188	4,064	56.5	2,183	828	37.9
1972[19]	23,144	7,710	33.3	21,116	6,841	32.4	7,125	4,139	58.1	2,028	870	42.9
1971[20]	22,784	7,396	32.5	20,900	6,530	31.2	6,398	3,587	56.1	1,884	866	46.0
1970	22,515	7,548	33.5	20,724	6,683	32.2	6,225	3,656	58.7	1,791	865	48.3
1969	22,011	7,095	32.2	20,192	6,245	30.9	5,537	3,225	58.2	1,819	850	46.7
1968	21,944	7,616	34.7	N	6,839	33.7	N	3,312	58.9	N	777	46.3
1967[21]	21,590	8,486	39.3	N	7,677	38.4	N	3,362	61.6	N	809	49.3
1966	21,206	8,867	41.8	N	8,090	40.9	N	3,160	65.3	N	777	54.4
1959	18,013	9,927	55.1	N	9,112	54.9	N	2,416	70.6	1,430	815	57.0

ASIAN ALONE OR IN COMBINATION

2019	22,440	1,588	7.1	19,366	1,026	5.3	1,822	291	16.0	3,026	562	18.6
2018	22,046	2,166	9.8	18,745	1,360	7.3	1,943	380	19.5	3,231	783	24.2
2017[1]	21,556	2,063	9.6	18,562	1,350	7.3	2,041	354	17.3	2,943	694	23.6
2017	21,511	2,104	9.8	18,484	1,379	7.5	2,086	338	16.2	2,963	720	24.3
2016	20,756	2,062	9.9	17,856	1,287	7.2	1,931	365	18.9	2,858	761	26.6
2015	20,037	2,234	11.1	17,183	1,361	7.9	1,675	254	15.2	2,762	839	30.4
2014	19,685	2,268	11.5	16,964	1,479	8.7	1,994	355	17.8	2,621	754	28.8
2013[2]	19,182	2,398	12.5	16,800	1,680	10.0	1,873	525	28.1	2,339	700	29.9
2013[3]	19,023	1,974	10.4	16,642	1,305	7.8	1,923	323	16.8	2,333	660	28.3
2012	18,173	2,072	11.4	15,751	1,467	9.3	1,756	374	21.3	2,334	580	24.8
2011	17,813	2,189	12.3	15,591	1,550	9.9	1,847	411	22.2	2,133	614	28.8
2010[4]	17,237	2,064	12.0	14,950	1,463	9.8	1,804	386	21.4	2,208	578	26.2
2009	15,272	1,901	12.4	13,403	1,361	10.2	1,539	290	18.9	1,826	527	28.8
2008	14,543	1,686	11.6	12,817	1,270	9.9	1,471	228	15.5	1,707	410	24.0
2007	14,430	1,467	10.2	12,527	1,012	8.1	1,421	250	17.6	1,837	426	23.2
2006	14,331	1,447	10.1	12,463	984	7.9	1,210	220	18.1	1,801	449	24.9
2005	13,731	1,501	10.9	11,931	1,039	8.7	1,223	220	18.0	1,771	457	25.8
2004[5]	13,291	1,295	9.7	11,661	876	7.5	1,190	170	14.3	1,599	417	26.1
2003	12,891	1,527	11.8	11,266	1,116	9.9	1,184	294	24.8	1,590	402	25.3
2002	12,487	1,243	10.0	10,742	816	7.6	1,146	175	15.3	1,708	417	24.4

ASIAN ALONE[25]

2019	19,926	1,464	7.3	17,134	946	5.5	1,576	254	16.1	2,752	518	18.8
2018	19,768	1,996	10.1	16,765	1,243	7.4	1,686	327	19.4	2,946	732	24.8

U.S. Census Bureau

Table B-5.
Poverty Status of People by Family Relationship, Race, and Hispanic Origin: 1959 to 2019—Con.

(Populations in thousands. Population as of March of the following year. For information on confidentiality protection, sampling error, nonsampling error, and definitions, see <https://www2.census.gov/programs-surveys/cps/techdocs/cpsmar20.pdf>)

Race, Hispanic origin, and year	All people			People in families						Unrelated individuals		
				All families			Families with female householder, no spouse present					
	Total	Below poverty		Total	Below poverty		Total	Below poverty		Total	Below poverty	
		Number	Percent		Number	Percent		Number	Percent		Number	Percent
2016	18,879	1,908	10.1	16,220	1,179	7.3	1,657	326	19.7	2,627	715	27.2
2015	18,241	2,078	11.4	15,597	1,260	8.1	1,455	222	15.5	2,556	784	30.7
2014	17,790	2,137	12.0	15,261	1,391	9.1	1,725	315	18.2	2,431	713	29.3
2013³	17,257	2,255	13.1	15,057	1,589	10.6	1,574	442	28.1	2,180	661	30.3
2013³	17,063	1,785	10.5	14,895	1,154	7.7	1,657	228	13.7	2,128	623	29.3
2012	16,417	1,921	11.7	14,190	1,357	9.6	1,515	309	20.4	2,156	547	25.4
2011	16,086	1,973	12.3	14,100	1,389	9.9	1,570	327	20.8	1,921	571	29.7
2010⁴	15,611	1,899	12.2	13,515	1,341	9.9	1,471	327	22.2	2,040	547	26.8
2009	14,005	1,746	12.5	12,296	1,244	10.1	1,353	250	18.5	1,673	491	29.3
2008	13,310	1,576	11.8	11,719	1,192	10.2	1,308	209	16.0	1,574	378	24.0
2007	13,257	1,349	10.2	11,471	930	8.1	1,256	217	17.3	1,720	391	22.7
2006	13,177	1,353	10.3	11,428	912	8.0	1,057	187	17.8	1,683	428	25.4
2005	12,580	1,402	11.1	10,911	970	8.9	1,059	189	17.8	1,645	427	26.0
2004⁵	12,231	1,201	9.8	10,734	812	7.6	1,024	135	13.2	1,472	388	26.3
2003	11,856	1,401	11.8	10,333	1,017	9.8	1,028	242	23.6	1,494	375	25.1
2002	11,541	1,161	10.1	9,899	763	7.7	1,019	155	15.2	1,613	390	24.2
ASIAN AND PACIFIC ISLANDER²³												
2001	12,465	1,275	10.2	10,745	873	8.1	1,333	198	14.8	1,682	393	23.4
2000⁶	12,672	1,258	9.9	11,044	895	8.1	1,231	289	23.4	1,588	350	22.0
1999⁷	11,955	1,285	10.7	10,507	1,010	9.6	1,201	275	22.9	1,415	270	19.1
1998	10,873	1,360	12.5	9,576	1,087	11.4	1,123	373	33.2	1,266	257	20.3
1997	10,482	1,468	14.0	9,312	1,116	12.0	932	313	33.6	1,134	327	28.9
1996	10,054	1,454	14.5	8,900	1,172	13.2	1,018	300	29.5	1,120	255	22.8
1995⁸	9,644	1,411	14.6	8,582	1,112	13.0	919	266	28.9	1,013	260	25.6
1994⁹	6,654	974	14.6	5,915	776	13.1	582	137	23.6	696	179	25.7
1993¹⁰	7,454	1,134	15.3	6,609	898	13.6	725	126	17.4	791	228	28.8
1992¹¹	7,779	985	12.7	6,922	787	11.4	729	183	25.0	828	193	23.3
1991¹²	7,192	996	13.8	6,367	773	12.1	721	177	24.6	785	209	26.6
1990	7,014	858	12.2	6,300	712	11.3	638	132	20.7	668	124	18.5

Year	Total	Below poverty — Number	Below poverty — Percent	Total	Below poverty — Number	Below poverty — Percent	Total	Below poverty — Number	Below poverty — Percent	Total	Below poverty — Number	Below poverty — Percent
1989	6,673	939	14.1	5,917	779	13.2	614	212	34.6	712	144	20.2
1988[3]	6,447	1,117	17.3	5,767	942	16.3	650	263	40.5	651	160	24.5
1987[7,3]	6,322	1,021	16.1	5,785	875	15.1	584	187	32.0	516	138	26.8
HISPANIC (ANY RACE)[26]												
2019	60,602	9,544	15.7	52,743	7,587	14.4	12,248	3,512	28.7	7,627	1,878	24.6
2018	59,957	10,526	17.6	52,041	8,368	16.1	11,939	3,716	31.1	7,645	2,047	26.8
2017[7]	59,051	10,816	18.3	51,651	8,760	17.0	12,155	4,274	35.2	7,063	1,946	27.6
2017	59,053	10,790	18.3	51,517	8,708	16.9	12,244	4,198	34.3	7,206	1,954	27.1
2016	57,556	11,137	19.4	50,525	9,200	18.2	11,926	4,136	34.7	6,697	1,793	26.8
2015	56,780	12,133	21.4	49,524	10,109	20.4	11,878	4,401	37.1	6,884	1,876	27.2
2014[3]	55,504	13,104	23.6	48,296	10,853	22.5	11,919	4,817	40.4	6,776	1,981	29.2
2013[3]	54,181	13,356	24.7	47,266	11,128	23.5	13,060	5,406	41.4	6,414	1,915	29.9
2013	54,145	12,744	23.5	47,254	10,536	22.3	11,679	4,860	41.6	6,545	2,063	31.5
2012	53,105	13,616	25.6	46,183	11,361	24.6	11,255	4,816	42.8	6,502	2,018	31.0
2011	52,279	13,244	25.3	45,781	11,125	24.3	11,368	4,996	44.0	6,096	1,882	30.9
2010[4]	50,971	13,522	26.5	44,612	11,376	25.5	10,719	4,748	44.3	5,846	1,863	31.9
2009	48,811	12,350	25.3	42,717	10,345	24.2	10,283	4,176	40.6	5,718	1,801	31.5
2008	47,398	10,987	23.2	41,732	9,303	22.3	9,265	3,751	40.5	5,417	1,577	29.1
2007	45,933	9,890	21.5	40,125	8,248	20.6	8,917	3,527	39.6	5,508	1,490	27.1
2006	44,784	9,243	20.6	39,177	7,650	19.5	8,652	3,189	36.9	5,317	1,468	27.6
2005[5]	43,020	9,368	21.8	37,759	7,767	20.6	7,868	3,069	39.0	4,971	1,451	29.2
2004[5]	41,690	9,122	21.9	36,438	7,705	21.1	7,825	3,072	39.3	4,971	1,293	26.0
2003	40,300	9,051	22.5	35,469	7,637	21.5	7,452	2,861	38.4	4,620	1,325	28.7
2002	39,216	8,555	21.8	34,598	7,184	20.8	7,013	2,554	36.4	4,364	1,255	28.8
2001	37,312	7,997	21.4	33,110	6,674	20.2	6,830	2,585	37.8	3,981	1,211	30.4
2000[6]	35,955	7,747	21.5	31,700	6,430	20.3	6,469	2,444	37.8	3,978	1,163	29.2
1999[7]	34,632	7,876	22.7	30,872	6,702	21.7	6,527	2,642	40.5	3,481	1,068	30.7
1998	31,515	8,070	25.6	28,055	6,814	24.3	6,074	2,837	46.7	3,218	1,097	34.1
1997	30,637	8,308	27.1	27,467	7,198	26.2	5,718	2,911	50.9	2,976	1,017	34.2
1996	29,614	8,697	29.4	26,340	7,515	28.5	5,641	3,020	53.5	2,985	1,066	35.7
1995[8]	28,344	8,574	30.3	25,165	7,341	29.2	5,785	3,053	52.8	2,947	1,092	37.0
1994[9]	27,442	8,416	30.7	24,390	7,357	30.2	5,328	2,920	54.8	2,798	926	33.1
1993[10]	26,559	8,126	30.6	23,439	6,876	29.3	5,333	2,837	53.2	2,717	972	35.8
1992[21]	25,646	7,592	29.6	22,695	6,455	28.4	4,806	2,474	51.5	2,577	881	34.2
1991[12]	22,070	6,339	28.7	19,658	5,541	28.2	4,326	2,282	52.7	2,146	667	31.1
1990	21,405	6,006	28.1	18,912	5,091	26.9	3,993	2,115	53.0	2,254	774	34.3
1989	20,746	5,430	26.2	18,488	4,659	25.2	3,763	1,902	50.6	2,045	634	31.0
1988[13]	20,064	5,357	26.7	18,102	4,700	26.0	3,734	2,052	55.0	1,864	597	32.0
1987[7,3]	19,395	5,422	28.0	17,342	4,761	27.5	3,678	2,045	55.6	1,933	598	31.0
1986	18,758	5,117	27.3	16,880	4,469	26.5	3,631	1,921	52.9	1,685	553	32.8
1985[4]	18,075	5,236	29.0	16,276	4,605	28.3	3,561	1,983	55.7	1,602	532	33.2

See footnotes at end of table.

Table B-5.
Poverty Status of People by Family Relationship, Race, and Hispanic Origin: 1959 to 2019—Con.

(Populations in thousands. Population as of March of the following year. For information on confidentiality protection, sampling error, nonsampling error, and definitions, see <https://www2.census.gov/programs-surveys/cps/techdocs/cpsmar20.pdf>)

Race, Hispanic origin, and year	All people			People in families									Unrelated individuals		
	Total	Below poverty		All families			Families with female householder, no spouse present						Total	Below poverty	
		Number	Percent	Total	Below poverty		Total	Below poverty						Number	Percent
					Number	Percent		Number	Percent						
1984[15]	16,916	4,806	28.4	15,293	4,192	27.4	3,139	1,764	56.2				1,481	545	36.8
1983	16,544	4,633	28.0	15,075	4,113	27.3	3,032	1,670	55.1				1,364	457	33.5
1982	14,385	4,301	29.9	13,242	3,865	29.2	2,664	1,601	60.1				1,018	358	35.1
1981[16]	14,021	3,713	26.5	12,922	3,349	25.9	2,622	1,465	55.9				1,005	313	31.1
1980	13,600	3,491	25.7	12,547	3,143	25.1	2,421	1,319	54.5				970	312	32.2
1979[17]	13,371	2,921	21.8	12,291	2,599	21.1	2,058	1,053	51.2				991	286	28.8
1978	12,079	2,607	21.6	11,193	2,343	20.9	1,817	1,024	56.4				886	264	29.8
1977	12,046	2,700	22.4	11,249	2,463	21.9	1,901	1,077	56.7				797	237	29.8
1976	11,269	2,783	24.7	10,552	2,516	23.8	1,766	1,000	56.6				716	266	37.2
1975	11,117	2,991	26.9	10,472	2,755	26.3	1,842	1,053	57.2				645	236	36.6
1974[18]	11,201	2,575	23.0	10,584	2,374	22.4	1,723	915	53.1				617	201	32.6
1973	10,795	2,366	21.9	10,269	2,209	21.5	1,534	881	57.4				526	157	29.9
1972[19]	10,588	2,414	22.8	10,099	2,252	22.3	1,370	733	53.5				488	162	33.2

N Not available.

[1] Estimates reflect the implementation of an updated processing system and should be used to make comparisons to 2018 and subsequent years.

[2] The 2014 CPS ASEC included redesigned questions for income and health insurance coverage. All of the approximately 98,000 addresses were eligible to receive the redesigned set of health insurance coverage questions. The redesigned income questions were implemented to a subsample of the 98,000 addresses using a probability split panel design. Approximately 68,000 addresses were eligible to recieve a set of income questions similar to those used in the 2013 CPS ASEC, and the remaining 30,000 addresses were eligible to receive the redesigned income questions. The source of these 2013

[15] Implementation of Hispanic population weighting controls and introduction of 1980 Census-based sample design.

[16] Implemented three technical changes to the poverty definition. See "Characteristics of the Population Below the Poverty Level: 1980" P60-133.

[17] Implementation of 1980 Census population controls.
Questionnaire expanded to show 27 possible values from 51 possible sources of income.

[18] Implementation of a new CPS ASEC processing system.
Questionnaire expanded to ask 11 income questions.

[19] Full implementation of 1970 Census-based sample design.

[20] Introduction of 1970 Census sample design and population controls.

estimates is the portion of the CPS ASEC sample that received the redesigned income questions, approximately 30,000 addresses.

[3] The source of these 2013 estimates is the portion of the CPS ASEC sample that received the income questions consistent with the 2013 CPS ASEC, approximately 68,000 addresses.

[4] Implementation of 2010 Census-based population controls.

[5] Data have been revised to reflect a correction to the weights in the 2005 CPS ASEC.

[6] Implementation of a 28,000 household expansion.

[7] Implementation of 2000 Census-based population controls.

[8] Full implementation of 1990 Census-based sample design and metropolitan definitions, 7,000 household sample reduction, and revised editing of responses on race.

[9] Introduction of 1990 Census sample design.

[10] Data collection method changed from paper and pencil to computer-assisted interviewing. In addition, the 1994 CPS ASEC was revised to allow for the coding of different income amounts on selected questionnaire items. Limits either increased or decreased in the following categories: earnings limits increased to $999,999; social security limits increased to $49,999; supplemental security income and public assistance limits increased to $24,999; veterans' benefits limits increased to $99,999; child support and alimony limits decreased to $49,999.

[11] Implementation of 1990 Census population controls.

[12] Estimates are revised to correct for nine omitted weights from the original 1992 CPS ASEC. See "Money Income of Households, Families, and Persons in the United States: 1992" P60-184.

[13] Estimates reflect the implementation of a new CPS ASEC processing system and are also revised to reflect corrections to the files after publication of the 1988 advance report "Money Income and Poverty Status in the United States: 1988" P60-166.

[14] Full implementation of 1980 Census-based sample design.

[21] Implementation of a new CPS ASEC processing system.

[22] Beginning with the 2003 CPS ASEC, respondents were allowed to choose one or more races. White alone refers to people who reported White and did not report any other race category. The use of this single-race population does not imply that it is the preferred method of presenting or analyzing the data. The Census Bureau uses a variety of approaches.

[23] For the year 2001 and earlier, the CPS ASEC allowed respondents to report only one race group.

[24] Black alone refers to people who reported Black and did not report any other race category.

[25] Asian alone refers to people who reported Asian and did not report any other race category.

[26] Because Hispanics may be any race, data in this report for Hispanics overlap with data for racial groups. Being Hispanic was reported by 15.6 percent of White householders who reported only one race, 5.0 percent of Black householders who reported only one race, and 2.5 percent of Asian householders who reported only one race. Data users should exercise caution when interpreting aggregate results for the Hispanic population and for race groups because these populations consist of many distinct groups that differ in socioeconomic characteristics, culture, and recency of immigration. Data were first collected for Hispanics in 1972.

Note: Before 1979, people in unrelated subfamilies were included as people in families. Beginning in 1979, people in unrelated subfamilies are included in all people but are excluded from people in families. An unrelated subfamily is defined as a married-couple family with or without children or a single parent with one or more own, never-married, children under the age of 18 living in a household and not related by birth, marriage, or adoption to the householder.

Source: U.S. Census Bureau, Current Population Survey, 1960 to 2020 Annual Social and Economic Supplements (CPS ASEC).

Table B-6.

Poverty Status of People by Age, Race, and Hispanic Origin: 1959 to 2019

(Populations in thousands. Population as of March of the following year. For information on confidentiality protection, sampling error, nonsampling error, and definitions, see <https://www2.census.gov/programs-surveys/cps/techdocs/cpsmar20.pdf>)

Race, Hispanic origin, and year	Under 18 years — All people under 18 years Total	Below poverty Number	Percent	Related children in families Total	Below poverty Number	Percent	18 to 64 years Total	Below poverty Number	Percent	65 years and over Total	Below poverty Number	Percent
ALL RACES												
2019	72,637	10,466	14.4	71,854	10,165	14.1	197,475	18,660	9.4	54,642	4,858	8.9
2018	73,284	11,869	16.2	72,425	11,491	15.9	197,775	21,130	10.7	52,788	5,146	9.7
2017	73,470	12,759	17.4	72,612	12,358	17.0	198,012	21,913	11.1	51,066	4,893	9.6
2017	73,356	12,808	17.5	72,532	12,439	17.1	198,113	22,209	11.2	51,080	4,681	9.2
2016	73,586	13,253	18.0	72,674	12,803	17.6	197,051	22,795	11.6	49,274	4,568	9.3
2015	73,647	14,509	19.7	72,558	13,962	19.2	197,260	24,414	12.4	47,547	4,201	8.8
2014	73,556	15,540	21.1	72,383	14,987	20.7	196,254	26,527	13.5	45,994	4,590	10.0
2013³	73,439	15,801	21.5	72,246	15,116	20.9	194,694	25,899	13.3	44,963	4,569	10.2
2013	73,625	14,659	19.9	72,573	14,142	19.5	194,833	26,429	13.6	44,508	4,231	9.5
2012	73,719	16,073	21.8	72,545	15,437	21.3	193,642	26,497	13.7	43,287	3,926	9.1
2011	73,737	16,134	21.9	72,568	15,539	21.4	193,213	26,492	13.7	41,507	3,620	8.7
2010⁴	73,873	16,286	22.0	72,581	15,598	21.5	192,481	26,499	13.8	39,777	3,558	8.9
2009	74,579	15,451	20.7	73,410	14,774	20.1	190,627	24,684	12.9	38,613	3,433	8.9
2008	74,068	14,068	19.0	72,980	13,507	18.5	189,185	22,105	11.7	37,788	3,656	9.7
2007	73,996	13,324	18.0	72,792	12,802	17.6	187,913	20,396	10.9	36,790	3,556	9.7
2006	73,727	12,827	17.4	72,609	12,299	16.9	186,688	20,239	10.8	36,035	3,394	9.4
2005	73,285	12,896	17.6	72,095	12,335	17.1	184,345	20,450	11.1	35,505	3,603	10.1
2004³	73,241	13,041	17.8	72,133	12,473	17.3	182,166	20,545	11.3	35,209	3,453	9.8
2003	72,999	12,866	17.6	71,907	12,340	17.2	180,041	19,443	10.8	34,659	3,552	10.2
2002	72,696	12,133	16.7	71,619	11,646	16.3	178,388	18,861	10.6	34,234	3,576	10.4
2001	72,021	11,733	16.3	70,950	11,175	15.8	175,685	17,760	10.1	33,769	3,414	10.1
2000⁶	71,741	11,587	16.2	70,538	11,005	15.6	173,638	16,671	9.6	33,566	3,323	9.9
1999⁷	71,685	12,280	17.1	70,424	11,678	16.6	171,146	17,289	10.1	33,377	3,222	9.7
1998	71,338	13,467	18.9	70,253	12,845	18.3	167,327	17,623	10.5	32,394	3,386	10.5
1997	71,069	14,113	19.9	69,844	13,422	19.2	165,329	18,085	10.9	32,082	3,376	10.5
1996	70,650	14,463	20.5	69,411	13,764	19.8	163,691	18,638	11.4	31,877	3,428	10.8
1995⁸	70,566	14,665	20.8	69,425	13,999	20.2	161,508	18,442	11.4	31,658	3,318	10.5
1994⁹	70,020	15,289	21.8	68,819	14,610	21.2	160,329	19,107	11.9	31,267	3,663	11.7
1993¹⁰	69,292	15,727	22.7	68,040	14,961	22.0	159,208	19,781	12.4	30,779	3,755	12.2
1992¹¹	68,440	15,294	22.3	67,256	14,521	21.6	157,680	18,793	11.9	30,430	3,928	12.9
1991¹²	65,918	14,341	21.8	64,800	13,658	21.1	154,684	17,586	11.4	30,590	3,781	12.4
1990	65,049	13,431	20.6	63,908	12,715	19.9	153,502	16,496	10.7	30,093	3,658	12.2

Year											
1989	64,144	12,590	19.6	63,225	12,001	19.0	152,282	15,575	10.2	29,566	3,363	11.4
1988[3]	63,747	12,455	19.5	62,906	11,935	19.0	150,761	15,809	10.5	29,022	3,481	12.0
1987[13]	63,294	12,843	20.3	62,423	12,275	19.7	149,201	15,815	10.6	28,487	3,563	12.5
1986	62,948	12,876	20.5	62,009	12,257	19.8	147,631	16,017	10.8	27,975	3,477	12.4
1985[14]	62,876	13,010	20.7	62,019	12,483	20.1	146,396	16,598	11.3	27,322	3,456	12.6
1984[15]	62,447	13,420	21.5	61,681	12,929	21.0	144,551	16,952	11.7	26,818	3,330	12.4
1983	62,334	13,911	22.3	61,578	13,427	21.8	143,052	17,767	12.4	26,313	3,625	13.8
1982	62,345	13,647	21.9	61,565	13,139	21.3	141,328	17,000	12.0	25,738	3,751	14.6
1981[16]	62,449	12,505	20.0	61,756	12,068	19.5	139,477	15,464	11.1	25,231	3,853	15.3
1980	62,914	11,543	18.3	62,168	11,114	17.9	137,428	13,858	10.1	24,686	3,871	15.7
1979[17]	63,375	10,377	16.4	62,646	9,993	16.0	135,333	12,014	8.9	24,194	3,682	15.2
1978	62,311	9,931	15.9	61,987	9,722	15.7	130,169	11,332	8.7	23,175	3,233	14.0
1977	63,137	10,288	16.2	62,823	10,028	16.0	128,262	11,316	8.8	22,468	3,177	14.1
1976	64,028	10,273	16.0	63,729	10,081	15.8	126,175	11,389	9.0	22,100	3,313	15.0
1975	65,079	11,104	17.1	64,750	10,882	16.8	124,122	11,456	9.2	21,662	3,317	15.3
1974[18]	66,134	10,156	15.4	65,802	9,967	15.1	122,101	10,132	8.3	21,127	3,085	14.6
1973	66,959	9,642	14.4	66,626	9,453	14.2	120,060	9,977	8.3	20,602	3,354	16.3
1972[19]	67,930	10,284	15.1	67,592	10,082	14.9	117,957	10,438	8.8	20,117	3,738	18.6
1971[20]	68,816	10,551	15.3	68,474	10,344	15.1	115,911	10,735	9.3	19,827	4,273	21.6
1970	69,159	10,440	15.1	68,815	10,235	14.9	113,554	10,187	9.0	19,470	4,793	24.6
1969	69,090	9,691	14.0	68,746	9,501	13.8	111,528	9,669	8.7	18,899	4,787	25.3
1968	70,385	10,954	15.6	70,035	10,759	15.3	108,684	9,803	9.0	18,559	4,632	25.0
1967[21]	70,408	11,656	16.6	70,058	11,427	16.3	107,024	10,725	10.0	18,240	5,388	29.5
1966	70,218	12,389	17.6	69,869	12,146	17.4	105,241	11,007	10.5	17,929	5,114	28.5
1965	69,986	14,676	21.0	69,638	14,388	20.7	N	N	N	N	N	N
1964	69,711	16,051	23.0	69,364	15,736	22.7	N	N	N	N	N	N
1963	69,181	16,005	23.1	68,837	15,691	22.8	N	N	N	N	N	N
1962	67,722	16,963	25.0	67,385	16,630	24.7	N	N	N	N	N	N
1961	66,121	16,909	25.6	65,792	16,577	25.2	N	N	N	N	N	N
1960	65,601	17,634	26.9	65,275	17,288	26.5	N	N	N	N	N	N
1959	64,315	17,552	27.3	63,995	17,208	26.9	96,685	16,457	17.0	15,557	5,481	35.2
WHITE ALONE[22]											
2019	52,494	6,443	12.3	51,866	6,209	12.0	149,832	12,535	8.4	45,760	3,534	7.7
2018	52,763	7,049	13.4	52,153	6,783	13.0	150,564	14,133	9.4	44,307	3,762	8.5
2017[1]	53,101	7,796	14.7	52,481	7,520	14.3	151,156	14,653	9.7	42,999	3,577	8.3
2017	53,022	8,041	15.2	52,412	7,772	14.8	151,259	15,027	9.9	42,991	3,368	7.8
2016	53,319	8,324	15.6	52,594	7,963	15.1	151,044	15,467	10.2	41,623	3,322	8.0
2015	53,550	9,204	17.2	52,786	8,838	16.7	151,731	16,325	10.8	40,254	3,057	7.5
2014	53,637	9,602	17.9	52,732	9,172	17.4	151,562	18,086	11.9	39,054	3,400	8.7
2013[2]	53,638	10,296	19.2	52,657	9,702	18.4	151,234	17,629	11.7	38,475	3,362	8.7
2013[3]	53,846	8,808	16.4	53,074	8,428	15.9	151,334	17,931	11.8	37,905	3,197	8.4
2012	54,066	9,979	18.5	53,201	9,547	17.9	151,042	17,946	11.9	37,039	2,891	7.8
2011	54,186	10,103	18.6	53,268	9,643	18.1	151,416	18,007	11.9	35,732	2,739	7.7
2010[4]	54,490	10,092	18.5	53,573	9,590	17.9	151,218	18,353	12.1	34,274	2,638	7.7

See footnotes at end of table.

Table B-6.
Poverty Status of People by Age, Race, and Hispanic Origin: 1959 to 2019—Con.

(Populations in thousands. Population as of March of the following year. For information on confidentiality protection, sampling error, nonsampling error, and definitions, see <https://www2.census.gov/programs-surveys/cps/techdocs/cpsmar20.pdf>)

Race, Hispanic origin, and year	All people under 18 years			Under 18 years — Related children in families			18 to 64 years			65 years and over		
	Total	Below poverty Number	Percent	Total	Below poverty Number	Percent	Total	Below poverty Number	Percent	Total	Below poverty Number	Percent
2009	56,266	9,938	17.7	55,397	9,440	17.0	152,367	17,391	11.4	33,414	2,501	7.5
2008	56,153	8,863	15.8	55,339	8,441	15.3	151,681	15,356	10.1	32,714	2,771	8.5
2007	56,419	8,395	14.9	55,483	8,002	14.4	150,875	14,135	9.4	31,839	2,590	8.1
2006	56,205	7,908	14.1	55,330	7,522	13.6	150,143	14,035	9.3	31,270	2,473	7.9
2005	56,075	8,085	14.4	55,152	7,652	13.9	148,450	14,086	9.5	30,905	2,700	8.7
2004[5]	56,053	8,308	14.8	55,212	7,876	14.3	146,974	14,486	9.9	30,714	2,534	8.3
2003	55,779	7,985	14.3	54,989	7,624	13.9	145,783	13,622	9.3	30,303	2,666	8.8
2002	55,703	7,549	13.6	54,900	7,203	13.1	144,694	13,178	9.1	29,980	2,739	9.1
WHITE[33]												
2001	56,089	7,527	13.4	55,238	7,086	12.8	143,796	12,555	8.7	29,790	2,656	8.9
2000[6]	55,980	7,307	13.1	55,021	6,834	12.4	142,164	11,754	8.3	29,703	2,584	8.7
1999[7]	55,833	7,639	13.7	54,873	7,194	13.1	139,974	12,085	8.6	29,553	2,446	8.3
1998	56,016	8,443	15.1	55,126	7,935	14.4	138,061	12,456	9.0	28,759	2,555	8.9
1997	55,863	8,990	16.1	54,870	8,441	15.4	136,784	12,838	9.4	28,553	2,569	9.0
1996	55,606	9,044	16.3	54,599	8,488	15.5	135,586	12,940	9.5	28,464	2,667	9.4
1995[8]	55,444	8,981	16.2	54,532	8,474	15.5	134,149	12,869	9.6	28,436	2,572	9.0
1994[9]	55,186	9,346	16.9	54,221	8,826	16.3	133,289	13,187	9.9	27,985	2,846	10.2
1993[10]	54,639	9,752	17.8	53,614	9,123	17.0	132,680	13,535	10.2	27,580	2,939	10.7
1992[11]	54,110	9,399	17.4	53,110	8,752	16.5	131,694	12,871	9.8	27,256	2,989	11.0
1991[12]	52,523	8,848	16.8	51,627	8,316	16.1	130,312	12,097	9.3	27,297	2,802	10.3
1990	51,929	8,232	15.9	51,028	7,696	15.1	129,784	11,387	8.8	26,898	2,707	10.1
1989	51,400	7,599	14.8	50,704	7,164	14.1	128,974	10,647	8.3	26,479	2,539	9.6
1988[13]	51,203	7,435	14.5	50,590	7,095	14.0	128,031	10,687	8.3	26,001	2,593	10.0
1987[11]	51,012	7,788	15.3	50,360	7,398	14.7	126,991	10,703	8.4	25,602	2,704	10.6
1986	51,111	8,209	16.1	50,356	7,714	15.3	125,998	11,285	9.0	25,173	2,689	10.7
1985[14]	51,031	8,253	16.2	50,358	7,838	15.6	125,258	11,909	9.5	24,629	2,698	11.0
1984[15]	50,814	8,472	16.7	50,192	8,086	16.1	123,922	11,904	9.6	24,206	2,579	10.7
1983	50,726	8,862	17.5	50,183	8,534	17.0	123,014	12,347	10.0	23,754	2,776	11.7
1982	50,920	8,678	17.0	50,305	8,282	16.5	121,766	11,971	9.8	23,234	2,870	12.4
1981[16]	51,140	7,785	15.2	50,553	7,429	14.7	120,574	10,790	8.9	22,791	2,978	13.1
1980	51,653	7,181	13.9	51,002	6,817	13.4	118,935	9,478	8.0	22,325	3,042	13.6
1979[17]	52,262	6,193	11.8	51,687	5,909	11.4	117,583	8,110	6.9	21,898	2,911	13.3

Year	(1)	(2)	(3)	(4)	(5)	(6)	(7)	(8)	(9)	(10)	(11)	(12)
1978	51,669	5,831	11.3	51,409	5,674	11.0	113,832	7,897	6.9	20,950	2,530	12.1
1977	52,563	6,097	11.6	52,299	5,943	11.4	112,374	7,893	7.0	20,316	2,426	11.9
1976	53,428	6,189	11.6	53,167	6,034	11.3	110,717	7,890	7.1	20,020	2,633	13.2
1975	54,405	6,927	12.7	54,126	6,748	12.5	109,105	8,210	7.5	19,654	2,634	13.4
1974[18]	55,590	6,223	11.2	55,320	6,079	11.0	107,579	7,053	6.6	19,206	2,460	12.8
1973	N	N	N	56,211	5,462	9.7	N	N	N	N	2,698	14.4
1972[19]	N	N	N	57,181	5,784	10.1	N	N	N	N	3,072	16.8
1971[20]	N	N	N	58,119	6,341	10.9	N	N	N	N	3,605	19.9
1970	N	N	N	58,472	6,138	10.5	N	N	N	N	4,011	22.6
1969	N	N	N	58,578	5,667	9.7	N	N	N	17,062	4,052	23.3
1968	N	N	N	N	6,373	10.7	N	N	N	16,791	3,939	23.1
1967[21]	N	N	N	N	6,729	11.3	N	N	N	16,514	4,646	27.7
1966	N	N	N	N	7,204	12.1	N	N	N	N	4,357	26.4
1965	N	N	N	N	8,595	14.4	N	N	N	N	N	N
1960	N	N	N	N	11,229	20.0	N	N	N	N	N	N
1959	N	N	N	N	11,386	20.6	N	N	N	N	4,744	33.1
WHITE ALONE, NOT HISPANIC[22]												
2019	36,391	3,030	8.3	35,976	2,886	8.0	116,810	8,321	7.1	41,442	2,801	6.8
2018	36,619	3,265	8.9	36,245	3,107	8.6	117,979	9,510	8.1	40,218	2,951	7.3
2017[1]	37,122	3,793	10.2	36,727	3,614	9.8	118,969	9,884	8.3	39,127	2,942	7.5
2017	37,047	4,026	10.9	36,655	3,860	10.5	119,078	10,230	8.6	39,131	2,737	7.0
2016	37,485	4,050	10.8	36,982	3,799	10.3	119,785	10,526	8.8	37,951	2,687	7.1
2015	37,859	4,563	12.1	37,342	4,301	11.5	120,908	10,812	8.9	36,682	2,411	6.6
2014	38,057	4,679	12.3	37,457	4,440	11.9	121,424	12,173	10.0	35,727	2,801	7.8
2013[2]	38,167	5,116	13.4	37,849	4,784	12.7	121,629	11,691	9.6	35,322	2,745	7.8
2013[3]	38,395	4,094	10.7	38,167	3,833	10.1	121,991	12,133	9.9	34,781	2,569	7.4
2012	38,759	4,782	12.3	38,322	4,510	11.8	122,221	11,833	9.7	34,131	2,324	6.8
2011	38,955	4,850	12.5	38,823	4,554	11.9	123,101	12,112	9.8	32,904	2,210	6.7
2010[4]	39,437	4,866	12.3		4,544		123,731	12,230	9.9	31,616	2,155	6.8
2009	40,917	4,850	11.9	40,319	4,518	11.7	125,511	11,658	9.3	30,736	2,022	6.6
2008	41,300	4,364	10.6	40,707	4,059	11.2	125,482	10,380	8.3	30,149	2,280	7.6
2007	41,979	4,255	10.1	41,304	3,996	10.0	125,161	9,598	7.7	29,442	2,179	7.4
2006	42,212	4,208	10.0	41,563	3,930	9.7	124,847	9,761	7.8	28,990	2,044	7.0
2005[5]	42,523	4,254	10.0	41,867	3,973	9.5	124,326	9,708	7.8	28,704	2,264	7.9
2004[5]	42,978	4,519	10.5	42,363	4,190	9.9	124,326	10,236	8.3	28,639	2,153	7.5
2003	43,150	4,233	9.8	42,547	3,957	9.3	123,110	9,391	7.6	28,335	2,277	8.0
2002	43,614	4,090	9.4	43,017	3,848	8.9	122,511	9,157	7.5	28,018	2,321	8.3
WHITE, NOT HISPANIC[23]												
2001	44,095	4,194	9.5	43,459	3,887	8.9	122,470	8,811	7.2	27,973	2,266	8.1
2000[6]	44,244	4,018	9.1	43,554	3,715	8.5	121,499	8,130	6.7	27,948	2,218	7.9

See footnotes at end of table.

Table B-6.
Poverty Status of People by Age, Race, and Hispanic Origin: 1959 to 2019—Con.

(Populations in thousands. Population as of March of the following year. For information on confidentiality protection, sampling error, nonsampling error, and definitions, see <https://www2.census.gov/programs-surveys/cps/techdocs/cpsmar20.pdf>)

Race, Hispanic origin, and year	Under 18 years						18 to 64 years			65 years and over		
	All people under 18 years			Related children in families								
	Total	Below poverty Number	Percent	Total	Below poverty Number	Percent	Total	Below poverty Number	Percent	Total	Below poverty Number	Percent
1999[7]	44,272	4,155	9.4	43,570	3,832	8.8	120,341	8,462	7.0	27,952	2,118	7.6
1998	45,355	4,822	10.6	44,670	4,458	10.0	120,282	8,760	7.3	27,118	2,217	8.2
1997	45,491	5,204	11.4	44,665	4,759	10.7	119,373	9,088	7.6	26,995	2,200	8.1
1996	45,605	5,072	11.1	44,844	4,656	10.4	118,822	9,074	7.6	27,033	2,316	8.6
1995[8]	45,689	5,115	11.2	44,973	4,745	10.6	118,228	8,908	7.5	27,034	2,243	8.3
1994[9]	46,668	5,823	12.5	45,874	5,404	11.8	119,192	9,732	8.2	26,684	2,556	9.6
1993[10]	46,096	6,255	13.6	45,322	5,819	12.8	118,475	9,964	8.4	26,272	2,663	10.1
1992[11]	45,590	6,017	13.2	44,833	5,558	12.4	117,386	9,461	8.1	26,025	2,724	10.5
1991[12]	45,236	5,918	13.1	44,506	5,497	12.4	117,672	9,244	7.9	26,208	2,580	9.8
1990	44,797	5,532	12.3	44,045	5,106	11.6	117,477	8,619	7.3	25,854	2,471	9.6
1989	44,492	5,110	11.5	43,938	4,779	10.9	116,983	8,154	7.0	25,504	2,335	9.2
1988[13]	44,438	4,888	11.0	43,910	4,594	10.5	116,479	8,293	7.1	25,044	2,384	9.5
1987[13]	44,461	5,230	11.8	43,907	4,902	11.2	115,721	8,327	7.2	24,754	2,472	10.0
1986	44,664	5,789	13.0	44,041	5,388	12.2	115,157	8,963	7.8	24,298	2,492	10.3
1985[14]	44,752	5,745	12.8	44,199	5,421	12.3	114,969	9,608	8.4	23,734	2,486	10.5
1984[15]	44,886	6,156	13.7	44,349	5,828	13.1	114,180	9,734	8.5	23,402	2,410	10.3
1983	44,830	6,649	14.8	44,374	6,381	14.4	113,570	10,279	9.1	22,992	2,610	11.4
1982	45,531	6,566	14.4	45,001	6,229	13.8	113,717	10,082	8.9	22,655	2,714	12.0
1981[16]	45,950	5,946	12.9	45,440	5,639	12.4	112,722	9,207	8.2	22,237	2,834	12.7
1980	46,578	5,510	11.8	45,989	5,174	11.3	111,460	7,990	7.2	21,760	2,865	13.2
1979[17]	46,967	4,730	10.1	46,448	4,476	9.6	110,509	6,930	6.3	21,339	2,759	12.9
1978	46,819	4,506	9.6	46,606	4,383	9.4	107,481	6,837	6.4	20,431	2,412	11.8
1977	47,689	4,714	9.9	47,459	4,582	9.7	106,063	6,772	6.4	19,812	2,316	11.7
1976	48,824	4,799	9.8	48,601	4,664	9.6	104,846	6,720	6.4	19,565	2,506	12.8
1975	49,670	5,342	10.8	49,421	5,185	10.5	103,496	7,039	6.8	19,251	2,503	13.0
1974[18]	50,759	4,820	9.5	50,520	4,697	9.3	101,894	6,051	5.9	18,810	2,346	12.5
BLACK ALONE OR IN COMBINATION												
2019	13,023	3,338	25.6	12,918	3,297	25.5	28,843	4,531	15.7	5,394	966	17.9
2018	13,222	3,773	28.5	13,061	3,704	28.4	28,423	4,948	17.4	5,180	975	18.8
2017[1]	13,163	3,903	29.7	12,999	3,816	29.4	28,231	5,216	18.5	4,942	930	18.8
2017	13,187	3,731	28.3	13,042	3,663	28.1	28,253	5,142	18.2	4,952	948	19.1

Year	Total (1)	Number (1)	Percent (1)	Total (2)	Number (2)	Percent (2)	Total (3)	Number (3)	Percent (3)	Total (4)	Number (4)	Percent (4)
2016	13,190	3,916	29.7	13,084	3,866	29.5	27,834	5,186	18.6	4,660	864	18.5
2015	13,128	4,146	31.6	12,944	4,052	31.3	27,653	5,835	21.1	4,447	816	18.4
2014	12,875	4,639	36.0	12,706	4,564	35.9	27,442	6,137	22.4	4,249	805	19.0
2013[2]	13,044	4,359	33.4	12,915	4,325	33.5	27,056	6,031	22.3	4,054	772	19.0
2013[3]	13,104	4,838	36.9	12,882	4,730	36.7	26,923	6,410	23.8	4,085	712	17.4
2012	13,108	4,815	36.7	12,908	4,675	36.2	26,482	6,265	23.7	3,993	730	18.3
2011	12,968	4,849	37.4	12,815	4,762	37.2	25,962	6,241	24.0	3,718	640	17.2
2010[4]	13,015	4,923	37.8	12,759	4,814	37.7	25,815	6,031	23.4	3,555	643	18.1
2009	12,655	4,480	35.4	12,445	4,349	34.9	24,815	5,441	21.9	3,405	655	19.2
2008	12,388	4,202	33.9	12,201	4,104	33.6	24,404	5,017	20.6	3,305	663	20.0
2007	12,380	4,178	33.7	12,227	4,106	33.6	23,968	4,742	19.8	3,215	748	23.3
2006	12,375	4,086	33.5	12,206	4,097	32.6	23,510	4,652	19.8	3,128	710	22.7
2005	12,159	4,074	33.5	11,975	3,972	33.2	23,338	4,735	20.3	3,053	708	23.2
2004[5]	12,190	4,059	33.6	12,012	3,962	33.0	22,842	4,638	20.3	3,005	714	23.8
2003	12,215	4,108	33.6	11,989	3,977	33.2	22,355	4,313	19.3	2,933	688	23.5
2002	12,114	3,817	31.5	11,931	3,733	31.3	22,170	4,376	19.7	2,922	691	23.6
BLACK ALONE[24]												
2019	10,851	2,865	26.4	10,761	2,831	26.3	26,857	4,261	15.9	5,257	947	18.0
2018	11,084	3,273	29.5	10,940	3,212	29.4	26,644	4,660	17.5	5,045	951	18.9
2017[1]	11,005	3,350	30.4	10,877	3,280	30.2	26,645	4,960	18.6	4,834	915	19.0
2017	10,991	3,184	29.0	10,882	3,134	28.8	26,648	4,877	18.3	4,561	932	19.3
2016	11,115	3,418	30.8	11,040	3,382	30.6	26,286	4,963	18.9	4,343	853	18.7
2015	11,087	3,651	32.9	10,928	3,571	32.7	26,194	5,568	21.3	4,143	801	18.4
2014	11,015	4,090	37.1	10,887	4,036	37.1	25,954	5,869	22.6	3,993	796	19.2
2013[2]	11,003	3,708	33.7	10,896	3,678	33.8	25,562	5,742	22.5	3,933	736	18.7
2013[3]	11,088	4,244	38.3	10,916	4,153	38.0	25,552	6,099	23.9	3,975	698	17.6
2012	11,078	4,201	37.9	10,931	4,097	37.5	25,154	6,002	23.9	3,893	708	18.2
2011	11,138	4,320	38.8	11,005	4,247	38.6	24,831	5,980	24.1	3,640	630	17.3
2010[4]	11,173	4,355	39.0	10,953	4,271	39.0	24,667	5,775	23.4	3,443	617	17.9
2009	11,282	4,033	35.7	11,102	3,919	35.3	23,953	5,264	22.0	3,320	647	19.5
2008	11,172	3,878	34.4	10,998	3,781	34.4	23,565	4,855	20.6	3,229	646	20.0
2007	11,302	3,904	34.5	11,174	3,838	34.3	23,213	4,602	19.8	3,150	731	23.2
2006	11,315	3,777	33.4	11,168	3,690	33.0	22,907	4,570	19.9	3,085	701	22.7
2005	11,136	3,841	34.5	10,962	3,743	34.2	22,659	4,627	20.4	3,007	701	23.3
2004[5]	11,244	3,788	33.7	11,080	3,702	33.4	22,226	4,521	20.3	2,956	705	23.8
2003	11,367	3,877	34.1	11,162	3,750	33.6	21,746	4,224	19.4	2,876	680	23.7
2002	11,275	3,645	32.3	11,111	3,570	32.1	21,547	4,277	19.9	2,856	680	23.8
BLACK[23]												
2001	11,556	3,492	30.2	11,419	3,423	30.0	21,462	4,018	18.7	2,853	626	21.9
2000[6]	11,480	3,581	31.2	11,296	3,495	30.9	21,160	3,794	17.9	2,785	607	21.8

See footnotes at end of table.

Table B-6.

Poverty Status of People by Age, Race, and Hispanic Origin: 1959 to 2019—Con.

(Populations in thousands. Population as of March of the following year. For information on confidentiality protection, sampling error, nonsampling error, and definitions, see <https://www2.census.gov/programs-surveys/cps/techdocs/cpsmar20.pdf>)

Race, Hispanic origin, and year	Under 18 years						18 to 64 years			65 years and over		
	All people under 18 years			Related children in families								
	Total	Below poverty		Total	Below poverty		Total	Below poverty		Total	Below poverty	
		Number	Percent		Number	Percent		Number	Percent		Number	Percent
1999[7]	11,488	3,813	33.2	11,260	3,698	32.8	21,518	4,000	18.6	2,750	628	22.8
1998	11,317	4,151	36.7	11,176	4,073	36.4	20,837	4,222	20.3	2,723	718	26.4
1997	11,367	4,225	37.2	11,193	4,116	36.8	20,400	4,191	20.5	2,691	700	26.0
1996	11,338	4,519	39.9	11,155	4,411	39.5	20,155	4,515	22.4	2,616	661	25.3
1995[8]	11,369	4,761	41.9	11,198	4,644	41.5	19,892	4,483	22.5	2,478	629	25.4
1994[9]	11,211	4,906	43.8	11,044	4,787	43.3	19,585	4,590	23.4	2,557	700	27.4
1993[10]	11,127	5,125	46.1	10,969	5,030	45.9	19,272	5,049	26.2	2,510	702	28.0
1992[21]	10,956	5,106	46.6	10,823	5,015	46.3	18,952	4,884	25.8	2,504	838	33.5
1991[12]	10,350	4,755	45.9	10,178	4,637	45.6	18,355	4,607	25.1	2,606	880	33.8
1990	10,162	4,550	44.8	9,980	4,412	44.2	18,097	4,427	24.5	2,547	860	33.8
1989	10,012	4,375	43.7	9,847	4,257	43.2	17,853	4,164	23.3	2,487	763	30.7
1988[13]	9,865	4,296	43.5	9,681	4,148	42.8	17,548	4,275	24.4	2,436	785	32.2
1987[13]	9,730	4,385	45.1	9,546	4,234	44.4	17,245	4,361	25.3	2,387	774	32.4
1986	9,629	4,148	43.1	9,467	4,037	42.7	16,911	4,113	24.3	2,331	722	31.0
1985[14]	9,545	4,157	43.6	9,405	4,057	43.1	16,667	4,052	24.3	2,273	717	31.5
1984[15]	9,480	4,413	46.6	9,356	4,320	46.2	16,369	4,368	26.7	2,238	710	31.7
1983	9,417	4,398	46.7	9,245	4,273	46.2	16,065	4,694	29.2	2,197	791	36.0
1982	9,400	4,472	47.6	9,269	4,388	47.3	15,692	4,415	28.1	2,124	811	38.2
1981[16]	9,374	4,237	45.2	9,291	4,170	44.9	15,358	4,117	26.8	2,102	820	39.0
1980	9,368	3,961	42.3	9,287	3,906	42.1	14,987	3,835	25.6	2,054	783	38.1
1979[17]	9,307	3,833	41.2	9,172	3,745	40.8	14,596	3,478	23.8	2,040	740	36.2
1978	9,229	3,830	41.5	9,168	3,781	41.2	13,774	3,133	22.7	1,954	662	33.9
1977	9,296	3,888	41.8	9,253	3,850	41.6	13,483	3,137	23.3	1,930	701	36.3
1976	9,322	3,787	40.6	9,291	3,758	40.4	13,224	3,163	23.9	1,852	644	34.8
1975	9,421	3,925	41.7	9,374	3,884	41.4	12,872	2,968	23.1	1,795	652	36.3
1974[18]	9,439	3,755	39.8	9,384	3,713	39.6	12,539	2,836	22.6	1,721	591	34.3
1973	N	N	N	9,405	3,822	40.6	N	N	N	1,672	620	37.1
1972[19]	N	N	N	9,426	4,025	42.7	N	N	N	1,603	640	39.9
1971[20]	N	N	N	9,414	3,836	40.4	N	N	N	1,584	623	39.3
1970	N	N	N	9,448	3,922	41.5	N	N	N	1,422	683	48.0

Year												
1969	N	N	N	9,290	3,677	39.6	N	N	N	1,373	689	50.2
1968	N	N	N	N	4,188	43.1	N	N	N	1,374	655	47.7
1967²	N	N	N	N	4,558	47.4	N	N	N	1,341	715	53.3
1966	N	N	N	N	4,774	50.6	N	N	N	1,311	722	55.1
1965	N	N	N	N	5,022	65.6	N	N	N	N	711	62.5
ASIAN ALONE OR IN COMBINATION												
2019	5,234	329	6.3	5,198	315	6.1	14,483	1,007	7.0	2,724	252	9.3
2018	5,158	538	10.4	5,095	508	10.0	14,348	1,334	9.3	2,559	294	11.6
2017¹	5,170	524	10.1	5,124	505	9.9	13,993	1,259	9.0	2,392	280	11.7
2017	5,133	537	10.5	5,088	524	10.3	13,970	1,303	9.3	2,408	263	10.9
2016	4,922	495	10.1	4,874	477	9.8	13,581	1,301	9.6	2,253	266	11.8
2015	4,728	539	11.4	4,611	489	10.6	13,133	1,390	10.6	2,176	252	11.6
2014	4,792	577	12.0	4,722	544	11.5	12,834	1,443	11.2	2,059	301	14.6
2013²	4,900	628	12.8	4,858	600	12.4	12,393	1,457	11.8	1,889	312	16.5
2013³	4,740	457	9.6	4,701	442	9.4	12,374	1,258	10.2	1,910	259	13.6
2012	4,557	570	12.5	4,485	533	11.9	11,913	1,291	10.8	1,703	211	12.4
2011	4,572	607	13.3	4,495	566	12.6	11,660	1,397	12.0	1,581	185	11.7
2010⁴	4,308	586	13.6	4,256	560	13.2	11,414	1,265	11.1	1,515	214	14.1
2009	3,996	531	13.3	3,946	507	12.9	9,898	1,154	11.7	1,378	216	15.7
2008	3,717	494	13.3	3,678	476	12.9	9,507	1,031	10.8	1,319	162	12.3
2007	3,606	431	11.9	3,558	402	11.3	9,531	892	9.4	1,293	144	11.2
2006	3,573	408	11.4	3,530	398	11.3	9,553	897	9.4	1,205	142	11.8
2005	3,472	359	10.3	3,435	352	10.2	9,115	999	11.0	1,144	144	12.6
2004⁵	3,406	329	9.7	3,367	311	9.2	8,780	819	9.3	1,104	147	13.3
2003	3,316	420	12.7	3,279	406	12.4	8,510	956	11.2	1,065	152	14.2
2002	3,199	353	11.0	3,159	338	10.7	8,292	804	9.7	995	86	8.7
ASIAN ALONE²⁵												
2019	3,916	286	7.3	3,887	272	7.0	13,373	932	7.0	2,638	246	9.3
2018	3,998	453	11.3	3,948	426	10.8	13,292	1,254	9.4	2,479	289	11.7
2017¹	4,058	420	10.4	4,023	405	10.1	13,120	1,193	9.1	2,348	277	11.8
2017	4,019	455	11.3	3,985	442	11.1	13,097	1,244	9.5	2,358	255	10.8
2016	3,875	430	11.1	3,839	412	10.7	12,796	1,217	9.5	2,209	261	11.8
2015	3,786	466	12.3	3,693	420	11.4	12,325	1,360	11.0	2,130	252	11.8
2014	3,750	524	14.0	3,681	492	13.4	12,012	1,314	10.9	2,029	299	14.7
2013²	3,766	555	14.7	3,746	538	14.4	11,646	1,393	12.0	1,845	307	16.7
2013³	3,651	367	10.1	3,621	354	9.8	11,531	1,162	10.1	1,881	256	13.6
2012	3,596	497	13.8	3,542	470	13.3	11,153	1,220	10.9	1,669	205	12.3
2011	3,657	494	13.5	3,600	466	13.0	10,873	1,297	11.9	1,555	182	11.7
2010⁴	3,431	494	14.4	3,399	477	14.0	10,696	1,191	11.1	1,484	214	14.4

See footnotes at end of table.

Table B-6.

Poverty Status of People by Age, Race, and Hispanic Origin: 1959 to 2019—Con.

(Populations in thousands. Population as of March of the following year. For information on confidentiality protection, sampling error, nonsampling error, and definitions, see <https://www2.census.gov/programs-surveys/cps/techdocs/cpsmar20.pdf>)

Race, Hispanic origin, and year	Under 18 years						18 to 64 years			65 years and over		
	All people under 18 years			Related children in families								
		Below poverty			Below poverty			Below poverty			Below poverty	
	Total	Number	Percent	Total	Number	Percent	Total	Number	Percent	Total	Number	Percent
2009	3,311	463	14.0	3,271	444	13.6	9,344	1,069	11.4	1,350	213	15.8
2008	3,052	446	14.6	3,016	430	14.2	8,961	974	10.9	1,296	157	12.1
2007	2,980	374	12.5	2,932	345	11.8	9,012	832	9.2	1,265	143	11.3
2006	2,956	360	12.2	2,915	351	12.0	9,039	851	9.4	1,182	142	12.0
2005	2,871	317	11.1	2,842	312	11.0	8,591	941	11.0	1,118	143	12.8
2004[5]	2,854	281	9.9	2,823	265	9.4	8,294	774	9.3	1,083	146	13.5
2003	2,759	344	12.5	2,726	331	12.1	8,044	907	11.3	1,052	151	14.3
2002	2,683	315	11.7	2,648	302	11.4	7,881	764	9.7	977	82	8.4
ASIAN AND PACIFIC ISLANDER[23]												
2001	3,215	369	11.5	3,169	353	11.1	8,352	814	9.7	899	92	10.2
2000[6]	3,294	420	12.7	3,256	407	12.5	8,500	756	8.9	878	82	9.3
1999[7]	3,212	381	11.9	3,178	367	11.5	7,879	807	10.2	864	96	11.1
1998	3,137	564	18.0	3,099	542	17.5	6,951	698	10.0	785	97	12.4
1997	3,096	628	20.3	3,061	608	19.9	6,680	753	11.3	705	87	12.3
1996	2,924	571	19.5	2,899	553	19.1	6,484	821	12.7	647	63	9.7
1995[8]	2,900	564	19.5	2,858	532	18.6	6,123	757	12.4	622	89	14.3
1994[9]	1,739	318	18.3	1,719	308	17.9	4,401	589	13.4	513	67	13.0
1993[10]	2,061	375	18.2	2,029	358	17.6	4,871	680	14.0	503	79	15.6
1992[11]	2,218	363	16.4	2,199	352	16.0	5,067	568	11.2	494	53	10.8
1991[12]	2,056	360	17.5	2,036	348	17.1	4,582	565	12.3	555	70	12.7
1990	2,126	374	17.6	2,098	356	17.0	4,375	422	9.6	514	62	12.1
1989	1,983	392	19.8	1,945	368	18.9	4,225	512	12.1	465	34	7.4
1988[13]	1,970	474	24.1	1,949	458	23.5	4,035	583	14.4	442	60	13.5
1987[13]	1,937	455	23.5	1,908	432	22.7	4,010	510	12.7	375	56	15.0
HISPANIC (ANY RACE)[26]												
2019	18,608	3,888	20.9	18,386	3,796	20.6	37,207	4,836	13.0	4,787	821	17.1
2018	18,739	4,436	23.7	18,479	4,316	23.4	36,673	5,205	14.2	4,544	884	19.5
2018[7]	18,595	4,643	25.0	18,319	4,525	24.7	36,136	5,446	15.1	4,320	726	16.8
2017	18,575	4,639	25.0	18,312	4,519	24.7	36,156	5,415	15.0	4,322	736	17.0
2016	18,385	4,890	26.6	18,129	4,764	26.3	35,113	5,542	15.8	4,057	706	17.4

Year												
2015	18,231	5,269	28.9	17,944	5,139	28.6	34,686	6,188	17.8	3,863	676	17.5
2014	17,995	5,745	31.9	17,636	5,522	31.3	33,873	6,701	19.8	3,636	658	18.1
2013[2]	17,898	5,907	33.0	17,496	5,638	32.2	32,839	6,746	20.5	3,443	704	20.4
2013[3]	17,837	5,415	30.4	17,559	5,273	30.0	32,903	6,654	20.2	3,405	676	19.8
2012	17,664	5,976	33.8	17,341	5,773	33.3	32,228	6,977	21.6	3,213	663	20.6
2011	17,600	6,008	34.1	17,276	5,820	33.7	31,643	6,667	21.1	3,036	569	18.7
2010[4]	17,371	6,059	34.9	16,964	5,815	34.3	30,740	6,948	22.6	2,860	516	18.0
2009	16,965	5,610	33.1	16,655	5,419	32.5	29,031	6,224	21.4	2,815	516	18.3
2008	16,370	5,010	30.6	16,138	4,888	30.3	28,311	5,452	19.3	2,717	525	19.3
2007	15,647	4,482	28.6	15,375	4,348	28.3	27,731	4,970	17.9	2,555	438	17.1
2006	15,147	4,072	26.9	14,907	3,959	26.6	27,209	4,698	17.3	2,428	472	19.4
2005[5]	14,654	4,143	28.3	14,361	3,977	27.7	26,051	4,765	18.3	2,315	460	19.9
2004[5]	14,173	4,098	28.9	13,929	3,985	28.6	25,324	4,620	18.2	2,194	403	18.4
2003	13,730	4,077	29.7	13,519	3,982	29.5	24,490	4,568	18.7	2,080	406	19.5
2002	13,210	3,782	28.6	12,971	3,653	28.2	23,952	4,334	18.1	2,053	439	21.4
2001	12,763	3,570	28.0	12,559	3,433	27.4	22,653	4,014	17.7	1,896	413	21.8
2000[6]	12,399	3,522	28.4	12,115	3,342	27.6	21,734	3,844	17.7	1,822	381	20.9
1999[7]	12,188	3,693	30.3	11,912	3,561	29.9	20,782	3,843	18.5	1,661	340	20.5
1998	11,152	3,837	34.4	10,921	3,670	33.6	18,668	3,877	20.8	1,696	356	21.0
1997	10,802	3,972	36.8	10,625	3,865	36.4	18,217	3,951	21.7	1,617	384	23.8
1996	10,511	4,237	40.3	10,255	4,090	39.9	17,587	4,089	23.3	1,516	370	24.4
1995[8]	10,213	4,080	40.0	10,011	3,938	39.1	16,673	4,153	24.9	1,458	342	23.5
1994[9]	9,822	4,075	41.5	9,621	3,956	41.1	16,192	4,018	24.8	1,428	323	22.6
1993[10]	9,462	3,873	40.9	9,188	3,666	39.9	15,708	3,956	25.2	1,390	297	21.4
1992[11]	9,081	3,637	40.0	8,829	3,440	39.0	15,268	3,668	24.0	1,298	287	22.1
1991[12]	7,648	3,094	40.4	7,473	2,977	39.8	13,279	3,008	22.7	1,143	237	20.8
1990	7,457	2,865	38.4	7,300	2,750	37.7	12,857	2,896	22.5	1,091	245	22.5
1989	7,186	2,603	36.2	7,040	2,496	35.5	12,536	2,616	20.9	1,024	211	20.6
1988[13]	7,003	2,631	37.6	6,908	2,576	37.3	12,056	2,501	20.7	1,005	225	22.4
1987[13]	6,792	2,670	39.3	6,692	2,606	38.9	11,718	2,509	21.4	885	243	27.5
1986	6,646	2,507	37.7	6,511	2,413	37.1	11,206	2,406	21.5	906	204	22.5
1985[14]	6,475	2,606	40.3	6,346	2,512	39.6	10,685	2,411	22.6	915	219	23.9
1984[14]	6,068	2,376	39.2	5,982	2,317	38.7	10,029	2,254	22.5	819	176	21.5
1983	6,066	2,312	38.1	5,977	2,251	37.7	9,697	2,148	22.5	782	173	22.1
1982	5,527	2,181	39.5	5,436	2,117	38.9	8,262	1,963	23.8	596	159	26.6
1981[16]	5,369	1,925	35.9	5,291	1,874	35.4	8,084	1,642	20.3	568	146	25.7
1980	5,276	1,749	33.2	5,211	1,718	33.0	7,740	1,563	20.2	582	179	30.8

See footnotes at end of table.

Table B-6.

Poverty Status of People by Age, Race, and Hispanic Origin: 1959 to 2019—Con.

(Populations in thousands. Population as of March of the following year. For information on confidentiality protection, sampling error, nonsampling error, and definitions, see <https://www2.census.gov/programs-surveys/cps/techdocs/cpsmar20.pdf>)

Race, Hispanic origin, and year	Under 18 years						18 to 64 years			65 years and over		
	All people under 18 years			Related children in families								
	Total	Below poverty		Total	Below poverty		Total	Below poverty		Total	Below poverty	
		Number	Percent		Number	Percent		Number	Percent		Number	Percent
1979[17]	5,483	1,535	28.0	5,426	1,505	27.7	7,314	1,232	16.8	574	154	26.8
1978	5,012	1,384	27.6	4,972	1,354	27.2	6,527	1,098	16.8	539	125	23.2
1977	5,028	1,422	28.3	5,000	1,402	28.0	6,500	1,164	17.9	518	113	21.9
1976	4,771	1,443	30.2	4,736	1,424	30.1	6,034	1,212	20.1	464	128	27.7
1975	N	N	N	4,896	1,619	33.1	N	N	N	N	137	32.6
1974[18]	N	N	N	4,939	1,414	28.6	N	N	N	N	117	28.9
1973	N	N	N	4,910	1,364	27.8	N	N	N	N	95	24.9

N Not available.

[1] Estimates reflect the implementation of an updated processing system and should be used to make comparisons to 2018 and subsequent years.

[2] The 2014 CPS ASEC included redesigned questions for income and health insurance coverage. All of the approximately 98,000 addresses were eligible to receive the redesigned set of health insurance coverage questions. The redesigned income questions were implemented to a subsample of the 98,000 addresses using a probability split panel design. Approximately 68,000 addresses were eligible to recieve a set of income questions similar to those used in the 2013 CPS ASEC, and the remaining 30,000 addresses were eligible to receive the redesigned income questions. The source of these 2013 estimates is the portion of the CPS ASEC sample that received the redesigned income questions, approximately 30,000 addresses.

[3] The source of these 2013 estimates is the portion of the CPS ASEC sample that received the income questions consistent with the 2013 CPS ASEC, approximately 68,000 addresses.

[15] Implementation of Hispanic population weighting controls and introduction of 1980 Census-based sample design.

[16] Implemented three technical changes to the poverty definition. See "Characteristics of the Population Below the Poverty Level: 1980" P60-133.

[17] Implementation of 1980 Census population controls.
Questionnaire expanded to show 27 possible values from 51 possible sources of income.

[18] Implementation of a new CPS ASEC processing system.
Questionnaire expanded to ask 11 income questions.

[19] Full implementation of 1970 Census-based sample design.

[20] Introduction of 1970 Census sample design and population controls.

[21] Implementation of a new CPS ASEC processing system.

[22] Beginning with the 2003 CPS ASEC, respondents were allowed to choose one or more races. White alone refers to people who reported White and did not report any other race category. The use of this single-race population does not imply that it is the preferred

[4] Implementation of 2010 Census-based population controls.

[5] Data have been revised to reflect a correction to the weights in the 2005 CPS ASEC.

[6] Implementation of a 28,000 household expansion.

[7] Implementation of 2000 Census-based population controls.

[8] Full implementation of 1990 Census-based sample design and metropolitan definitions, 7,000 household sample reduction, and revised editing of responses on race.

[9] Introduction of 1990 Census sample design.

[10] Data collection method changed from paper and pencil to computer-assisted interviewing. In addition, the 1994 CPS ASEC was revised to allow for the coding of different income amounts on selected questionnaire items. Limits either increased or decreased in the following categories: earnings limits increased to $999,999; social security limits increased to $49,999; supplemental security income and public assistance limits increased to $24,999; veterans' benefits limits increased to $99,999; child support and alimony limits decreased to $49,999.

[11] Implementation of 1990 Census population controls.

[12] Estimates are revised to correct for nine omitted weights from the original 1992 CPS ASEC. See "Money Income of Households, Families, and Persons in the United States: 1992" P60-184.

[13] Estimates reflect the implementation of a new CPS ASEC processing system and are also revised to reflect corrections to the files after publication of the 1988 advance report "Money Income and Poverty Status in the United States: 1988" P60-166.

[14] Full implementation of 1980 Census-based sample design.

method of presenting or analyzing the data. The Census Bureau uses a variety of approaches.

[23] For the year 2001 and earlier, the CPS ASEC allowed respondents to report only one race group.

[24] Black alone refers to people who reported Black and did not report any other race category.

[25] Asian alone refers to people who reported Asian and did not report any other race category.

[26] Because Hispanics may be any race, data in this report for Hispanics overlap with data for racial groups. Being Hispanic was reported by 15.6 percent of White householders who reported only one race, 5.0 percent of Black householders who reported only one race, and 2.5 percent of Asian householders who reported only one race. Data users should exercise caution when interpreting aggregate results for the Hispanic population and for race groups because these populations consist of many distinct groups that differ in socioeconomic characteristics, culture, and recency of immigration. Data were first collected for Hispanics in 1972.

Note: Before 1979, people in unrelated subfamilies were included as people in families. Beginning in 1979, people in unrelated subfamilies are included in all people but are excluded from people in families. An unrelated subfamily is defined as a married-couple family with or without children or a single parent with one or more own, never-married, children under the age of 18 living in a household and not related by birth, marriage, or adoption to the householder.

Source: U.S. Census Bureau, Current Population Survey, 1960 to 2020 Annual Social and Economic Supplements (CPS ASEC).

About the Author

PETER THALHEIM HAS brought his experience from sixty-one years of life starting as a two-year-old immigrant coming to America in 1963 to this book. He attended K–12 public school and obtained a bachelor's degree in European history and later a law degree. Admitted to the bars of the states of Connecticut and New York, he practiced commercial litigation, general corporate law, and residential real estate, among other matters. At the same time, he developed his skills as a home builder and contractor by doing some of the work with his own hands and back. He has traveled around the world, visiting the Soviet Union twice before it disappeared, and has visited Communist China three times in addition to his backpacking through Southeast Asia. He has also spent considerable time traveling and visiting in Europe, where he has employed his average knowledge of German, basic knowledge of French, and rudimentary knowledge of Russian to get about and converse. An enthusiastic American who loves the great outdoors, he has driven across the great country of the United States numerous times.

One of his proudest accomplishments was joining the United States Army Reserve as a JAG officer after starting work in New York City as a litigator. These years in the reserves shaped what would become Check "American!" More recently, Mr. Thalheim ran unsuccessfully for governor of the state of Connecticut in 2017–2018, which was inspired by the positive message of "life, love, liberty" of Faith Tabernacle Missionary Baptist Church, an African American Baptist church in Stamford, Connecticut, that Mr. Thalheim regularly attends. During his campaign, Mr. Thalheim was introduced to the National Association for the Advancement of Colored People and has since been elected to the executive committee of the NAACP, Stamford, Connecticut, branch, in January 2020, a nonpartisan civil rights organization. In 2022, Mr. Thalheim was elected chair of the Education Committee of the NAACP's Stamford branch.

CPSIA information can be obtained
at www.ICGtesting.com
Printed in the USA
LVHW031027070223
738747LV00001B/3